Beyond EU-Enlargement
Volume 2

Wim van Meurs (ed.)

Beyond EU-Enlargement

Volume 2
The Agenda of Stabilisation
for Southeastern Europe

Bertelsmann Foundation Publishers
Gütersloh 2001

Die Deutsche Bibliothek – CIP-Einheitsaufnahme

A data set for this publication is available at
Die Deutsche Bibliothek.

2ⁿᵈ edition 2001
© 2001 Bertelsmann Foundation Publishers, Gütersloh
Responsible: Cornelius Ochmann
Cover design and illustration: werkzwei, Lutz Dudek, Bielefeld
Typesetting: digitron GmbH, Bielefeld
Printing: Rihn GmbH, Blomberg
ISBN 3-89204-549-6

Contents

Strategy Paper

Strategic Challenges and Risks of EU Eastern Enlargement

Iris Kempe, Wim van Meurs

1 Risks of EU Enlargement

The break-up of the Soviet Union, the dissolution of the Warsaw Pact and Comecon as well as the fall of the Berlin Wall marked the end of a historical era in Europe. Europe is no longer divided into two parts for ideological reasons or because of opposing systems. There is an opportunity to establish a new, common European order. Enlargement of the European Union (EU) towards the east is a step toward creating security and stability beyond the borders of present day "Europe". The new opportunities at the same time also carry some new risks and political challenges. These emanate on the one hand from economically and politically unstable neighbouring states, and on the other hand from follow-up questions beyond the current requirements of EU enlargement towards the east.

As the title says, this report will for the first time deal with the potential and risks at the eastern and southeastern borders of the European Union that will be there "beyond enlargement", "beyond" in a threefold sense:
- *Geography* as regards those states and border regions for which the EU has not formulated accession prospects so far, and which will thus find themselves beyond and outside the European integration process in the medium term as well;
- *Time* as regards the follow-up questions of enlargement towards the east from 2005 onwards for various policy areas;
- *Quality* as regards the questions of principle to be derived from enlargement towards the east and the discernible finality of the Union.

These three dimensions are not only relevant for the analyses on Eastern and Southeastern Europe presented in the two accompanying volumes, but also for future policies which will be geared towards all of Europe, along and beyond the borders of the EU. As far as the regions beyond the future EU borders are concerned, the key questions of exporting stability without importing instability, of permeability and control, of enlargement process and foreign policy, are unavoidable. At the moment these states can be divided into two groups: The successor states of the former Soviet Union, which after EU eastern enlargement will come to share a border with the Union, and the Southeast European region. Both regions confront European decision-makers with new tasks in the area of security policy, caused by the whole spectrum of transformation problems, ranging from economic crises to minority conflicts escalating into violence. In this context, the EU is required like no other organisation in Europe to play a role as stabiliser in the transformation process and also as soft-security provider. In formulating its policies, the EU has up to now opted for various forms of co-operation that do not offer the perspective of accession: In its co-operation with Belarus, Moldova, Ukraine and Russia, accession has been excluded for the time being. Relations with states that will be in Direct Neighbourhood to the enlarged EU are limited to partnership and co-operation. For the regions of acute crisis in the "Western Balkans", on the other hand, the "window of opportunity" for prospective accession has been opened, and is supported by a Stability Pact as well as the Stabilisation and Association Process.

Despite numerous differences, the security and stability problems in both regions can be approached by a comparison of four core areas:

1. Minority problems and legacies of the past;
2. Questions of visa and customs procedures;
3. Regional and cross-border co-operation;
4. Pan-European security.

With these topics in mind, the regions of the future eastern border (Direct Neighbourhood) as well as the future southeastern border were investigated in order to identify risks and follow-up questions resulting from the process of enlarging the EU towards the east. Conclusions and consequences can be found in the subsequent policy recommendations.

1.1 Direct Neighbourhood and risks along the eastern borders

Up to now, EU decision-makers have made substantial efforts to achieve institutionalised regulations for their relations with their future neighbour states. As successor states of the former Soviet Union, Russia, Ukraine, Belarus and Moldova are members in the Organisation for Security and Co-operation in Europe (OSCE). The admission of these states to the Council of Europe (CoE) is a sign of progress, but also reveals problems in the democratic development of the countries concerned: The guest status of Belarus, for example, has been suspended since 1997 because of the problematic domestic situation. In order to be able to criticise Russia's role in the second Chechenyan war, the parliamentary assembly of the CoE has temporarily repealed Russia's right to vote.

The European Union has signed Partnership and Co-operation Agreements (PCA) with Russia, Ukraine, Belarus and Moldova. With the exception of Belarus, the agreements have been ratified by all countries and taken effect. Drawn up along the same lines, the agreements reflect Western interest in bilateral political co-operation on democratic foundations as well as Eastern interest in economic co-operation. If the possibilities provided for in the agreements are completely implemented, this will create a broad range of opportunities for political dialogue and economic co-operation on various levels, from summits to concrete working groups, and in the case of economic co-operation may even lead to the establishment of free trade zones. The Partnership and Co-operation Agreements with Ukraine and Russia are supplemented by Common Strategies for each, instruments of the EU's Common Foreign and Security Policy. The difference to relations with the East and Central European countries is that none of the current strategies envisages EU membership.

The country reports on relations between the Russian Federation, Ukraine, Belarus and Moldova and the European Union published in the documentation point toward distinct deficits and potentials insufficiently explored. One major point of criticism is raised in the country reports on Ukraine and Moldova. By way of a strategic answer, *Ukraine* and *Moldova* passed policy statements of their own on their relations to the EU. These are aimed at an early association and the inherent promise of prospective membership. This has to be seen in conjunction with the foreign policy aim to distance themselves from the hegemony of Russia and to strengthen national sovereignty. While Kiev and Chisinau think of prospective membership as a factor stabilising the transformation process, Brussels regards the fact that the transformation tasks have only been very insufficiently fulfilled up to now as one of the main obstacles to formulating membership prospects. While the East European side perceives the continuing lack of membership prospects as a risk leading to loss of stability throughout Europe, the West European side fears that even a debate about possible accession might endanger internal security and stability in Western Europe.

There is a lack of normative and institutional concepts to shape the whole of Europe, though the challenge in this context lies more with the EU than with the OSCE or the CoE. Unlike the other organisations, the EU links stability and security and thus has the potential to manage the extended, i.e., beyond military, risks to security caused by economic and social upheavals. The more manifest the membership prospect, the greater the chances for the EU to exert its influence. This can be seen in the countries that are membership candidates, where the Copenhagen Criteria and the *acquis communautaire* have achieved priority status in domestic development. The imbalance between the Ukrainian and Moldovan positions on the one side and the European position on the other leads to a strategic vacuum.

In view of the dilemma created by the lack of EU membership prospects and unsolved transformation problems, there is a danger that Ukraine and Moldova will remain politically and economically "risky neighbours". Should Poland be among the first East-Central European members of the EU, the asymmetries along this border will continue to grow. It has to be assumed that the security and stability problems will increase too.

Complete or partial failure of the Ukrainian and Moldovan transformation would at the same time influence relations with the Russian Federation. In both cases, the countries concerned are ethnically and economically weakly consolidated nation-states. Because of its economic structure and ethnic make-up, Ukraine has traditionally been divided into a Russian-dominated east and the genuinely Ukrainian west. As a result of its uncertain relations with Romania and separatist Transnistria, Moldova is also suffering from the consequences of a fragile national consolidation.

Russian dominance over the so-called "near abroad" also becomes manifest in economic dependencies, in particular the almost complete dependence on energy supplies. Not only are the enormous debts owed to Russia for energy supplies a sensitive factor but also the routes of the pipelines. By leading the Jamal pipeline through Belarus, Russia is making a point of bypassing Ukraine. This decision not only violates the interests of Kiev, it is also regarded as a sensitive issue by Poland. Ukraine's national independence and economic strength are of strategic concern to Poland. Through consolidation in the core of Europe, the Polish government is trying to make the Russian influence more calculable. In case of Poland's EU accession, the conflict about energy between Russia and Ukraine would also put a burden on European-Russian relations, especially as Russia's political and economic interests overlap considerably in the gas and oil sector.

The relationship between the EU and *Belarus* is even more difficult than relations with Ukraine and Moldova. The official foreign policy of the Lukashenko regime concentrates on intensifying relations with Russia, even going so far as to support tendencies towards a Russian-Belarus Union. Improvement of the extremely frosty relations with Europe is occasionally used as a punching ball in domestic policy.

The main risk, however, emanates from the domestic and economic policies of the Lukashenko regime. In spite of the deteriorating economic situation, the office holder is not prepared to abide by democratic minimum standards like free elections, economic reforms and orientation towards Europe. Because of the violations of human rights and democracy, the current very low economic attractiveness and sometimes even aggressive behaviour in dealing with Western representatives, international organisations and representatives of the West have distanced themselves from Minsk. The EU has not set up a delegation, but only a technical office responsible for the Tacis programme. Compared with the other CIS countries, the commitment of Western organisations and foreign foundations is also low. The only activities that stand out in this context are the activities of the local OSCE office.

As a consequence of the insufficient interest shown by the EU and other international players, the opposition in Belarus and forces within the Lukashenko regime that are interested in reform are hardly ever noted. Even if this group of players may seem small when seen from the outside, their capacity to act should not be underestimated, and could even be increased by targeted support from the outside. This is particularly true because orientation towards Europe carries a high symbolic and normative value for the representatives of reform in Belarus. It is symptomatic, and in this respect similar to developments in Ukraine and Moldova, for a dissociation from Russian hegemonial tendencies in the area and for orientation of the system transformation towards the West.

Unlike Southeastern Europe, with its conflicts caused by minority problems, Belarus does not have a serious potential for ethnic conflicts. The potential threats emanating from Belarus are in the first place based on asymmetries in relation to its Polish and Lithuanian neighbours. The continuing economic downturn and overdue democratisation turn Belarus into the European regime most characterised by dictatorial components. The emergence of new dividing lines as a consequence of EU eastern enlargement will increase this tendency and at the same time make Belarus an even more difficult neighbour. Apart from the domestic and economic policy components mentioned, the geopolitical situation of the country is also very important for common European security. Continued national sovereignty is an important factor for the relationship between the Eastern Central European countries and Russia. A reunification of Moscow and Minsk would not only be a burden on national stability, it would, moreover, also not be in the interest of Europe as a whole.

In the relations between the *Russian Federation* and the EU, there is a consensus that in the medium term an accession of Russia is neither a feasible prospect, nor one worth striving for. Under the presidency of Mr. Putin, the importance of the EU has increased: While the Russian side regarded the political role of the EU as comparatively insignificant even as late as 1997, the Russian government at present sees the EU as an influential political player. The reason for this change in attitude is that the EU is increasingly gaining a foreign and defence policy profile over and beyond its economic importance. This has led Russian decision-makers to the conclusion that there is a multilateral alternative to the current unilateral world order dominated by the USA. This position held by the Russian government deviates from the fundamental convictions of European decision-makers. The EU shapes its policy towards Russia as a complement to its trans-atlantic relations.

In contrast to their critical attitude towards NATO enlargement, Russian decision-makers as a rule welcome the EU eastern enlargement; at least they voice this position in political declarations of intent. The Russian position on some details important for EU enlargement towards the east differs fundamentally from this statement, however. There are uncertainties and differences regarding sensitive specific aspects. Once Poland and Lithuania have become members of the EU, the Russian exclave of *Kaliningrad* will be surrounded by EU member states. Goods and passenger traffic in the region will be cut off from the mother country even more than now. Despite some efforts to design a Kaliningrad strategy within the framework of the EU's *Northern Dimension* initiative-there are still neither European nor Russian concepts for the visa issue or the integration of economic development in the Kaliningrad region in an overall concept for the Baltic Sea region, which would give due consideration to Russian security concerns. The requirements to be met by a common European strategy for Kaliningrad are increasing because of the region's structural economic weakness, and the strategic interest of some Russian decision-makers to utilise Kaliningrad as a stronghold against NATO and EU enlargement towards the east.

A whole range of risks results from relations with the *Baltic states*. The new national security doctrine of the Putin government strongly underlines Russia's role as protector of the Russian population in Estonia and Latvia. In accordance with this position, the Russian government, but also the general public and the media, are very sensitive about the situation of the Russian-speaking population in Estonia and Latvia. Points of criticism are deficits in the legislation regulating citizenship, the Latvian language laws, and the generally difficult social and economic living conditions. In some points the Russian criticism corresponds with the OSCE assessment and the Progress Reports by the EU. A greater problem for future neighbourhood relations, however, is Russia's policy to exploit the situation of the Russian-speaking population in the Baltic states for its own political ends, and instrumentalise it as a way to manifest Russian claims. On the basis of this position, Russian decision-makers and analysts have repeatedly claimed a say in the accession negotiations between the EU and Estonia and Latvia. This may lead to a potential conflict between the enlargement process and relations with Russia.

The as yet unratified Estonian-Russian and Latvian-Russian border treaties are a further lever used by the Russian government to try and influence the speed of EU enlargement, as clarification of open border issues is a precondition for EU accession. This instance illustrates particularly well that the Baltic States have become a test case for relations between the EU and Russia far surpassing normative declarations of intent. Thus it is far from sufficient that the Russian government is in favour of EU enlargement towards the east. Rather the degree of approval is measured against the treatment of critical issues like agreement on the border treaties or evaluation of the situation of the Russian-speaking population in Estonia and Latvia.

Up to now sensitive aspects like Kaliningrad and the question of relations between Russia and the Baltic states have not been sufficiently taken into account in EU strategies. The Union leaves the responsibility up to the Baltic states, without taking into account that even a partially acceptable solution to this problem, so closely related to Eastern enlargement might in the future also lead to conflicts between Europe and Russia.

Apart from the risks emanating from inadequate EU strategies, the situation in Russia also contains numerous risks for the Union. According to optimistic estimates, the increase in GDP, which has grown again for the first time in more than a decade, and the rise in industrial production could be interpreted as signs for structural successes of the Putin presidency. In this interpretation, the rise in industrial production and the GNP will be followed by the urgently needed structural reforms and institutional changes in procedures for political decisions. Critics point out, however, that the social basis for Mr. Putin's efforts at reform is too slim. The open conflicts he is engaged in at the moment with oligarchs, the media and regional elites, as well as in the Caucasus may be welcome on a certain level, but they require a broad measure of support. The latter is largely missing, however, as Mr. Putin's policy is mostly backed by representatives of the middle ranks of the administration and the secret service. And the ordinary man in the street, who is largely preoccupied with finding the means for survival, neither has the feeling of being represented in politics nor any opportunities for social involvement.

As long as transformation of the Russian system has not consolidated sufficiently within Russian society, Russia is bound to remain a risk factor for Europe. It is true that in view of its nuclear arms potential, Russia claims the status of a superpower. The modest economic potentials put a narrow limit to the practical importance. The economic crises, social problems and political instabilities not only hamper the ability to act in the field of foreign policy, they also increase the asymmetries between Russia and Europe. The mere promise of EU accession has led to an improvement of the investment climate and economic stabilisation in the Eastern and Central European Countries. Should this tendency continue on both sides, Europe as a whole will increasingly be split into a stable and a risky space.

1.2 Strategy recommendations on Direct Neighbourhood

Differentiation strategy: In formulating policy recommendations, one can distinguish between approaches that focus comprehensively on one complete region, and approaches that concentrate on specific sensitive aspects. By concentrating on the criterion of membership or non-membership, the policy of the European institutions arrives at insufficiently differentiated forms of relations with the so-called "outs". Russia, Moldova and Ukraine are members of the CoE and the OSCE. Thus these institutions recognise the progress made by the CIS states in their domestic transformation and foreign policy reorientation. With respect to the EU as the institution most important for economic stability and political integration in Europe, the situation is different: In its strategies and declarations of intent any prospects for membership beyond the borders of what is today Central and Eastern Europe have been rejected. The arguments are largely technical and institutional, focusing on non-compliance with the Copenhagen Criteria for EU membership. The development of relations with Turkey, the "Western Balkans" or the Southeast European accession countries has shown, however, that crises and conflicts may well create political scope to act in the interpretation of the conditions for accession.

Setting aside the Copenhagen Criteria, the Ukrainian as well as the Moldavian government make their point for EU membership prospects, with the intention, among others, to consolidate their states internally and to maintain their sovereignty vis-à-vis the powerful Russian neighbour. Declarations claiming Russia's interest in EU membership, however, are limited to spontaneous political exclamations which are not reflected in the corresponding doctrines. This means that the criteria concerning what is expected of the EU are completely different, although all CIS countries suffer from political instability and economic crises. By reducing its decisions to a Yes or No on association and membership, the EU limits its own potential to create security and stability in Europe. The result is a risk-charged vacuum of non-policy. In order to fill this vacuum, it would be necessary to have a strategy of differentiated relations. Beyond the *acquis communautaire,* Ukraine's and Moldova's present European self-perception should be seen as a chance. Beyond the "in" and "out" debate, the differences between the future neighbour states have to be perceived in a politically adequate and differentiated way, and strategically implemented accordingly.

EU prospects for Ukraine and Moldova: European policy vis-à-vis CIS countries intent on becoming members of the EU should be to convert the current No on accession into a Yes, in principle. This is the only way in which the potential of the European standard-setting policy can be used as an instrument for conflict prevention and domestic stabilisation even beyond the future borders of the EU. In order to counteract excessive expectations, the European Commission and the governments of the members states will at the same time have to underline that association and accession depend on the success of the domestic transformation process.

In the sense of the fundamental considerations outlined above, EU prospects may be introduced into the political debate. Under the premise of a possible association, the opportunities for co-operation already contained in the Partnership and Co-operation Agreements and in the Common Strategy, could be used in a more intensive manner. The same should apply to the co-operation between the current membership candidates and neighbour states willing to accede. Supported by European programmes and funds, this could not only help to transfer experiences with the transformation process, it could also bring up the topic of relations between candidate states and the European Commission for discussion. The correlation between success in managing the transformation tasks and prospects for EU association should also be pointed out in programmes for technical co-operation like Tacis and Transform by including references to the adoption of the *acquis communautaire* in the terms of reference. Efforts and successes in transforming the system would thus be directly linked to prospects for EU membership.

Involving Russia in the follow-up questions of eastern enlargement: In the case of the Russian Federation, there are fewer strategic deficits because neither is working toward Russian membership in the Union. There are, however, strategic deficits resulting from specific sensitive aspects of EU enlargement towards the east that concern Russia directly or indirectly. First of all, it must be the task of the EU to define, together with the Russian government and in their common interest, sensitive aspects of EU enlargement towards the east, and outline the limits to which Russia can be allowed to exert its influence. This would mean that Russian decision-makers and analysts would no longer give the impression of being a party to the membership negotiations, as this is a matter between the Commission and the membership candidates.

Kaliningrad strategy: Establishing a committee on the topic of EU enlargement towards the east should be discussed within the current framework of Russian-European co-operation, for instance in the political dialogue. On its agenda, such a committee should have those items that touch upon the direct interests of Russia as well as those of the Union and the candidate states. On top of the agenda would be drawing up a Kaliningrad strategy. In the process it would be possible to take up existing Russian and EU initiatives. Starting from there, the more sensitive issues of visa regulation, regional development of Kaliningrad and Russian security interests would have to be discussed. According to political signals from Brussels and the member states, there will not be any exceptions for visa regulations to and from Kaliningrad. Nevertheless there are extensive technical and administrative possibilities: Issuing a transit visa within the region must be made as easy and quick as possible by establishing additional consulates. Visa charges and additional insurance should be abolished.

A second pillar of the Kaliningrad strategy must be based on the internal stabilisation of the region. In addition to the EU, the Russian government as well as the regional decision-makers are called on to draw up and implement innovative concepts in this process. In the European context, the most urgent political requirement is maximising cross-border co-operation with the neighbouring states of Poland and Lithuania as well as giving support via programmes of technical assistance. Kaliningrad should be granted the status of first-priority funding region on both levels. On the Russian side it is particularly important to minimise military-strategic concerns and maximise investments for national and international investors. Developing Kaliningrad into a centre for technical innovation should be discussed. Avoiding or diminishing asymmetries between Kaliningrad and the neighbouring future EU member states is the most comprehensive guarantee for security. The problem most difficult to solve on the European side is Russian decision-makers endeavouring to instrumentalise the strategic-military potential of Kaliningrad as a stronghold against NATO and EU enlargement towards the east. This risk can only be diminished by ensuring that the stabilisation of Kaliningrad through international co-operation, investment and innovation is beneficial to the Russian economy.

Democratisation of Belarus: The difficult neighbourhood in relation to Belarus is not only caused by the dictatorial character of the Lukashenko regime, but also by the fact that Belarus is almost completely ignored in international relations. Removing this strategic vacuum is a necessity, even if only for the sole purpose of not letting go all chances for democratisation and Europeanisation of Belarus that are unused at the present. The development of Serbia may serve as an example: Targeted support of oppositional forces and regional players from the outside contributed to the regime and to the creation of the preconditions for democratic and market-economic reforms. A similar strategy should also be pursued in the case of Belarus. Concessions to Lukashenko must only be made under the premise that he initiates structural change. The release of political prisoners, for instance, should not be regarded as a structural change. Examples for structural change would be the introduction of a democratic right to vote, giving the opposition access to the mass media, or the democratisation of the government system.

The foremost aim of the West should be to Europeanise and strengthen civil society in Belarus. An important mainstay for the Europeanisation of Belarus is the presence of European institutions, above all the EU. The technical office currently working there should be developed into a full-fledged EU delegation. This proposal is not primarily directed at co-operation with the Belarus government, but rather at co-operation with non-government organisations, universities and business representatives interested in reform. In combination with the installation of as many diverse communication channels as possible, information and knowledge about European institutions should be increased.

First priority in economic co-operation must be given to supporting the privatisation process. Economic competence can be transferred through co-operation with companies from EU member states as well as candidate states. On the other hand the presence of Western advisors in Belarus should not only be continued but expanded as well. This kind of policy can transfer Western competence to largely isolated Belarus in a targeted way, in order to increase the basis for economic reform in the medium term.

Relations between Belarus and Europe as well as the Europeanisation of Belarus can in addition be intensified through an extension and intensification of relations between institutions of the civil society and the educational system. The list of possible schemes is long. It starts with establishing joint training programmes at the universities, continues with a co-operation between institutes of private education and the support of the opposition parties and independent trade unions, and continues through training and co-operation with independent journalists and critical representatives of regional self-government.

Just as in the case of Belarus, support of the development of civil society in Russia, Moldova and Ukraine constitutes a core element of overall democratisation, economic reform and transformation. It has to be pointed out at the same time, though, that this is only one element of European strategy vis-à-vis the countries concerned. Support of civil society must not be used as an excuse for postponing urgently needed political decisions.

1.3 Stabilisation and risks along the southeastern borders

The "Western Balkans" are *the* crisis region in Europe, for both economic transformation and state consolidation. Despite significant differences, the ten transformation countries from Estonia to Bulgaria have all made sufficient progress in their transformation towards a pluralist democracy and an efficient market economy since 1989/1991 to be granted the status of EU accession states under the Copenhagen Criteria. In comparison, the countries of the "Western Balkans" have a much bigger backlog in the transformation process and worse starting conditions after ten years of war, expulsion and instability than before. The most important economic indicators in all states of Southeastern Europe are below the level of 1989, and apart from the violent disintegration of the Yugoslav Federation, Albania, Romania and Bulgaria also experienced state crises in the 1990s.

The Reasons for the increasing *falling behind of the "Western Balkans"* may be grouped into four tightly interwoven risk areas, or rather development deficits which partly reach much further back than the post-communist transformation or even the decades of communist rule: (1) the ethnic conflicts and the lack of state consolidation in the region with their consequences for regional stability; (2) the weakness and instability of the political regimes; (3) the deficits in the development of the civil society; and, last but not least, (4) mismanagement of the economic transformation, which on the one hand, starts at a level much lower than in Eastern and Central Europe and shows many elements of a developmental rather than a transformation process, and is, on the other hand, exceedingly misdirected by widespread corruption and criminalisation.

Unlike the potential for conflict along the eastern borders, the potential for conflict in the "Western Balkans" could not be regionally and politically controlled. Unlike the *frozen conflicts* along the eastern border, the ethnic conflicts following the disintegration of the Federal Republic of Yugoslavia escalated and forced the international community to intervene, leading to the war in Kosovo in spring 1999. Apart from the protection of human and minority rights, this *humanitarian intervention* also put the prestige and integrity of NATO at stake. In view of these dangers, the Europeans were very firm in their approach, after the phase of military intervention, to stabilise the region permanently and to rule out such escalations of violence at the future borders of the EU and within the developing common European security area.

The international community with leading roles for the USA as the only global power and the European Union as regional power – has covered the "Western Balkans" with a network of initiatives, strategies and programmes. The list is almost endless – KFOR, SFOR, Partnership for Peace, Stability Pact, SECI, Black Sea Co-operation, Balkan Conference for Stability and Co-operation in Southeastern Europe, OBNOVA, UNPREDEP, UNMIK, Stabilisation and Association Process, and reaches from diplomatic mediation, military intervention, economic assistance or trade support to reconstruction and administration in the protectorates. The overall balance of Western commitment after ten years of war, expulsion, impoverishment and destabilisation is mixed. It is true that the end of the Milosevic regime in Serbia has improved the prospects for the region, but in view of the structural deficits mentioned and the negative consequences of the past ten years, this can only be seen as a precondition for change, not a panacea.

Consequently, the EU has decided to apply not only its emerging foreign and security policy capacities to stabilise the region, but above all its tried and tested instruments as a regional power: Massive support for the process of democratic and economic transformation with EU membership prospects as an incentive. The prospects were first acceded to the countries of the "Western Balkans" in the Stability Pact – a commitment which was explicitly made at the European Councils in Helsinki and in Feira. At the same time the roles of Romania and Bulgaria as stabilisers in the Southeast European region were strengthened through the start of membership negotiations (although the economic criteria were only met in part). Overall the stabilisation of the region is now based on qualitatively different preconditions than during *Operation Allied Force,* and the region is being integrated into the common European economic and security area.

1.4 Regional risks and strategic deficits

The list of potential instability risks in the Southern European region and the resulting strategic requirements or rather deficits, however, is equally substantial. In important areas these risk potentials do not even only result from the structural preconditions inherited from the pre-socialist and socialist era or from the post-1989 conflicts, but are caused by external control, or rather European approaches to solve the problems, as shown by a summary of some important risk potentials.

The unsolved question of the national and territorial status quo in the region continues to be an essential obstacle to regional co-operation as well as to transformation of the national economies. This is true for the restructuring of the Federal Republic of Yugoslavia, or rather its dissolution, the question of independence for Montenegro and/or Kosovo, and the status of "protectorate" for Bosnia-Herzegovina and Kosovo pushed through by the international community. The open question regarding the status of Kosovo in particular constitutes a substantial instability factor for the region. While the status quo as a protectorate is basically unacceptable to both parties of the conflict, each option for a solution would lead to reactions and follow-up questions, and a new escalation of violence could not be excluded. Under international law, the condition of protectorate status furthermore collides with the requirements of political consolidation and a fresh economic start in Kosovo.

As the international community prefers as a solution (at least for the time being) a continuation of the protectorate to the two options – with escalation potential, and valuable time and energy that ought to be spent on the necessary development and transformation policy is lost. There is a real danger that the national question remains a dominant issue or may be instrumentalised politically as a substitute for transformation, not only in Kosovo but also in Serbia and the FRY.

In the area of economic development, two risks for the future development of the region, which have in part already materialised, must not be underestimated: *Aid addiction* and *criminalisation of the economy.* The fact that chances for economic development in Kosovo, Bosnia and Montenegro were limited from the start and have been even further reduced by the war (the term "economic reconstruction" is misleading) implies that the capacity needed to absorb massive Western aid in a controlled, effective and sustainable way will simply not be there. If this cannot be assured, however, financial aid could often only benefit a small political-economic establishment and increase social disparities. The national economy would become dependent on foreign support and international presence. Accordingly, parts of the political and economic elite are not interested in optimal economic transformation and legal-institutional restructuring, but in a continuation of the opportunities to profit from unregulated economic development. Hand in hand with this development, there will also be criminalisation of several business sectors and intermingling of political and entrepreneurial interests.

A strategic dilemma rather than a risk is caused by the heterogeneity of Southeastern Europe itself and the resulting friction between the EU principles of regionality and conditionality. Although the Southeastern European countries find themselves in the bottom half of the East European ranking for all transformation criteria, the structural differences and potentials within the region are considerable.

The preconditions of the various steps of approaching the EU have thus led to a division of the region in two respects: As a result of EU conditionality (the preconditions that have to be met with each step), the institutional and contractual relations between the EU and every country of the region are different, ranging from Co-operation Agreements to Stability Pact and SAP candidature up to Europe Agreements, a state of affairs that does nothing for regional co-operation, and even diminishes the willingness to co-operate on a regional level. On the other hand, the instruments of a bilateral approach to the EU have a positive effect on economic development and political stability, which will inexorably lead to increasing disparities and rifts opening in the development within the region.

Thus, the EU principles of *conditionality* and *regionality* collide when put into practice. With the implementation of the most important EU strategies – Stability Pact on the one hand and the Stabilisation and Association Process on the other – this will become increasingly manifest. The Stability Pact depends on the concept of comprehensive regional co-operation and has to meet only a basic set of conditions (protection of minority and human rights, recognition of borders, willingness to establish good-neighbourly relations). The logic of the Stabilisation and Association Process on the other hand is based on conditionality, an incremental sequence of bilateral contractual relations with the EU in conjunction with correspondingly increasing conditions ranging from the basic conditionality of the Stability Pact up to the comprehensive *acquis communautaire* of EU membership.

1.5 Optimisation and convergence of EU Balkans policy

Since the Kosovo war and especially since the Helsinki European Council, the self-definition of the European Union has changed. A decisive impulse for these changes was given by the war in Kosovo, but the consequences reach far beyond the Balkan region. As a regional power, the EU increasingly bears responsibility for a Europe that is bigger than its 15 member states, and reaches even beyond the twelve or thirteen accession states. This means synchronising Europe as an economic power, Europe as a stabiliser in the transformation process and Europe as a fledgling foreign and security policy player.

Convergence of the existing EU strategies means first of all a leading role of the European Union in the mega-project of stabilising Southeastern Europe. If the long-term objective is integration into the Union, then it would be useful to structure its first interim stop, the Stability Pact, as an EU institution. This would also benefit sequentialisation and the transition from the Stability Pact to the Stabilisation and Association Process.

As dominant initiative, the Stability Pact will also determine the shape of the emerging region. Accordingly, the inclusion of Romania and Bulgaria is to be seen as a positive move. On the one hand, the division between these two accession states and the "Western Balkans", which have several structural problems in common, is artificial, and on the other, Romania and Bulgaria could take over certain regional stabilisation or vanguard functions. At the same time, the idea to admit Moldova to the Pact could release this state from its position between the CIS and the Balkans, and join it up with the region to which it belongs in terms of history and its present development. Generally speaking, this means that because of the internal heterogeneity of Southeastern Europe and of the experiences in Central and eastern Europe, co-operation should be prompted but subordinated to political-strategic EU integration and its conditionality. The course of differentiated rather than accelerated pre-accession of Southeastern Europe could then be geared to functional considerations and regional associations of the "willing and able" instead of striving to include every country.

EU membership prospects for the Balkan countries and a strategy of differentiated pre-accession should be pursued in parallel with the process of enlargement towards the East. A successful first round of enlargement in 2005 would be the best of all possible guarantees for stability and transformation in Southeastern Europe. Nevertheless the nexus between Eastern enlargement and geopolitical interests or security issues can hardly be denied: The Kosovo war has had a substantial influence on the decisions of Helsinki, which proves that the EU standards of the *acquis communautaire* are not the only decisive criteria in enlargement negotiations. The capacities and security interests of the union should be recognised as factors, too.

23

2 Regional risks and European strategies

2.1 A European strategy for minority and border issues

Although the relationships between ethnic majority and minority in many of the transition countries are not without problems, and some unsettled border issues continue to exist, the European balance of achievements is rather positive in this respect. With no intention of diminishing the existing risks, it is justified to point out that the worst-case scenario after the break-up of the Soviet Union and the Eastern Bloc ten years ago has not come true.

Scenarios for the future of the *Baltic states* after 1991 – especially for Latvia and Estonia – often forecast either expulsion/emigration of the stateless Russian-speaking population or a civil war-like escalation. Instead, the high proportion of stateless Russian-speaking residents and the model of an ethnic democracy in Latvia and Estonia led to considerable tensions between the titular nation and minority as well as between national governments and European organisations. In the past couple of years, however, citizenship, language and other minority laws have been changed considerably and have thus been largely adjusted to European standards. It is true that this has not as yet led to a massive speed-up in nationalisation and integration, but the danger of an escalating ethnic conflict has been reduced. Unfortunately, the same cannot be said of the border issues, which despite lengthy negotiations, have not yet been resolved by treaty.

The danger potential inherent in minority and border conflicts in *Central and eastern Europe* was estimated to be much lower from the outset, as on the one hand, the mutual minorities were not as large and were better integrated, and on the other hand, the ethnic-historical legacies and regional concepts of an enemy were less pronounced. Nevertheless, it has to be taken as a positive sign that there has never been a serious attempt at reversing the numerous border changes made in the wake of the Second World War. Bilateral basic treaties ensure the borders and the protection of minorities in this region.

Although there are also positive developments in *Southeastern Europe*, like government participation for the Hungarian minority in Romania, the Turkish minority in Bulgaria or various nationalities living side by side in one state as in Bosnia or Macedonia, the overall picture is still overshadowed by the Albanian and Serbian questions, and the corresponding violent dissolution of the Yugoslav Federation in the past ten years. As a consequence, many conflict potentials concerning minorities and borders on the "Western Balkans" could only be contained by means of massive international commitment, political, diplomatic and military intervention. On balance, the Europeans achieved few successes and many defeats in this region. Even after the war in Kosovo, there still remains a long list of unsolved ethnical-historical claims and persistent enemy figures: the *de facto* division of Bosnia, the Serb minority in Kosovo, the Albanian minority in southern Serbia, the first stages of a repatriation of refugees, etc. Furthermore, the promising tendencies in the neighbouring states are much too fragile to rule out regional consequences from the conflict potential on the "Western Balkans".

Overall, the importance of minority and border issues for the transformation and accession countries has decreased significantly, from a domestic policy as well as from an international perspective. Implementation of the laws and social integration of minority groups are challenges still to be met. There are no signs of an escalation of violence or a destabilisation of the national economy and society in any region, and in none of the minorities. The inherent tensions and competition between majority and minority are mainly fought by means of the legal institutions and procedures provided for that purpose, and often have converted themselves into questions of socio-economic or regional disadvantages.

Despite some reservations, this positive overall balance is due to the direct and indirect work of several European organisations, whose division of labour is part of the secret for success. The European Union contributed substantially to the success of the transformation to market economy and democracy by means of support from the outside, and since 1993, the Copenhagen Criteria have provided an almost unsurpassable incentive for the transformation countries and their political elites to adjust their minority policy and legislation to "European standards". This is also the point where the institutional division of labour started: While the EU limited itself in the *acquis* to relatively basic requirements, which mainly comprised generally accepted human and minority rights as well as the recognition of European borders, the CoE and the OSCE took on the task of formulating legal norms and the transfer and implementation of these norms. While the CoE formulated important legal norms laid down in the Framework Convention for the protection of national minorities and the European Charter for Regional and Minority Languages, OSCE missions mediated in minority conflicts in Tallinn, Riga, on the Balkans, as well as in Chisinau or Tbilisi.

2.1.1 *Present and future risks*

In spite of the success story outlined above, four big risk areas can be identified for the years prior to and after a (phased) enlargement of the EU towards the east:
1. The requirement of a solution to the minority and border conflicts as a *condition for EU and NATO membership* undoubtedly has its justification and its uses from a European-security perspective. The dangers of this conditionality, however, are just

as straightforward: States opposing the EU or NATO membership of their neighbours are given additional political means to exert pressure, and an incentive to keep up conflict-laden issues or even to create them and to torpedo constructive approaches to a solution. While the potential Moscow is able to mobilise among the Russian-speaking population in the Baltic states is steadily decreasing in the run-up to EU membership (not, however, the emotional power and capacity for political instrumentalisation of this question on the Russian side of the border), the lack of border treaties is gaining sensitivity and leverage. Not for nothing are the expectations and rates of assent for EU membership among the Russian-speaking population in the Baltic states often higher than among Baltic nationals. For Moscow, however, the minorities in the Baltic states and unsolved border issues remain a compelling argument for a say in the process of enlargement towards the east.

2. The question of *"European responsibility" for national minority policy* also creates the danger that governments and/or political parties might be tempted in their domestic policy to pass off the adjustment of minority rights to European standards as the unavoidable price for the advantages of EU membership, thus washing their hands of all responsibility, with the resulting consequences for the implementation of the laws and long-term multi-ethnic integration. There may be less cause for alarm because of the dynamism developing in the minority and integration policy of the accession countries in the last couple of years: the ambitious integration projects in Estonia and Latvia, as well as a certain snub of nationalist rhetoric in the politics of other accession states.

3. As a rule, the EU accession of each country will inexorably lead to further stabilisation and development of the national economy, which in turn will increase the economic and social asymmetries along the outer borders. From a European perspective, the possibly increasing asymmetries between ethnic minorities and their home states (or vice versa) caused by this development are less important than the sometimes fatal ethno-political *nexus between nationalities policy and transformation policy* within the accession countries themselves. Often ethnic minorities are concentrated in regional, sectoral, social, or economic areas, which makes transformation decisions in the corresponding policy fields particularly sensitive and may even prevent decisions. The structural, regional and social policies of the EU are also acquiring an additional dimension. On the one hand, the EU has been given instruments to counterbalance social and regional disparities and thus make a positive contribution to the reduction of potential for ethnic conflict, while on the other hand, ethnic arguments and motives may have a negative influence on the implementation of these EU programmes.

4. Within the framework of the general dilemma between *permeability and border*

control, special attention should be paid to transnational minorities. While there is a widely accepted opinion that state borders might lose their separating effect and turn into bridges between peoples and states within a supranational European framework, decreasimg the separation between the minority and its neighbouring mother country, an unmodified implementation of the Schengen rules would have a counter-productive effect at, respectively, the temporary and the future outer borders of the EU. After enlargement, the outer border of the EU might impede contact between members of ethnic minorities and their respective homelands. The general paradox of this situation is the fact that the price to be paid for optimising the opportunities for contact and integration across national borders *within* the European Union would have to be paid by the transnational minorities on both sides of the *outer borders* of the EU. Thus the Schengen acquis and the bilateral border treaties proposed by the EU collide.

While some of the risks mentioned would become obsolete with the signatures to the Act of Accession, others would only then unfold their destabilising potential. Generally this leads up to the question – no longer hypothetical since the "Austrian crisis" – of an EU strategy in case the legislation of a new member deviates widely from the European standards in the area of minority policy, or fails to implement the laws and international treaties, e.g., because of a change in government or a domestic policy crisis.

2.1.2 *A European framework for minority and border issues*

In view of the successes of the past, the recommendations will be directed at how to prepare for the challenges posed by aligning and integrating Southeastern Europe, and for dealing with the effects of destructive elements in Baltic-Russian relations, on European relations with Russia, and vice versa.

In the run-up to enlargement towards the East, the *Baltic region* will become a point of friction between Europe and Russia. Here regional conflicts turn into European issues. Without conceding a say in the accession proceedings of individual candidate countries to Moscow, there are two ways in which a constructive involvement of Russia could be achieved in order to prevent an indirect blockade, which would furthermore (because of the lack of border treaties) toward the EU policy of cross-border co-operation. Organisations like the OSCE, the Baltic Sea Council or the CoE with a membership beyond the future EU borders to the East, offer a forum and a framework for co-operation which include the neighbouring countries in a constructive way and which allow first steps to turn *border regions* into *sub-regions*. On the other hand, a timely decision about date and extent of a first round of enlargement would allow for finding ways to clarify and, wherever possible, limit in a joint effort between Brussels, the border countries involved and the East Slavonic neighbours the negative consequences (e.g., the question of visas, border traffic, transitory regulations, trade policy) of enlargement towards the east for the latter where there is a justified interest.

On the condition that consolidation is achieved in *Southeastern Europe* and especially in the "Western Balkans" that translates the minority questions from the area of military and civil war violence into questions of national legislation and international treaties, it would be possible to continue the tried and tested division of labour among EU, OSCE and CoE.

When all is said and done, the EU will make its biggest contribution towards a solution of the minority and border conflicts indirectly through the normative power of the accession process and the stabilising power of funding programmes, and economic union. It is right in limiting its normative role in the nationality and citizenship policy, which is one of the core areas of national sovereignty, to some few fundamental principles based on a consensus that consists of recognised basic rights and democratic principles. As even the EU-15 have hardly been able up to now to agree on farther-reaching binding agreements, it would be presumptuous for the EU to take the vanguard role in this area. Especially in view of their specific aims, their intergovernmental mode and their broader membership, the OSCE and CoE are better equipped to regulate minority conflicts, even beyond the borders of the ten accession candidates. It will be a special challenge for the EU in view of this pan-European responsibility to use its various economic and political instruments in a flexible way, also with respect to political and social developments, while at the same time bearing its own stability interests and geopolitical aspects in mind, instead of approaching this matter unilaterally in a prescriptive way along strictly normative lines. This requires a strengthening of the Common Foreign and Security Policy.

2.2 Pan-European security

2.2.1 *Regional conflicts as European risks*

The security policy challenges in Europe resemble an equation with two variables: On the one hand there are numerous regional risks in the future neighbouring countries, which are often difficult to identify and to regulate from the outside because of the multitude of interests and players involved, and on the other, the European players only have limited foreign and security policy capacities and competencies at their disposal.

Instrumentalisation of frozen conflicts: This is a special type of conflict which may be characterised as frozen conflict. This type of conflict serves to compensate deficits in shaping the transformation. A striking example is provided by the conflict in Chechenya: Without a concept for economic and political reforms, the escalation and de-escalation of the Chechen conflict has repeatedly been a central topic for Russian election campaigns. Pre-modern, because ethnically dominated, conflict lines are to replace the really sensitive issues of a sustainable implementation of the transformation process.

The only insufficiently accomplished tasks of the transformation process in the future neighbouring countries contain a twofold security risk: On the one hand ethnic tensions, weak national consolidation, dependence on Russian raw material supplies, economic problems and social conflicts are causing extended security risks. Even if the development up to now has been much more peaceful than expected at the beginning of the transformation process, there are still regional trouble spots. This means that further escalation cannot be excluded. In addition, the growing asymmetries with Western Europe are increasing the risk potential. On the other hand, there is the fear that political decision-makers will contribute to the escalation of regional conflicts in order to distract from the failures of transformation and demonstrate national strength to the outside world. Given such a scenario, the interest in a lasting solution of regional problems would be limited in so far as they are being instrumentalised for political and economic aims beyond crisis management.

With progressing EU enlargement towards the east, a part of these frozen conflicts would move into direct neighbourhood to the EU. Despite some progress in the integration of the Russian-speaking part of the population, Russian decision-makers and the media still claim that Russian interests in Estonia and Latvia are only insufficiently protected. Against Ukraine, too, Putin is taking an increasingly offensive course by demanding settlement of the energy debts and at the same time rerouting pipelines to bypass Ukraine. This policy is being criticised not only in Kiev, but also increasingly in Warsaw. If Poland and the Baltic States are admitted in the first round of enlargement, these conflicts would mean immediate security risks for the EU.

Better than any other border region in Europe, Southeastern Europe demonstrates the linkage between hard and soft security risks and thus the value of a combined strategy of CFSP, regional economic power, and membership prospects that could only be offered by the European Union. The nexus between national conflicts, transformation deficits, state crises as well as regional, ethnic and social disparities requires a set of instruments for as broad a range as possible. While NATO and the USA have taken on the burdens and the responsibility for the military phase in the Kosovo conflict, their instruments, or rather their capacities, for involvement in the comprehensive and long-term phase of reconstruction after the war are limited. The EU as a regional power inherently carrying out its Balkans policy without an exit strategy would be in a position to use its economic prosperity and political stability to good effect in this context, together with EU prospects flanked by the Stability Pact, as well as stabilisation and association processes as long-term, credible commitment.

Nevertheless, the presence of the European economic space and the geographical proximity of enlargement towards the East also contain new risks for Southeastern Europe. Massive guidance form the outside always implies the danger of "aid addiction" and an excessive expansion of economic crime and state corruption at the expense of the civil society, state consolidation and self-supporting development of the national economy.

The dilemma resulting from this constellation and EU strategy is the contradiction between conditionality of eastward enlargement (and the stabilisation and association process) on the one hand and the security and stability tasks of the EU beyond its own borders on the other. Consequently not only are the efforts at transformation rewarded but also, if the worst comes to the worst, transformation failures and regional instability.

European security and defence policy: The currently existing security conflicts along the eastern and southeastern borders highlight the European institutions' insufficient potential to act. Despite progress in the European security and defence policy, the power of the European organisations is limited to conflict prevention and the setting of norms from the outside. The security and defence policy competence of the EU and the OSCE may in the first place be characterised as peacemaking and norm-setting policy. Consequently their field of action is limited to the prevention of conflicts that have not yet erupted into violence and to rebuilding stability once the military conflict is over.

In contrast to American foreign policy, the EU has the advantage that the Eastern European players see it as a regulating power without claims to dominance. The European institutions have correspondingly few possibilities to cope with conflicts that have already erupted into violence. They do not correspond to the threat potential of future neighbourly relations. The imbalance between security policy tasks and the European institutions' still limited possibilities to act can however be seen as follows: The new challenges will give important impetus to the intensification of integration and to the extension of security policy competencies in the European institutions.

2.2.2 *Strategic elements for an extension of European security policy*

The combined strength of the OSCE, the CoE and above all the EU lies in the numerous options available to them for conflict prevention. In view of the new security policy challenges in the context of EU enlargement towards the east, it is necessary to extend and specify these competencies in accordance with the given circumstances. The instruments of setting standards through prescribing aims and of supporting the transformation process should be used as far as possible to reduce the asymmetries along the lines of the future outer border of the EU. This recommendation is based on the findings of peace and conflict research that growing asymmetries lead to increasing security risks.

This policy has to be seen realistically, though: The range in which standards can be set is defined through the possibilities of linking them to positive or negative sanctions. The biggest influence can be exerted in the phase before accession, when the adherence to Western standards is a condition for accession.

In view of the difficulties of the transformation and the limited possibilities of setting norms from the outside, it is only realistic to assume that economic crises and political instabilities will continue to exist. In order to be able to institutionalise the resulting relations in the medium term, recourse can be drawn from experiences during the East-West conflict, when relations were less a partnership between equal players than among unequal players. Despite this inequality, it was nevertheless possible to find institutional regulations for particular aspects of relations. This experience of the creation of – relative – security in spite of asymmetrical starting conditions is to be utilised in the security policy approach towards neighbourhood relations by the enlarged EU. This approach should be supplemented by the development and implementation of a European early warning system for regional conflicts. The intensified co-operation in security and defence matters agreed at the EU-Russia summit in Paris on 30 October 2000 is a step in the right direction. In view of the high degree of inscrutability in the transformation, the security risks and the players, an effective policy of conflict prevention can only function on the basis of regular and wide-ranging risk reports.

Far beyond the present possibilities for conflict prevention, EU enlargement towards the east also represents a security policy challenge which should give European integration a push in the direction of a Common Security and Defence policy.

2.3 Visa policy and border control

2.3.1 The risk of new dividing lines

The European Union has been given the historical chance to create a new order in Europe. This task, however, threatens to drift off into the dilemma of diverging interests: On the one hand, Europe is no longer in principle divided into East and West by opposing systems. On the other hand, the disintegration of the old system of power leads to new borders being created. Dividing lines no longer threaten to develop from ideological differences but rather from economic and social asymmetries. Like no other European organisation, the EU is taking on a double function in this context. It is seen as the guarantor of economic stability and modernisation. At the same time it defines its integration area on the inside, and establishes common outer borders through the creation of common asylum, immigration and visa law. The introduction of visa regulations figures among the politically sensitive topics of EU enlargement towards the east, and has additional implications for the new European order. Western decision-makers are faced with the dilemma of divergent interests between asylum, immigration and visa policy on the one side, and foreign and security policy aspects on the other. In normative declarations of intent, treaties and summit meetings, the players underline the importance of extending cross-border co-operation, and it is emphasised that enlargement towards the east should be shaped in as open a manner as possible.

Internal security and common European stability: Contrary to these proclaimed aims, the political decisions of the EU are much more dominated by the real or assumed pressure of migration from the outside and the maintenance of internal security: As a precondition for accession, the candidate states have to adjust their visa policies to EU regulations.

With forming and consolidating new national states, decision-makers are confronted with new problems of establishing borders, border control and visa regulations. On the rhetorical level at least the Central and Eastern European countries agree with the position of the EU; they aim at avoiding new dividing lines through EU enlargement towards the east. They differ in the way in which they translate this aim into political decisions. The following factors are important in this process: Orientation towards EU standards aimed at accession as early as possible, historical legacies in relations with the eastern neighbours, questions of national sovereignty and identity, and national minorities in the neighbour states. This list makes clear that the introduction of visa regulations touches upon numerous other interests above and beyond the technical-administrative issues.

Concrete formulation and the resulting need for action can best be illustrated by taking examples from the regions concerned. The countries closest to the EU position as regards the introduction of visa regulations are the *Baltic states*. In order to enter Estonia, Latvia or Lithuania from Russia, Belarus or the Ukraine, it is necessary to get a visa. Some few exceptions are limited to regular border traffic and special regulations for public holidays, political dialogue and family matters. As there is a high proportion of Russian-speaking inhabitants in Estonia and Latvia in particular, and in addition frontier regions with unsolved border issues or even divided cities like Narva-Ivangorod, these regulations lead to social hardship and economic problems in individual cases. The difficulties are mainly emphasised by regional decision-makers, who are directly concerned with these problems. The overall picture shows that the introduction of restrictive entry regulations, but creates follow-up problems at the same time. The limited cost-benefit ratio of this policy is demonstrated by the fact that smuggling and cross-border crime continue to be problems in all Baltic states, despite these regulations.

Deterioration of bilateral relations: The greatest caution in the introduction of visa regulations can be found in Polish-Ukrainian relations: According to the current regulations, Ukrainian nationals may enter Poland without a visa for a maximum period of three months, which means that the candidate country Poland deviates from the present visa regulations of the EU vis-à-vis Ukraine. The introduction of visa regulations would not only make the relations more complicated on the administrative level; players on both sides also interpret them as indicators for new dividing lines. At the same time, Poland belongs to the first round of EU applicants, which would according to current EU policy, mean an end to visa-free travel with Ukraine. In order to do justice to both sides, so to speak, the Polish government is postponing the introduction of visa regulation to as late a date as possible. At the same, time individual decision-makers vote for the implementation of exceptional rules or even uphold the maximum claim of visa-free travel. The case of Poland illustrates how the unresolved contradictions between stability beyond the future borders of the EU on the one hand and internal security on the other may condense to a dilemma for Direct Neighbourhood.

Against it, Southeastern Europe is not developing into a duty and visa-free zone; there is rather an abundance of intransparent and inconsistent bilateral regulations, between the states and political entities of the region and the EU countries as well as within the region itself. Yet it is an undisputed fact that greater effectiveness, optimisation and wherever possible loosening of the border regulation would strongly contribute to greater understanding between the peoples, cross-border co-operation, reduction of regional and ethnic conflict potentials and strengthening of economic activities.

Risk of an aggravation of minority problems: In addition to unresolved questions of nationhood, minority interests also influence the content of the visa regulations. In order to adjust its regulations to EU requirements, the Romanian government has tightened its entry regulations for nationals of neighbouring *Moldova*, effective 1 July 2000. Now it is necessary to present a passport upon entry into Romania. In order to circumvent these formalities, many Moldovan citizens used the possibility to apply for Romanian citizenship in addition to their Moldovan citizenship. Should Romania enter the EU, Moldovan citizens with double nationality would also obtain EU citizenship.

Special problems arise in all those cases, where minorities live in a neighbouring country which would come under EU visa regulations in the course of EU enlargement towards the east. Should Romania not be among the accession candidates in the first round of enlargement, the Hungarian minority would be separated from its home state through a visa border. Neither Hungary nor Romania is interested in straining the political climate through travel restrictions for minorities if they want to travel into their mother countries, or even causing minority conflicts.

The list of empirical cases illustrates the variety of constellations and interests, showing that visa regulations embody highly sensitive issues connected with EU enlargement towards the east, over and beyond the technical-administrative aspect of issuing visa, passport and border control. The introduction of visa regulations in accordance with the Schengen agreement will, however, by no means meet all expectations put into it. Cross-border crime, smuggling and migration can only be contained through tightened visa regulation to a certain extent. Questions of minority and citizen rights may be so contradictory to visa regulations that they contribute to circumventing EU regulations. Yet visa regulations need not necessarily lead to the erection of a new Iron Curtain. The important issue is to recognise the political options in time and to use them accordingly.

2.3.2 A European strategy for controlled permeability

Up to now the visa strategy of EU eastern enlargement has been restricted to the requirements of the *acquis communautaire*. Seen in isolation, this is a transparent as well as stringent approach for the accession countries. There is great need for an active visa policy which would go beyond the technical, standardised aspects of the Schengen regulations. In view of strategic requirements, the EU has assumed a great deal of responsibility for maintaining safety and stability in Europe as a whole. Beyond pure norm setting, the EU should take a proactive stance in shaping the process. This approach can be divided into more technically-oriented and more politically co-operative aspects.

Technical-administrative optimisation: Technical regulations for visa requirements must be aimed at making issuing visas and entry formalities as simple and cost-efficient as possible. As is already the case at the moment, Phare and Tacis funds may be used to establish and extend border crossings and consular departments according to Western standards. Apart from the financial support, eastern border officials should be trained in the west, and western experts sent to the future outer borders of the EU. These processes could already be started before the accession procedures. The co-operation on the level of customs and visa policy should also be extended to a kind of common migration policy with the future neighbouring countries.

The more the process of issuing visas follows the criteria of efficiency and transparency and avoids incurring extra cost, the less the Schengen border will be regarded as a new Iron Curtain.

With the help of a targeted information policy, the introduction of technical regulations should be made as transparent as possible. By making the administrative procedures for visas less complicated, it would be possible even today to improve the negative image of the Schengen regulations. The administrative procedures for issuing visas to members of minorities who want to visit their mother countries and to residents of the Kaliningrad region should be made particularly easy.

Demands for standardisation or even annulment of the visa and customs regulations in the "Western Balkans", however, are still unrealistic and premature. Not only are some weaker states dependent on direct revenues from duties and similar incomes, the new entrepreneurs in particular also profit from the low degree of institutionalisation of the market economy. A future EU border will moreover cut through this region and in the process integrate the more successful and more stable transformation countries and separate them from the region. The asymmetrical trade concessions for the "Western Balkans" recently declared by the EU are an indication of the new cost-benefits calculations regarding the region's integration with the EU, and a European economic area featuring differentiated integration.

Cross-border co-operation: Even a perfect technical and organisational introduction of visa regulations will necessarily lead to new dividing lines being drawn. In order to counteract this process, EU and Council of Europe should establish a second pillar of active visa policy based on measures for cross-border co-operation. This would comprise the whole range of cross-border and inter-regional co-operation, starting with economic co-operation via student exchanges up to co-operation between border administrations. Special attention should be paid to those economic and social initiatives of cross-border co-operation which promise spill-over effects for other areas of co-operation.

The political postulate must be to alleviate the consequences of the erection of visa-related dividing lines through as comprehensive a European support as possible for social, economic and political relations reaching beyond future EU borders.

2.4 Regional and cross-border co-operation

2.4.1 *The potential of co-operation*

Multilateral, interstate co-operation and cross-border, sub-state co-operation have similar political and social potential, but they also generate similar resistance and contradictions in the European context. While the continuing process of European integration and the abolition of internal borders create security risks and create new requirements for securing the outside borders, an exclusion of the direct neighbours from this Europe integrating itself would in turn contain a risk potential. Enlargement towards the east thus has stabilising and destabilising consequences at the same time.

This issue of finding a balance between the export of stability and import of instability, between internal and external security as well as between border control and permeability is an issue for the EU as a whole but also for the individual states. In this sense it is important for Europe to guarantee a certain institutional plurality, which would reach across the emerging geographical finality of the EU, by way of regional co-operation. The Baltic Sea Council and Black Sea Co-operation are outstanding regional examples for stabilising forums of multilateral and interstate co-operation. For the nation states sub-state, cross-border co-operation has a comparable function. Very often border regions are not only traditionally peripheral and structurally underdeveloped, but have also been hit especially hard by the changes in function and permeability of particular borders in the past ten years, by the disintegration of the Eastern Bloc and the Soviet Union to start with, and now by the process of EU enlargement towards the east. It would therefore serve the purpose of furthering cross-border co-operation to counteract the increase of economic asymmetries and disparities and to utilise synergy effects across the borders, in order to decrease the corresponding potentials for conflict. Thus regional and cross-border co-operation are not only key factors of European prosperity, but also of European security, in the sense of soft security.

"Regionality" is one of the fundamental principles of EU policy. The East Central European experience since 1989 has shown, however, that the attractiveness of EU membership and competition on the way to full membership have had rather detrimental effects on regional co-operation between the accession states, in particular across the "future" external border. The development up to now has shown that the East Central European countries' commitment to accession has been harmful rather then helpful for political as well as economic co-operation between the candidate countries, and has in addition led to an excessive reduction of forms of economic and political co-operation with respect to the neighbours to the east. Often the commitment to regional co-operation across EU borders will only return after EU accession, in an effort to establish a regional counterbalance, also with respect to foreign policy competence, to the "core of Europe".

This is why the EU is the driving force behind projects of multilateral regional co-operation. Co-operation in the Baltic Sea region is an excellent example: On a Finnish initiative, the EU supports co -operation among the countries bordering the Baltic Sea in the fields of energy, natural resources, environment, border control transport and infrastructure in the *Northern Dimension*. This is on the one hand aimed at increasing the coherence of EU policy in these fields, on the other hand at binding Russia closer to the

European structures. By using this instrument, the EU succeeds in implementing incentives for cross-border co-operation as a supplement to the focus on accession negotiations in the candidate countries. The successful co-operation in the Baltic Sea area at the same time demonstrates the weaknesses of regional co-operation in East Central Europe. Co-operation between Poland and Ukraine is limited to bilateral commitments. The partly impressive results are only insufficiently taken up by European politics. Potential for EU norm- setting policy remains unused.

Despite the more than considerable financial framework supplied and the great number of successful projects carried out, especially in the area of cross-border co-operation, there are still obstacles and deficits to be found in the insufficient co-ordination and adjustment of programmes and funding schemes for cross-border co-operation. Border regions along the future external borders of the EU are beyond the brief of the EU General Directorates. With respect to East Central Europe they come under the heading of enlargement policy, while the border regions in East and Southeastern Europe are treated as part of the EU foreign relations. The funding programmes mirror this distinction: The Phare programme should improve the accession capacity of the EU-associated countries, while Tacis should help stabilise the transformation process in the successor states of the former Soviet Union. Applications for projects of cross-border co-operation have to meet the requirements of Phare as well as Tacis. This is not always possible without frictional losses. The new CARDS programme for Southeastern Europe will certainly also include an important component for cross-border co-operation. After Phare already had been converted from *demand-driven* to *programme-driven* in 1997 (i.e., funding of measures increasing accession capacity), this prioritisation would also present itself for the other programmes. This would mean, e.g., concentrating the programmes especially in Russia (which is different from the small and enclosed Balkans region) on the region of the western border. In this way it would be possible, bearing in mind the capacity limits of the EU, to reduce the asymmetries and follow-up questions of enlargement towards the east along this border in an optimal way: In the interest of Russia, but also in the interest of stability in Europe.

2.4.2 *Policy recommendations for regional and cross-border co-operation*

At the core of the recommendations in the area of sub-state cross-border co-operation is the recognition of the contradiction inherent in the policy goals and accession requirements for law enforcement and domestic policy on the one hand, and the funding programmes for cross-border co-operation on the other. From an institutional point of view, Phare belongs to the General Directorate (GD) for Enlargement and Tacis to the GD for Foreign Relations, whereas border protection belongs partly to the process of accession negotiations and partly to the GD Justice and Home Affairs. With the approach of the first round of accession in eastern enlargement – presumably 2005 – and the long-term movement of the "Western Balkans", including Yugoslavia, towards accession prospects, the question of an institutional and procedural separation between Interreg-CBC, Phare, CARDS and Tacis increasingly arises.

In supporting measures for cross-border co-operation, it is advisable to have a close look at which measures promise which success. Experience has shown that economic and social approaches also offer possibilities to overcome obstacles to co-operation like difficult political conditions or historical enmities. This kind of co-operation may then generate spill-over effects for a reduction of the number of politically sensitive aspects.

Based on the positive results of the *Northern Dimension*, this approach should be translated to Central Europe in the sense of providing a model for best practice. With a kind of "East Central European Dimension" the EU could make it clear that the fears felt by decision-makers in Kiev and Warsaw concerning new dividing lines are unfounded. At the same time the links between Ukraine and Europe would become more stable, which could contribute to the strategy of EU prospects for Ukraine.

The European Union's role and balance of achievements with respect to regional and cross-border co-operation have not been realised in an optimal way up to now; however, because the different functions of the Union as security provider, economic community and political alliance collide with each other in exactly those policy areas.

3 Beyond EU Enlargement – the Agenda

With its enlargement towards the east, the EU contributes to ensuring stability, and preventing conflicts in today's Europe. Despite the historic importance of this process, European politics has by no means reached its final peak. On the contrary, enlargement towards the east entails new risks, but also new chances. Continuing instabilities in the neighbourhoods of the EU – the Direct Neighbourhood of Ukraine, Russia, Belarus and Moldova for whom the Union has not formulated accession prospects so far, and the trouble spot Southeastern Europe with promises of EU prospects – challenge the Union in its capacity for setting norms.

The European security risks increase the pressure to establish a European regional power in the area of foreign and defence policy. New challenges are to be faced by synchronising various policy areas, requirements to act and European self-perception. These challenges are emerging especially in those areas where EU integration, enlargement towards the east and foreign relations overlap.

1. The European Union is increasingly taking over responsibility for *security and stability* in a far-ranging concept of Europe which not only comprises the accession states but also regions beyond the future external borders of the EU, whose instability has or may have repercussion on Europe. As a consequence, however, the other "mega-projects" of the EU, like enlargement towards the east, can no longer be dealt with in a purely normative way along the conditionality of the Copenhagen Criteria and the *acquis communautaire* but have to be seen in the broader context of regional stabilisation and geopolitics – as was recognised in Helsinki where the accession negotiations with Romania and Bulgaria were "brought forward". The contradiction between the normative conditionality of the accession process and the regional security policy requirements of a regional power, between quality and speed of enlargement towards the east is of a structural nature. However, as a consequence, it is not only the transformation efforts that are rewarded, but also, in the worst case, transformation failure and regional instability.

2. One strategic deficit of the policy of the European Commission vis-à-vis the CIS is its insufficient differentiation. Decisions must not be made along the lines of system transformation, but in addition also have to take the European self-determination of the states into account. The basic No to accepting CIS states willing to become members entails the risk of increasing instability caused by the rejection. At the same time the norm-setting policy of the EU loses its attractiveness and influence, as movement towards Europe or overcoming the problems of transformation respectively no longer carry the promise of positive sanction. In order to eliminate the strategic deficit of the basic No to EU accession of Ukraine and Moldova, the European Commission should formulate *EU prospects for Ukraine and Moldova*. The implications of this reversal of policy will, however, be limited to rhetoric until the states willing to accede can prove that they have made real progress in their transformation processes. This makes it even more important for the EU to emphasise the conditionality of the Copenhagen Criteria in its dialogue with the states concerned. In the Tacis projects to support the transformation process it is also important to point towards the *acquis communautaire* of the European Union in the sense of a normative aim.

3. As long as Belarus is dominated by the Lukashenko regime, it will remain a risky neighbour. It is in the European interest to contribute to securing stability through a *democratisation of Belarus*. Following the experiences in Serbia, it is necessary to support regional players and supporters of economic reform to bring about domestic change in Belarus and in this way to tighten the country's links to Europe. Apart from numerous possibilities of co-operation, it is first of all necessary to increase the presence of European institutions in Minsk.

4. In the relations between Russia and Europe, there is an important need for drawing up a *Kaliningrad strategy* in the context of EU enlargement towards the east. Technical questions regarding traffic of goods and people to and from Kaliningrad into the rest of Russia need to be treated in accordance with the EU regulations; solutions must, however, be easy to administer. The regional climate for investment in and around Kaliningrad must be improved through an extension of regional co-operation with the future EU members Poland and Lithuania. Russian decision-makers should strive to ensure political and legal stability. Under the proviso that Russia benefits from the innovations in the region, Moscow's isolationist and security policy reservations will also diminish.

5. In the case of Southeastern Europe the dilemma between the two EU principles of *regionality and conditionality* is much stronger than in the case of the ten present East European accession countries. In view of the attractiveness of EU membership and the heterogeneity of the neighbouring regions (e.g., "Western Balkans") regional co-operation will realistically come second behind a conditional, bilateral convergence with and integration into the European Union. Regional co-operation should accordingly be supported as a supplement to rather than as an alternative to EU integration.

6. By the same token, it is necessary to synchronise *EU integration and multilateral regional co-operation* in sub-regions which could eventually stretch across the external border. Organisations for interstate regional co-operation offer a constructive forum for dialogue and co-operation throughout Europe, especially where their aims, or rather their membership, reaches across present and/or future EU borders: *Northern Dimension, Black Sea Co-operation, Baltic Sea Council* and *OSCE*. On the other hand they serve as an important counterbalance for centripetal tendencies in Europe and turn peripheral border regions into European sub-regions.

7. Especially in the area of *cross-border co-operation*, it is imperative to subordinate the institutional-procedural framework to the functionality of the respective funding programme. Accordingly an adjustment or rather a merger of the EU programmes for cross-border co-operation – Interreg-CBC for EU members, Phare for accession countries, Tacis for CIS states, CARDS for the "Western Balkans" – would be appropriate for the state of the European integration and enlargement. As a model for interregional and cross-border co-operation, the EU initiative *Northern Dimension* should be translated into the form of an *East Central European Dimension* to relations between Poland and Ukraine.

8. Prioritising cross-border co-operation also requires a reconciliation with the requirements set for accession candidates by the *Schengen criteria*. While in view of the visa requirements, the erection of new dividing lines and thus an increase in the

asymmetries along these borders is unavoidable, the negative consequences, especially for the border regions, can be limited with the corresponding preparation and commitment. An *effective visa strategy* must consist of a dovetailed approach combining an optimum of technical-administrative procedures with measures of cross-border co-operation.

Overall it is part of the open self-definition of the EU not to pursue a foreign policy in the classical sense vis-à-vis its neighbours, but to offer conditional accession prospects. Up to now the inner prosperity and stability of the EU as well as the attractiveness of this accession offer have proved to be highly effective instruments in relations with the neighbouring transformation countries.

The debate about limits to enlargement should, however, give more consideration to the time dimension and the capacity of the EU to integrate new members. A Union which would, e.g. offer accession prospects to Ukraine – with the corresponding expectation management and time tables – can contribute more to a long-term reduction of national instability and transformation deficits of this neighbour. At the same time, guaranteeing the quality and the capacity of the union to integrate new members requires a more concrete concept for enlargement towards the east. Realistic expectations of management as well as the best-possible arrangements for follow-up issues in connection with the future neighbours, not least Russia, require an early setting of the date and the names for a first round of enlargement. If the EU were to come to a decision soon, this would on the one hand curb unrealistic expectations on the side of the candidate countries, and on the other hand leave enough preparation time to cushion the consequences of a temporary concrete exclusion for accession countries and third countries beyond the union. Typically, this will lead to a differentiated political and economic integration, in order to counterbalance destabilising asymmetries along the external border. Moreover, the process of reform and integration within the EU, Closer Co-operation as well as the gradual integration of the ten accession states will, in any case, bring the paradigm of differentiation to the fore in Europe. Differentiated integration were to acquire a particular urgency for security issues, if a new NATO enlargement were to occur prior to a first round of EU eastern enlargement. Differentiated integration overall requires a strengthening of CFSP, as apart from the "norm-setting" function, it is above all also the reactive capacity to decide and competence to act which will decide about the success of EU objectives for stabilising Europe as a whole.

Regional Reports

Southeastern Europe and the European Union: Problems, Actors, Policies

Martin Brusis, Nathan Galer

I Introduction

This chapter provides an overview of political, economic and social developments in Southeastern European countries from the perspective of the European Union. It is confined to the heterogeneous group of countries of the region that do not have the status of an EU member state or of an accession candidate, i.e., the countries referred to by the EU as the "Western Balkans": Albania, Bosnia-Herzegovina, Croatia, the Federal Republic of Yugoslavia (Serbia, Montenegro and Kosovo) and the Former Yugoslav Republic of Macedonia (FYROM). This chapter outlines the most relevant aspects of the transitions and conflicts related to the collapse of the former Yugoslavia, the current state of relations between the countries and the policies of important domestic actors towards the EU, in an effort to identify strategic actors the EU should address in its efforts to stabilise the region. The core argument is that the EU needs a differentiated strategy that reflects the wide diversity of actor and problem constellations in the countries and entities, ranging from milieu-shaping objectives and techniques in Albania, Bosnia-Herzegovina and FYROM to methods of directive intervention in Serbia, Kosovo, Montenegro and Croatia. In setting out these differences, this chapter considers each country/entity individually.

Beginning with Albania, section II identifies the key elements of the transition process in Southeastern Europe, focusing on its political, economic and social dimensions. In this respect, implications that this process has had for the European Union are also elucidated. After a brief overview of the Stability Pact and the envisaged Stabilisation and Association Agreements, section III continues by discussing the current contractual and political relationship between the aforementioned countries and the EU. Section IV deals with strategic actors in the Western Balkans, and identifies the direction and scope of their positions towards the EU, the integration process, and the general political interests of the West. The penultimate section explicates the implications of its predecessors in terms of policy priorities and recommendations for EU decision-makers.

II The political, economic and social transition in Southeastern Europe and its impact on the EU

This section commences by describing the main determinants of the comprehensive transition process the countries of Southeastern Europe have undergone since the demise of communism. Unlike the transition in Central and Eastern Europe, the development of the Southeastern European countries has been overshadowed by the wars in Croatia, Bosnia-Herzegovina and Kosovo.

During the Kosovo war, *Albania* had to cope with accommodating more than 450,000 refugees from Kosovo. Although the Albanian economy has profited from the demand generated by the Kosovo refugees, the deployment of NATO troops and the Western assistance operations, it is still lacking stable institutions and legal regulations required for a functioning market economy. Albania remains the poorest country in Europe with one of the highest shares of agricultural labour force, showing all the signs of structural backwardness that characterise less developed countries. The government has made progress in combating the armed criminal groups that gained power in large areas of the country after the breakdown of public order in 1997. However, the deficiencies of the judiciary system and widespread corruption constrain a more efficient prosecution of criminals. Due to the uncertain security situation, Albania remains one of the most important springboards for migrants trying to enter the EU. In 1999 the Italian Police caught 49,000 illegal immigrants on its Adriatic coastline; the number of Albanian citizens among them, however, amounted to only 7,000.[1]

The Kosovo war has not triggered a broad nationalist movement for a "Greater Albania". The current socialist government has declared its willingness to respect the existing borders and to support a solution of the Kosovo problem in the framework of more open borders and regional integration. The socialist party leaders intend to improve economic and cultural links between the ethnic Albanian communities in Kosovo, FYROM and Albania by facilitating cross-border trade, freedom of movement and co-operation between the education systems. Their victory in the local elections of October 2000 has strengthened the constituency they require to implement this policy.

---

1   ICG report No. 87: Albania: State of the Nation, 1 March 2000, p. 20.

Bosnia-Herzegovina had its own devastating war that destroyed the unique multi-ethnic structure of Bosnian society and territory. The quasi-protectorate of the High Representative, based upon the Dayton Peace Agreement of November 1995, has failed to construct a sustainable institutional arrangement for inter-ethnic co-existence. The joint institutions of Bosnia-Herzegovina – the Presidency, the Parliamentary Assembly, the Council of Ministers, and the Constitutional Court – exist only on paper, and their functioning is usually blocked by principal conflicts between the representatives of the three ethnic groups. About one half of the 2.1 million refugees and displaced persons have not returned to their homes. Returns of persons who constituted an ethnic minority in a given area mostly failed due to political and violent resistance of the local ethnic majorities. The High Representative in November 1999 issued laws that entitled refugees to claim the return of their flat/house and oblige the local administration to ensure the return of refugees if they desire so. Despite this reinforced commitment to a "minority return", the UNHCR meanwhile also considered the integration of refugees at their current place of residence as a second-best but viable option.[2]

The joint Bosniak-Croat-Serb presidency signed a declaration on 15 November 1999 that envisaged, inter alia, the establishment of a state border service, a Permanent Secretariat for the Joint Presidency, a new structure for the Council of Ministers, and the Presidency's support for a new electoral law. In the local elections on 8 April 2000, the Social Democratic Party won in Sarajevo and several other cities against the Bosniak Party of the Democratic Action, indicating a certain shift towards a political organisation with a non-ethnic orientation. However, this trend did not materialise in Republika Srpska and in parts of the Federation with ethnic Croat majorities, where the nationalist Serbian Democratic Party and the Croatian Democratic Community remained successful. Economic development is hampered by high tax burdens and a rapidly increasing amount of public debt. Massive inflows of foreign aid after the Dayton Agreement induced a high initial GDP growth that was interrupted by the Kosovo war, particularly in Republika Srpska. Industrial restructuring, the consolidation of the banking system and the expansion of a competitive private sector are the most important tasks ahead.[3]

After the death of President Franjo Tudjman, a significantly new political constellation has emerged in *Croatia*. In the parliamentary elections on 3 January 2000, the Croatian Democratic Community (HDZ) was defeated by a coalition of six opposition parties. This coalition consists of the Social Democratic and the Social-Liberal Parties,

---

2   Neue Zürcher Zeitung, 13/14 November 1999.

3   International Monetary Fund, Bosnia and Herzegovina: Selected Issues and Statistical Appendix. Staff Country Report No. 00/77, June 2000.

and of an alliance of the Croatian National Party, the Peasant Party, the People's Party and the Istrian Democratic Alliance. In the presidential elections on 7 February 2000, a constellation similar to a cohabitation emerged as the former Communist and HDZ politician Stipe Mesic defeated the candidate of the main governing party, the Social Democratic Party. While the Government and the President agree in principle on a constitutional amendment curtailing the President's powers, Mesic wants to retain the right to appoint ambassadors and the head of the secret service and to command the army. It is uncertain whether these claims can be reconciled with the weak role of the president preferred by the prime minister.[4] The new government strives to respect the freedom of media, cooperate with the International Tribunal in The Hague, participate in the Stability Pact and consider the Herzegovinian Croat community as an integral part of Bosnia-Herzegovina. In February 2000, the government prepared a plan to resettle 16,500 ethnic Serbian refugees. The Croatian foreign minister signed a common declaration with the prime minister of Republika Srpska on the mutual return of refugees. On 6 May 2000, Croatia concluded an agreement with the Bosniak-Croat Federation that provided a transparent regulation of Croatia's financial support for the Federation, entailing substantial curtailments. On 11 May 2000, the Croatian parliament re-instated the constitutional law on the protection of national minorities and adopted a law on the official use of and teaching in minority languages. Croatia joined the Partnership for Peace programme and the Euro-Atlantic Partnership Council on 24 May and the WTO on 17 July 2000.

Although Croatia has the strongest economy in the region, the decline of revenues from Adriatic coast tourism and the delay of structural and institutional reforms negatively affected its economic performance during the Tudjman era. Insider privatisation had a detrimental effect for the corporate governance structure of state-owned enterprises. Since 1997, the increasing volume of non-performing loans has endangered the stability of the banking system. In March 2000 the National Bank established direct control of the Istrian Bank in order to prevent its collapse. This intervention induced a political conflict in the governing coalition when the chairman of the Istrian Democratic Alliance and Minister of European Integration threatened to both leave the government and demand far-reaching autonomy for the Istrian peninsula. Croatia's exports to the EU amount to 49 per cent of its overall exports, imports from the EU comprise 57 per cent (1999), and the balance of trade with the EU is negative.[5]

Contrary to many expectations, the Kosovo war did not lead to a breakdown of the fragile democracy in the *Former Yugoslav Republic of Macedonia* (FYROM). However,

---

4   Frankfurter Allgemeine Zeitung, 13 April 2000.
5   COM(2000)311 of 24 May 2000.

the war and the massive influx of refugees imposed high burdens on the state and its population, and the embargo restricted the growth prospects of the economy. The parliamentary elections on 18 October and 1 November 1998 were won by a "Coalition for Change" consisting of the "Internal Macedonian Revolutionary Organisation-Democratic Party for Macedonian National Unity" (VMRO-DPMNE), the Democratic Party of the Albanians and the Democratic Alternative (DA). In December 1999, Boris Trajkovski of the VMRO-DPMNE won the presidential elections with the support of the ethnic Albanians. The local elections in September 2000 shifted voters' allegiances towards the opposition parties, i.e., the Social Democratic Union of Macedonia and the ethnic Albanian Party for Democratic Prosperity.

Suffering from the blockade of transit routes during the Kosovo war and from political instabilities in the neighbouring countries, the Macedonian economy has failed to improve its growth prospects and to overcome its inherited structural weakness. The unemployment rate is still extremely high, foreign direct investment stagnates at a low level, and the current account deficit is increasing. A large share of non-performing loans endangers the stability of the banking system. Initiating bankruptcy procedures against debtor enterprises is difficult and risky because some of the enterprises own shares of the banks that have loaned them money. To modernise enterprises, the government established an Agency for Reconstruction and Development in December 1998. FYROM's deficit in the balance of trade with the EU decreased from 1997 to 1998.

As a consequence of the war, Serbia's former autonomous province of *Kosovo* has come under UN administration, while formally remaining a part of the Federal Republic of Yugoslavia, whose borders remained unchanged. This ambiguous status is challenged by both Kosovo Albanian leaders who consider it as a pre-independent status and Belgrade which insists on its territorial integrity and which, in several cases, refused to accept visas issued for Kosovo by the United Nations Interim Administration Mission (UNMIK). The UN-led Interim Administration is composed of four pillars: humanitarian assistance (managed by the UNHCR), civil administration (UN), institution building (OSCE) and economic reconstruction, the task performed by the EU. UNMIK has gradually re-organised public institutions and normalised daily life Kosovo.

The economy of Kosovo is slowly recovering from war damage and the constraints on economic activities imposed by Serbian quasi-colonial rule in Kosovo. Until the war, the most important economic sectors were mining and agriculture. Furthermore, in 1998 private sector activity amounted to 80 per cent of GDP, and the per-capita GDP was estimated at US-$ 400. The war damaged approximately half of the 250,000 houses in Kosovo, led to a 65 per cent reduction of agricultural production in 1999, and nearly terminated industrial production. The assistance strategy of UNMIK and other international organisations aims at encouraging private sector activities in housing and agricultural production. Meanwhile, most of the private enterprises existing prior to 1999 have resumed operation, agricultural production has nearly reached the volume of pre-war years, and the construction sector is booming. UNMIK has permitted the use of DM as an official currency and established customs administration, public utilities and banking activities.[6] As the re-invigoration and expansion of the private sector is not linked to re-launching the previously state-owned enterprises, Kosovo Serbs, who were almost exclusively employed in the state sector, are losing their economic basis.[7]

Irrespective of the declarations and efforts of UNMIK and Kosovo Albanian leaders to preserve the multi-ethnic character of Kosovo, the bulk of the Kosovo Serb population left the area. The relations between Kosovo's ethnic Serbian and Albanian communities are characterised by persisting inter-ethnic violence: Ethnic Serbs loyal to Milosevic staged a protest against the alleged pro-Albanian policy of KFOR in the town of Kosovska Mitrovica that led to violent clashes between both communities. The climate of violence threatened the work of independent journalists who were intimidated by former members of the Kosovo Liberation Army (UCK) in several cases. Although Kosovo Albanian leaders condemned the violence against ethnic minorities, there appear to be groups of radical Kosovo Albanians that want to deter Kosovo Serbs from remaining in or returning to the area and have been intimidating moderate ethnic Albanian politicians. Apart from these struggles within Kosovo, an ominous Liberation Army for Presevo, Bujanova and Medvedja has attacked the Serbian Police in the Southwest Serbian region bordering Kosovo where a considerable ethnic Albanian minority lives. This army seems to aim at uniting the Albanian-populated area with Kosovo. In addition, several shootings have occurred on the Kosovo-Macedonian border.

While the UCK leaders formed a "provisional government" in April 1999, the government of the former Kosovo Albanian shadow state led by "President" Ibrahim Rugova still considers itself the legitimate representative of the Kosovar people. After the dissolution of the UCK in September 1999, most of its supporters created their own political party, the Party of Democratic Progress of Kosovo. On 21 May 2000, a first party congress renamed the party as Democratic Party of Kosova (PDK) and re-instated Hashim Thaci as the chairman of the Party. The UCK structures have been transformed into the Kosovo Police Service and the Kosovo Protection Corps. The ambiguous proto-army status of the Protection Corps indicates, on the one hand, the international community's interest in successfully demilitarising the UCK by providing UCK members

---

6   Report of the Secretary General on the United Nations Interim Administration Mission in Kosovo, S/2000/538 of 6 June 2000.

7   B. Haxhiu: Comment: The Unrealistic Dream of a Multi-Ethnic Kosovo, in: Balkan Crisis Report No. 144, 31 May 2000.

an alternative activity. On the other hand, the Corps enables UCK to persist as a nucleus of a future army for the independent Kosovo.

On 15 December 1999, UNMIK agreed with the Kosovo Albanian parties to abolish the provisional governments and the shadow state structures and to replace them with a Joint Interim Administrative Structure (JIAS) and a Kosovo Joint Interim Administrative Council. The JIAS functioned as an executive, and the Council was a representative body of political parties and ethnic groups in Kosovo. While Kosovo Serbs loyal to Milosevic refused to participate in the Council, the Serbs supporting Bishop Artemije and Momcilo Trajkovic made their co-operation contingent upon an effective protection of remaining and returning Kosovo Serbs.

Montenegro has increased its political and economic distance to Belgrade since the reform socialist politician Milo Djukanovic won presidential elections against Milosevic and the current federal prime minister, Momir Bulatovic, on 19 October 1997. The reform-oriented party coalition DZB (Da Zivimo Bolje) led by Djukanovic also won the parliamentary elections on 31 May 1998. During the Kosovo war Montenegro did not support the Milosevic regime and provided support for Kosovo Albanian refugees. On 5 August 1999 the Montenegrin Government proposed a "Platform for the Redefinition of State-Legal Relations between Montenegro and Serbia". This so-called Platform Proposal envisages that the two Yugoslav republics should be equal partners in a confederation and maintain independent foreign relations. Djukanovic has supported the Alliance for a Change founded by the democratic opposition in Serbia. Whereas the government is expecting Belgrade to offer negotiations on its Platform Proposal, separatist political actors in Montenegro are urging the government to hold a referendum on independence. An opinion poll conducted in February 2000 showed that 28 per cent of the questioned Montenegrins wanted to keep Yugoslavia in its current form, 23 per cent supported the confederation model proposed by the DZB and 36 per cent preferred to have an independent and sovereign state. Only 6 per cent of the respondents were in favour of uniting Montenegro with Serbia.[8] This split in the Montenegrin population was also reflected in the results of the local elections on 11 June 2000 which demonstrated a majority support for the DZB in Podgorica but a majority for the pro-Yugoslavia coalition in Herceg-Novi. As the Belgrade leadership imposed changes of the federal constitution in July 2000 against the will of Montenegro, abolishing the equal representation of the smaller republic in the second chamber of the federal parliament, the Djukanovic government called for a boycott of the federal elections in September 2000 that was supported by most Montenegrins. Consequently, Djukanovic did not

8   ICG report No. 89: Montenegro: In the Shadow of the Volcano, 21 March 2000, p. 11.

acknowledge Vojislav Kostunica as the new president of FRY – while accepting him as a leader of Serbia's democratic opposition.

The difficult economic situation facing Montenegro results from the subsequent wars that have isolated Yugoslavia's economy, hampered foreign and domestic investments, caused additional state expenditures for the war burdens and reduced the revenues from Adriatic coast tourism. These factors have been clearly recognised by the government which, in advocating its confederation model, also attempts at decoupling its economy from Serbia. As a first step towards more economic independence, the government introduced the DM as a second legal currency in November 1999. The objective behind the dual currency was to avoid the inflation of the Dinar, and was thus a response to the Yugoslav Central Bank policy of issuing Dinars to finance the costs of the Kosovo war and the reconstruction efforts. As a response, Belgrade suspended money transfers between both republics and imposed a trade blockade against Montenegro by closing the borders to traffic of goods in March 2000. The new Yugoslav President Kostunica lifted these blockades immediately after he had taken office. The introduction of the dual currency system has meanwhile slowed down inflation, but unemployment has risen, with an official unemployment rate hovering around 37 per cent. While the international community provided some aid, there was a lack of substantial support because donors hesitated to build relations with Montenegro as a non-sovereign entity and investors were put off by the political uncertainty. An increasing number of Serb paramilitaries entered Montenegro, and several confrontational incidents occurred between the Yugoslav army forces stationed in Montenegro and the Montenegrin police force.

In *Serbia,* a general strike and repeated demonstrations culminating in the occupation of the federal parliament on 5 October 2000 attained the resignation of President Slobodan Milosevic and the recognition of Vojislav Kostunica's victory in the federal presidential elections of 24 September 2000. The new president and the electoral coalition of opposition parties (DOS) that won the federal parliamentary elections, the municipal elections in Serbia and the elections for the assembly of the Vojvodina are faced with numerous difficult political and economic tasks. They have to organise the supply of sufficient energy and food for Serbia's population. The country's infrastructure was neglected during a decade of conflicts and economic regression, it suffered severe material damage during the Kosovo war and needs to be reconstructed. According to estimates of the G-17 group of independent economists, the per-capita income of Serbia fell from US-$ 2,941 (1989) to US-$ 950 in 2000, only slightly higher than the level of Albania, and the damage caused by the NATO attacks amounted to US-$ 30 billion.[9] The eco-

9   G17, http://www.g17.org.yu/english/index.htm; Frankfurter Allgemeine Zeitung, 9 October 2000.

nomic transformation needs to be continued, entailing many conflicting reform steps. The new political leadership has to re-define Serbia's relations with Montenegro, Kosovo, Vojvodina and Republica Srpska, with each of these "entities" posing highly controversial issues of Yugoslav-Serb state organisation and Serb national identity. Issues of justice, including the crimes of the Milosevic regime and the co-operation with the International Tribunal for War Criminals in the Hague will have to be addressed. The most challenging task for DOS leaders is probably to ensure the consolidation of democratic institutions and a democratic political culture in Serbia.

Despite its auspicious opinion polls, the electoral victory of the DOS coalition was far from safe. While the political protest movement launched immediately after the military defeat lost its momentum at the end of 1999, President Slobodan Milosevic managed to stabilise his power base in the Socialist Party of Serbia, the Army and the state apparatus. Forced constitutional changes in July 2000 introduced the direct election of the president and of the second chamber of the federal parliament, ensuring Milosevic' re-election and depriving Montenegro of its ability to block legislation on the federal level. The then strongest opposition party, the Serbian Renewal Movement (SPO), refused to co-operate with DOS in the electoral campaign. It was only the students' movement OTPOR, established after 1999, that emerged as a powerful political actor, combining its decentralised organisational structure with non-conventional forms of protest to effectively deconstruct the symbols and stereotypes of the regime.

One of the most imminent threats to the cohesion of the opposition leadership and the social movement that brought it to power is that Serbia's constitutional arrangement as a state has become highly problematic. The international administration in Kosovo has reduced Serbia's sovereignty over the former Autonomous Province of Kosovo to the control of Kosovo's external borders. Although the prospect of uniting Republika Srpska with Serbia has vanished with the international community's insistence on maintaining Bosnia-Herzegovina as an independent state, nationalists in Serbia and Republika Srpska continue to strive for a "Greater Serbia". Regionalist and ethnic minority parties in Vojvodina and Sandzak demand more autonomy to protect their cultural rights.[10] Opposition-led municipalities argue for a decentralisation that would enable them to solve the mounting economic and social problems themselves. Relations with Montenegro have been severely strained by the forced change of the federal constitution. These statehood conflicts and their symbolic importance may lead to the break-up of DOS since the coalition is composed of very heterogeneous political groups with rather different views on the conflicts.

---

10 For example, the Democratic League of Vojvodina in February 2000 demanded to transform Vojvodina into a constitutive Republic of FRY.

Table 1: Economic indicators (1998)[11]

	Albania	Bosnia-Herzegovina	Croatia	FYR of Macedonia
GDP (%)	8.00	18.00	2.30	2.90
GDP per capita (US-$)	930	972	4,820	1,548
Current account balance (m US-$)	−186	−1,097	−1,554	−318
Unemployment (%)	17.70	n.a	17.20	34.50
Inflation (%)	20.60	5.38	5.70	0.60
Private sector (% of GDP)	75.00	35.00	55.00	60.00

Reliable data for the Federal Republic of Yugoslavia are not available. GDP: estimated change in real terms; unemployment: estimated share of registered unemployed in labour force, annual average; inflation: estimated annual average change of consumer prices (data for Bosnia-Herzegovina distinguish between the Federation and the Republika Srpska); private sector: share of privatised and domestic private firms, as estimated by the EBRD (data for Bosnia-Herzegovina refer to estimates of the year 1999).

III Current relations of the Southeast European states with the EU

This section describes the current state of contractual and political relations between the Southeast European states and the EU, starting with a brief overview on the Stability Pact for Southeastern Europe. With its Stability Pact, the EU has committed itself to a much more substantial engagement for the long-term stability and prosperity of the region.[12] Apart from the political negotiation process initiated by the round tables, concrete and visible aid projects have been agreed on. Three donors' conferences in July 1999, November 1999 and March 2000 have mobilised more than US-$ 5 billion in aid commitments for approximately 300 projects.[13] About two-thirds of the sum will be spent on infrastructure projects. In view of the substantial EU aid and under diplomatic pressure from the EU, Romania and Bulgaria on 27 March 2000 agreed to build a Danube river bridge that will allow trans-Balkan traffic an alternative route to the Belgrade-Nis-Skopje motorway.

On 21 June 1999, the Council decided to offer Stabilisation and Association Agreements to all the Southeast European states. On 20 June 2000, the European Council

---

11 EBRD Transition Report 1999.
12 Cf. also the contribution of F. Schmidt and M. Uvalic in this volume.
13 The first conference yielded aid commitments of € 2.1 billion; the second donors' conference on 17 November 1999 attained a commitment of US-$ 1.35 billion for the reconstruction of Kosovo; on 29/30 March 2000 a third donors' conference mobilised US-$ 1.75 billion for approx. 300 projects.

in Feira for the first time stated that all former Yugoslav Republics are potential candidates for EU membership. The membership perspective is linked to the Copenhagen Criteria, i.e., the development of stable democratic institutions (rule of law, human and minority rights), a functioning market economy, the capacity to cope with competitive pressures inside the single market and the ability to adopt the acquis, accepting the aims of political, economic and monetary union. On 18 September 2000, the Council adopted a regulation that was envisaged to open the EU market completely to some industrial and agricultural products (except beef, wine and some types of fish) from Albania, Bosnia-Herzegovina, Croatia, FYROM and Kosovo. EU imports from Albania, Bosnia and Croatia are negligible, accounting for 0.6 per cent of total EU imports.[14]

In addition, the EU provides numerous forms of assistance to the countries of the region. It grants autonomous trade measures, provides economic and financial assistance, inter alia in the framework of Phare and OBNOVA, helps to stabilise the state budget and balance of payments, provides support for democratisation and civil society, participates in humanitarian assistance for refugees and returning people, offers co-operation in judicial and domestic policy and conducts a political dialogue. Among the Southeast European countries, Albania and FYROM have the most developed relations with the EU since they both have Trade and Cooperation Agreements and participate in the Phare programme. More than 80 per cent of the trade of the countries with the EU is duty-free. As far as relations with the Council of Europe are concerned, Albania, Croatia and FYROM became members in the mid-1990s. Bosnia-Herzegovina retains a Special Guest status, and FRY currently has no formal relations with the Council (see Table 2).

Since 1 December 1992 the Trade and Cooperation Agreement between the EU and *Albania* has been in effect. The Trade Agreement only envisaged most-favoured nation status. In the framework of the Agreement, four working groups have been established which are concerned with alignment and reform of legal regulations, customs co-operation, economic and financial questions, and agriculture and infrastructure. A separate agreement on textiles was in force between 1992 and 1995. On the basis of a Common Declaration of the EC and its member states a bilateral political dialogue was launched. Until 1999 four meetings on the level of ministers and five inter-parliamentary meetings were organised. Albania requested an Association Agreement in 1995, but the Commission in June 1995 did not consider the economic conditions appropriate for a Europe Agreement. According to the Commission,[15] Albania's problems were mainly the lack

14 Commission Press Release IP/00/586 of 7 June 2000.
15 COM(1999)599.

of institutional stability and its weak and dependent economy; establishing a free trade zone appeared to be problematic because the Albanian state drew high customs revenues from EU imports.

On 29 July 1999 the Council adopted a regulation on the regulation of imports from Albania and modified regulation No. 2820/98 on the General Customs Preferences with Albania. This regulation envisages additional autonomous trade preferences, transforming the Trade and Cooperation Agreement into an agreement similar to that for FYROM. The new trade preferences comprised an abolition of customs duties and quota for industrial goods (customs ceilings continue to be applied to some goods). The regulation stipulates specific customs ceilings for textiles and concessions for fishery products.

The Trade and Cooperation Agreement between *FYROM* and the EU has been in effect since 1 January 1998. The Agreement contains preferential regulation for imports of industrial goods from FYROM into the EU, some customs ceilings and concessions for agricultural products and an evolutionary clause envisaging further development of contractual relations towards an association agreement. Transport and textile agreements have been in effect since 28 November 1997 and 1 January 1997, respectively. Since April 1997 regular meetings have taken place between FYROM and the EU on the level of ministers, civil servants and parliamentary deputies.

On 24 January 2000 the Council adopted guidelines for negotiations on a Stabilisation and Association Agreement. According to the Conclusions of the European Council, this Agreement will include economic and financial assistance and co-operation, political dialogue, alignment with EU legislation, co-operation in other policy areas and free trade. The Commission aims to establish a free trade zone within 10–12 years by an asymmetrical liberalisation of tariffs and quotas for industrial and agricultural commodities.[16] On 7 March 2000 the Commission and the Macedonian government began negotiations on the agreement.

The EU has included *Bosnia-Herzegovina* among those countries with a perspective of a Stabilisation and Accession Agreement but due to the lack of progress in complying with the Dayton Agreement, no steps have been undertaken to establish contractual relations. Bosnia-Herzegovina participates in the OBNOVA programme.

Relations between the EU and *Croatia* have rapidly improved since the new Croatian government has taken office. The EU intends to directly conclude a Stabilisation and Association Agreement with Croatia, refraining from first agreeing to a Trade and Cooperation Agreement as in the cases of Albania and FYROM. As early as two months after the elections, the Council of Ministers invited the European Commission to elabo-

16   COM(1999)300.

rate a feasibility study to prepare negotiations with Croatia on a Stabilisation and Association Agreement. A Joint Consultative Task Force of the EU and Croatia met for the first time in order to support the technical preparation of Croatia for the negotiations on the Stabilisation and Association Agreement. In late Summer 2000 the Council mandated the Commission to negotiate a Stabilisation and Association Agreement with Croatia.

Relations with the EU and *Kosovo* are confined to the responsibilities of the EU within the framework of UNMIK. The EU has established the European Agency for Reconstruction in order to manage the implementation of economic reconstruction aid. The Agency is also charged with the task of facilitating the return of refugees into Kosovo. The Council included Kosovo into the OBNOVA programme that is applied in Bosnia-Herzegovina.[17]

Since the change of Government in *Montenegro*, the EU has tried to treat Montenegro differently from Serbia in its policy towards FRY. In October 1999 the Council decided to exempt Montenegro and Kosovo from the flight ban and the oil boycott imposed against FRY.[18] Since 1998 the EU has provided more than 100 million Euros in humanitarian, technical and financial assistance to Montenegro. Montenegro has opened a diplomatic mission in Brussels with the support of the EU. The European Investment Bank plans to grant a loan to Montenegro. In September 2000, the Council granted limited tariff quotas for Montenegrin aluminium products, which constitute an important export commodity of the Republic.

In its relations with *Serbia*, the EU quickly reacted to Vojislav Kostunica's appointment as President of Yugoslavia by lifting all sanctions imposed on FRY since 1998, with the exception of those measures targeted at Milosevic and his associates.[19] The Council invited FRY to participate in the Stabilisation and Association Process. The EU intended to set up a "Joint EU/FRY Task Force" preparing a Stabilisation and Association Agreement, to offer asymmetrical trade preferences to FRY, and to extend its aid and reconstruction programmes as well as the activities of the Kosovo-based European Agency for Reconstruction to FRY. The European Council of Biarritz provided immediate aid of 200 million Euros to Serbia. This rapid change of policy was not only induced by the interest in signalling EU support for the democratic change in Serbia, but can also be understood as a reflection of the increasing doubts over the efficacy of sanctions among EU member states.

17 EC Regulation No. 1628/96 of 25 July 1996, modified by the Council on 15 November 1999.
18 EC Regulation No. 1064/99 of 21 May 1999.
19 General Affairs Council of 9 October 2000: Declaration by the European Union on the FRY, Press Release No. 12123/00, http://ue.eu.int/Newsroom.

Until Kostunica's election, the EU had applied a diversified regime of economic, financial and political sanctions that became subsequently more targeted on representatives of the Milosevic regime. The Council barred selected Yugoslav citizens related to the Milosevic regime from receiving EU visas, extending its list in December 1999 and February 2000. While imposing extensive restrictions on oil and products to most of Serbia,[20] the EU supplied opposition-led towns with heating oil and asphalt in the framework of the initiative "Energy for Democracy".[21] The EU and the US also developed a trilateral co-operation with opposition representatives.[22]

In May 1999 the Council froze foreign accounts owned by the governments of FRY and Serbia as well as by companies and institutions controlled by, and persons related to, the governments of FRY/Serbia, banned new investments in Serbia, restricted the export of any goods, services, and technologies serving to repair equipment damaged by the air strikes, and prohibited public finance for privatisation in Serbia.[23] This was supplemented by the so-called 'White List' of 190 companies in Serbia to be excluded from the financial sanctions regime. It was expected to better target the financial sanctions against the governments of FRY and Serbia. In August 2000, approximately 300 Serb companies had applied for consideration, and a first provisional list of 240 companies was drawn up. However, this form of positive discrimination became increasingly criticised since the listed companies faced repressive actions by the Serbian government. Reacting to the changes in Serbia, the Council lifted the flight ban and the restrictions on the sale of oil products on 9 October 2000.[24] The embargos on arms sales and sales of material that might be used for internal repression and terrorism, however, remained in force.[25]

---

20 EC Regulation No. 900/99 of 30 April 1999, incorporated by EC Regulation No. 2111/99 and amended by EC Regulation No. 607/2000 of 20 March 2000.

21 EC Common Position 691/99 of 22 October 1999.

22 These meetings were attended by representatives of the Democratic Party, New Democracy, the Social Democratic Party, and the Civic Alliance, but not by the SPO.

23 Common Position of 10 May 1999 and Regulation No. 1294/99 of 15 June 1999, reinforcing previous Regulations. Montenegro and Kosovo were exempted from these restrictions (Common Positions 604/99 and 056/2000).

24 The ban had already been suspended on 20 March 2000 (EC Regulation No. 607/2000 of 20 March 2000).

25 Common Positions of 26 February 1996 and of 19 March 1998.

Table 2: Relations between the Western Balkan countries/entities and European institutions

Country/entity	EU	Council of Europe
Albania	Trade and Cooperation Agreement in force since 1 December 1992 Phare programme	Member since 13 July 1996
Bosnia-Herzegovina	OBNOVA programme since 1996	Special Guest status since 28 January 1994
Croatia	OBNOVA programme since 1996	Member since 11 November 1996
FYROM	Trade and Cooperation Agreement in force since 1 January 1998 Phare programme	Member since 9 November 1995
Kosovo	OBNOVA programme since 1999	–
Montenegro	–	–
Serbia/FRY	–	Expected to apply for Special Guest status

IV How strategic actors address EU concerns

This section describes the policies key political actors in the countries of Southeastern Europe have adopted with respect to the EU, European integration and the political interests of the EU in the region.

Although the primary political actors in *Albania* share the common goal of EU accession and integration into other Western institutions (such as NATO), the political spectrum has been characterised by inter- and intra-party division and antagonism. The Democratic Party, headed by former President Sali Berisha, boycotted the parliamentary vote of confidence for the newly appointed socialist government (lead by Fatos Nano), attempted a coup d'etat in September 1998, and has repeatedly called for early elections. However, within the Socialist Party the former Prime Minister Pandeli Majko represents a moderate alternative (in the sense that he is less likely to capitalise on extremist positions) to Nano, and critics of Berisha within the Democratic Party established a group called "Democratic Alternative" in November 1999. These rifts in both parties indicate that fundamentalist positions are giving way to more compromise-oriented and pragmatic political alternatives that may be able to rid Albanian politics of its divisive legacy.[26] Hopes for development of these moderate strains were dashed in

---

26   F. Schmidt: Generationskonflikte in Albaniens großen Parteien, in: Südosteuropa, 49 Heft 1–2/2000, pp. 32–50.

late 1999 when both Nano and Berisha successfully held off their younger challengers and maintained control of their parties.

However, the current socialist government, headed by the young and energetic Prime Minister Ilir Meta, has repeatedly demonstrated a willingness to push for Western integration through the framework of the Stability Pact and regional co-operation. Their continuing emphasis on open borders and integration seems promising in the wake of the "Albanian question". Indeed, Fatos Nano has emphasised the fact that there is no need to redraw the borders in the Balkans but to "make them irrelevant."[27] In contrast, the more problematic and politically destabilising attitude of the tough-talking DP fundamentalist Berisha is demonstrated by his October 1999 threat of an "Albanian Federation" to counter discrimination of ethnic Albanians in the region.

In *Bosnia-Herzegovina*, the 1998 general elections and the 2000 elections have again confirmed the legitimate powers of those Croat and Serbian parties that advocated ethnic cleansing, i.e., the Croatian Democratic Community (HDZ) in the ethnic Croat majority areas of the federation and the Serbian Democratic Party (SDS) in Republika Srpska. While this proved the failure of the international efforts to replace nationalist leaders with more moderate elites, a closer analysis of the municipal election results shows that moderate nationalists such as Haris Silajdzic in the Bosniak areas and Mladen Ivanic in Republika Srpska have successfully expanded their constituencies.[28] Yet, for the time being, there is no political majority that would represent a policy approach compatible with the objectives of the EU or the Dayton Peace Agreement. Neither the increasingly interventionist strategy of the High Representative, nor the perspective of EU association and membership was able to induce a fundamental change of political elites. The situation has changed in so far as nationalist Croat and Serb political actors in Bosnia-Herzegovina currently can rely less on economic support from their respective homelands. The new Croat government reduced its assistance for the shadow state structures of Herceg-Bosna. Belgrade's capacity to support Republika Srpska is restricted by its preoccupation with the domestic political changes. Pro-European actors in Bosnia-Herzegovina will probably only emerge in the form of a business community that is dependent on, and interested in, regional economic integration.

The new *Croatian* government has declared its willingness to comply with the Dayton Peace Agreement, facilitate the return of ethnic Serb refugees, participate in the Stability Pact and stop supporting the separatism of Herzegovinian Croats. While this policy coincides with the objectives of the EU more than the ambivalent policy of the

---

27   ICG interview with F. Nano, Tirana, 28 November 1999.
28   International Crisis Group: Bosnia's Municipal Elections 2000: Winners and Losers, ICG Balkans Report No. 91, 27 April 2000.

Tudjman government and the HDZ, it remains to be seen whether the heterogeneous governing coalition can maintain its cohesiveness over controversial domestic issues. Right-wing organisations have already staged a wave of protest and tried to instigate conflicts in ethnic Serb minority areas. Parts of the army have objected to the efforts to identify and send war criminals to the International Tribunal. Nevertheless, the new Croatian government is more committed to integration with the EU, envisages progress in EU integration as a major indicator for its performance, and can be addressed by the policy instruments of the EU. This opens a window of opportunity for the EU to use the upgrading of relations with Croatia as an example for Serbia and Bosnia-Herzegovina. The Racan government has been actively trying to strengthen its bilateral relations with Slovenia, Albania, Montenegro and Bosnia-Herzegovina in order to improve regional co-operation.

The *Macedonian* government has striven to build closer relations with the EU and to meet EU expectations, although many observers had considered two of its constituent parties, the VMRO-DPMNE and the ethnic Albanian DPA, as more nationalist and radical than the previous governing coalition. As long as closer co-operation with the EU does not lead to significant improvements in the economic situation in FYROM, this pro-European policy risks being subjected to nationalist strategies that play on the Albanian-Macedonian rift or on the threats to FYROM's statehood posed by the neighbouring countries.

FYROM is a highly centralised state, both politically and in terms of strategic actors. Regions or municipalities have little authority and scarce financial resources. Corruption, criminality, and legal inadequacies have prevented the development of a substantial private sector. In light of these circumstances, it makes most sense to focus on Skopje, and thus on the current ruling coalition, for the relevant actors with an orientation towards the West. All major parties in FYROM, including the long-ruling Social Democrats, have long shown a determinacy for the goal of integration in Western structures.

Most important in Western orientation is the senior partner in the ruling coalition, the VMRO-DPMNE, which is headed by Ljubco Georgievski and newly-elected President Boris Trajkovski. Through an ambitious and extensive election platform, the VMRO-DPMNE carefully avoided ethnic issues, pragmatically focusing instead on three key issues: the alignment of the economy with Western standards, the fight against corruption and organised crime in the region and the alignment of legal standards with EU requirements. In terms of foreign policy, Georgievski has been the most prominent advocate of Western institutions, claiming plans for membership in the EU, NATO, CEFTA, OECD, and WTO. Furthermore, he has pledged to develop close and friendly relations with FYROM's neighbouring "four wolves" and to work towards regional stability.

The remaining two coalition members, DPA leader Arben Xhaferi and DA leader Tupurkovski, have been quieter with broad rhetoric on Western integration. Although it is obvious that they do support such an orientation, each has preferred to spend more time focusing first on domestic issues. Xhaferi, on the one hand, seems to consider ethnic equality more important than integration towards the West, maintaining in a recent interview for the periodical Nova Makedonija that attempts towards political and economic improvement are useless without the resolution of ethnic tension. On the other hand, Tupurkovski has committed himself to economic reconstruction and development. Through the chairmanship of a self-created agency, Tupurkovski seems determined to attract and retain the involvement of the foreign community in FYROM in order to accelerate progress towards stability and prosperity.

However, much of this determination has remained rhetorical, and a significant portion of the stated reform has yet to be implemented. FYROM appears to be caught in stagnation, and in this loss of drive it is increasingly appearing as though the economic focus of the government may not be the most appropriate assessment or strategy for accession to the EU. This has been further demonstrated by continuing foreign policy difficulties with its four neighbours, as well as continuing ethnic tensions between Macedonians and Albanians.

The *Kosovo* Albanian political elite, like most other major political movements and parties in the region, generally supports Kosovo's integration into the EU but attaches a clear priority to the creation of an independent Kosovo. The PDK and the group around the prime minister of the provisional government, Hashim Thaci, and Rugova together with his party, the Democratic League of Kosova (LDK), were the main political forces competing for votes in the local elections of 28 October 2000.[29] As the constellation of political forces is still in flux, one can hardly assess whether the UCK-offspring PDK and Thaci or the LDK and its leader Rugova will develop a more EU-oriented policy. Thaci and Rugova continue to be clearly committed to an independent state of Kosovo.

Montenegro's political parties may be classified as Montenegrin separatists (LSCG, Miodrag Zivkovic), supporters of reform-oriented confederationist parties (DZB, consisting of the Social Democratic Party (SDP), Democratic Party of Socialists (DPS, Djukanovic), People's Party (NS), the pro-Yugoslav Socialist People's Party (SNP, Bulatovic) and Serb nationalists (SRS and Serb People's Party (SNS)). In the last parliamentary elections, most of the ethnic Albanians and ethnic Bosniaks voted for the DZB. The DZB is strongly interested in improving Montenegro's relations with the EU and uses any political gestures of the EU to demonstrate the success and expediency of its policy compared with the isolation of Belgrade. In contrast, the SNP and the Serb

---

29   S. Lipsius: Vorbild UCK: Albaner in Serbien gründen UCPMB, in: Südosteuropa 49 Heft 3–4/2000, pp. 133–143.

Nationalists take a critical stance towards the EU and the Western countries, accusing them of destroying Yugoslavia. The government has begun to develop its relations with Albania and Croatia. With Albania, concrete projects were agreed on to improve transportation, trade and telecommunication links. The Montenegrin President undertook a first step towards reconciliation with Croatia and apologised for the war damage inflicted by Montenegro when the Yugoslav Federal Army attacked Croatia in 1991. The Montenegrin government plans to participate fully in the Stability Pact framework and in 20 projects of the Pact.

In *Serbia*, the DOS coalition that supported the new President Kostunica and won both the federal parliamentary and the Serbian municipal elections consists of liberal and moderate nationalist parties. While sharing the general objective of a complete reintegration of Serbia into the international community, the parties seem to diverge with respect to issues affecting Serbian statehood and national interest. When DOS leaders rejected Montenegrin demands to become an independent state, they took a political position that, although driven by their objective to consolidate FRY, corresponded with the international interest of avoiding the creation of new states in the region. In order to induce the Montenegrin leadership to renounce its aim of independence, the new Yugoslav leadership has to address Montenegrin concerns, rebuild confidence in the other republic and, as a minimal concession, revert the changes of the federal constitution imposed by the Milosevic regime. This implies that a relationship of equality will be established for all dimensions of federal and inter-republican co-operation, thus arriving at a model that may contradict notions of a more integral state preferred by Kostunica and his associates on the one hand, and liberal representatives of the opposition movement on the other. The former seem to favour the project of a unitary, homogenizing Serb nation state designed according to the French example, the latter have shown a preference for a classical model of liberal democracy and rule of law that envisages strongly protected individual rights but no special rights for ethnic groups or territories.

In contrast with Serb-Montenegrin relations, Serb-Kosovo Albanian relations are far more difficult to mend, since the war and the atrocities of Serb troops in Kosovo have destroyed any Kosovo Albanian willingness to consider common statehood with Serbia. A rapprochement presupposes that Serbian society will come to terms with, and accept its responsibility for, the war crimes committed by the Milosevic regime. In addition, a dialogue with the Kosovo Albanians on the future status of Kosovo in relation to Serbia/FRY is impeded by the integral concept of a Serbian nation state prevailing among the DOS politicians, excluding any model of a loose (con-)federation of two plus one (Kosovo) or two (Vojvodina) republics. While there does not seem to be any viable settlement of the Kosovo conflict in sight, the DOS leaders will clearly refrain from questioning the de facto sovereignty of UNMIK, but continue to insist on the de jure sovereignty of FRY over Kosovo as stipulated in UN Security Council Resolution 1244. In their perspective, compliance will facilitate the re-entry of FRY into international organisations, and the international responsibility for Kosovo will relieve them from an additional burden during the period of economic and political transformation.

The DOS leaders of course know that an attempt at Serb nation-state building through an association with or integration of the Bosnian Serb entity Republika Srpska would violate the Dayton Agreement and jeopardize the international re-integration of FRY. However, given the project of a "Greater Serbia" that most of the moderate nationalist DOS members and their constituency have adhered to, struggles can be expected. It is unclear whether the opposition coalition will clearly prioritise international re-integration or link its "return to Europe" to closer relations with or political demands of the Bosnian Serb community. In comparison with these issues, the conflict on the distribution of debts and assets of the former Yugoslavia among its successor states seemed to allow for a resolution since, in the first weeks after his appointment, Kostunica indicated that the opposition leadership was willing to waive the claim of FRY to be the only successor state to the former Yugoslavia. Kostunica and other DOS politicians showed less openness towards a collaboration with the International War Crimes Tribunal in The Hague, raising doubts about its legitimacy and favouring a trial against Milosevic in Serbia. This restraint was partly due to concerns about a backlash of authoritarian forces during the first weeks after the overthrow of the regime.

V Policy priorities in Southeastern Europe

This section attempts to identify the different strategic challenges each country poses for the EU and the strategic priorities the EU has to set in order to achieve its objectives.

In *Albania*, the younger and more moderate Albanian politicians appear to be the most important strategic asset for the development of regional stability. In a number of speeches to the West, pragmatic and compromising Prime Minister Ilir Meta has reiterated full support for the stabilisation of Southeastern Europe through the framework of the Stability Pact, and has characterised Albanian foreign policy as the philosophy of "good neighbourliness" with countries like Greece, Montenegro, FYROM and Bulgaria.[30] This positive attitude towards Europe has been coupled with a commitment to and gradual improvement in law enforcement, the fight against corruption and the push for economic stability.

---

30 Cf. recent speeches by I. Meta to the Kennedy School of Government and the Council of Europe in April and May 2000.

As homeland to the ethnic Albanian communities in the Southern Balkans, Albania contributes to stability in the region – yet, sadly enough, such stability seems plagued by internal political discord and the failure to develop stable democratic institutions. Albania has enjoyed support from the West in the wake of Kosovo; the key now is to support those elements that may be capable of developing the economy, infrastructure and public administration of the country. The local elections in October 2000 reinforced the position of the socialist government and improved its subsequent ability to steer the region towards stability. If the West manages to support the development of interparty co-operation (most likely through the younger and more pragmatic moderates), Albanian politics may finally get over its legacy of divisiveness and return to the real issue at hand: stability in Albania and beyond.

In *Bosnia-Herzegovina*, the experience of the devastating ethnic war has left its lasting imprint on the divisive structure that shapes the formation and interest representation of political actors. The EU should accept that the three ethnic communities of the countries – in their overwhelming majority – perceive their interests to be represented best by ethnic nationalist parties and politicians. Increased pressure of the High Representative or the loss of a supportive homeland government in Croatia does not lead citizens to vote for non-ethnic political forces and results, at best, in a change from war-time nationalists to pragmatic nationalists. The implication for an EU strategy is to abandon any hope of short-term changes, such as landslide electoral shifts that would bring European-minded political actors to power (as occurred in Croatia).

Rather, the EU should follow a long-term approach and aim at changing Bosnian society. The most important instrument of such a strategy is to foster economic development, foreign investment and border-crossing trade both within Bosnia-Herzegovina and with the neighbouring states. The Bosnian economy, however, may become caught in a trap of aid-dependency – a dilemma that can only be overcome by revising and re-focusing Western assistance policies. Economic development needs to be supplemented by a broad-based qualification policy that provides international experience and professional know-how to young Bosnians and by institutional safeguards for free media. This economic "opening" strategy will bring about a generational change in the mid- to long-term, a new political and economic elite, and, as a probable result, a de-ethnicisation of Bosnian politics. Until the results of this strategy materialise, the current constitutional structures work appropriately in so far as they separate powers and provide a wide-ranging segmental autonomy to the entities and the ethnic communities that fits into the interest representation pattern of the moderate nationalist elites that have gained strength in the country. A more integrationist constitutional model would probably be confronted with even more resistance from the dominating elites, as can be concluded from the failure of the integrationist policy of encouraging minority returns of refugees. Moderate nationalists may also be more amenable to the dual policy of positive and negative sanctions the High Representative recently introduced when he warned Bosnian politicians that the refusal to implement legislation of the joint institutions may result in the withdrawal of Western aid.

The success of the Western-oriented *Croatian* government largely depends on its ability to deliver socio-economic improvements for the majority of the population – an objective in conflict with the need to implement those costly and overdue economic reforms that were neglected by the Tudjman government. The EU should clearly realise that the current constellation provides a window of opportunity to establish a functioning market economy and a consolidated democracy in Croatia. However, as indicated by the growing social protest activities buttressed by the widespread, persisting nationalist sentiment and organised by right-wing parties, this window may not be very large. A re-integrated right-wing opposition on the one hand, the internal heterogeneity of the governing coalition and the Mesic-Racan rivalry on the other may reduce the political capacity of the government to carry on with its reforms. In view of these risks, the EU should continue to reward the steps taken by the current government, thereby demonstrating the expediency of its chosen path. This political strategy should be combined with an economic strategy that facilitates growth and enables the government to compensate the losers of the transformation. The success of the current government is crucially important because it entails the opportunity for Croatia to become a regional stabilisation factor, particularly for Bosnia-Herzegovina. If the West could rely on a Croatian government that complies with the Dayton Agreement and the objectives of the international community, the diplomatic and political instruments to stabilise the Bosniak-Croat Federation would be greatly enhanced.

The key to the remarkable and somewhat enigmatic institutional stability of *FYROM* seems to consist of two factors. First, the sustained high involvement of the international community has provided a security presence (UNPREDEP), facilitated good governance and supported institutional models of inter-ethnic co-existence.[31] The EU should maintain the international presence and buttress it by a much more substantial involvement of private investors from EU member states. Second, the ruling elites have managed to establish practices of a consociationalist model that survived the change of government in 1998. This is particularly remarkable in view of the turbulent changes in the surrounding region, but should not be conceived as consolidated or concrete. While the EU does not have the means to, and should not, intervene in the operative practices of this power-

---

31 Indeed, FYROM may be the sole country in the Balkans where a multiethnic society need not be territorially divided for the sake of peace; it may thus demonstrate how democracy can hope to function in the Balkans some day – perhaps this form of democracy may be based upon the sort of power-sharing co-operation as advocated by Xhaferi, rather than the divisive and liberal "Montesquieuian" form which characterises Western politics.

sharing model, it can and should support a "freezing" of the institutional arrangements of consociationalist governance by strengthening their legal nature. This implies that the EU should focus on those actors in the government and society that will promote and develop the rule of law and the legal control of political discretion, such as judges and lawyers, public administration experts, civil servants and public sector employees. It is important to strengthen corporate or intermediate structures that may restrict rapid policy changes with potentially harmful effects for the fragile equilibrium of powers. The costs of this freezing strategy should be borne by the EU, and will most likely materialise due to a more gradual pace of economic reform and a public sector oversized in comparison with FYROM's level of economic development. Whereas the first cost component is caused by the need to build broad-based reform coalitions, distributing losses more equally, the second cost component results from requirements of ethnic proportionality rules in public functions and the general stabilising function of public sector employment.

Specific identification of strategic actors focuses on the political scene. In Skopje, a key actor appears to be the leader of the DA and former Macedonian representative for the rotating Yugoslav presidency, Vasil Tupurkovski. Of primary importance is the fact that Tupurkovski will almost certainly become FYROM's next head of state. His current central and mediating location between the 'radical' right of the VMRO-DPMNE and the left's DPA may indicate a strong ability to rally support from both poles of Macedonian society. Aside from these internal advantages, he seems set on creating and capitalising on foreign ties, as well as on promoting international involvement in FYROM. Another strategic actor is the head of the DPA, Arben Xhaferi. Though commanding only one of four ethnic Albanian parties in FYROM, Xhaferi seems pragmatically oriented towards equal opportunity and seems realistic in knowing how to best achieve the support of ethnic Albanians for reform to Western standards. His increasingly compromise-oriented attitude may be a key in securing a long-term settlement of ethnic tensions in FYROM; a settlement which, if successful, may be applicable to the rest of the region.

In addition to these key actors, there may be an important role to play in the various municipalities and regions in FYROM. In order to create a more effective administration, particularly with regard to issues that can best be solved at the local level, the EU should promote a certain degree of decentralisation of state structure. Such a move would have a twofold effect. First, a degree of decentralisation may be the key to opening up the country both to itself as well as to the West, so that actors of strategic importance (most notably those now notably absent, such as those from the private sector) can be identified and encouraged. Secondly, and perhaps more importantly, it may help alleviate ethnic tensions by encouraging a co-operative and transethnic democracy at the local level, essentially by allowing local politicians to deal with local issues.

For two reasons, the strategic interest of the EU is to institutionalise the current status situation of *Kosovo*. First, it is impossible to transform Kosovo into an independent state since this option would neither be supported by a post-Milosevic, democratic government of Serbia, nor would the necessary alteration of UN Security Council Resolution 1244 be approved by China or Russia. An independent Kosovo would be rejected by the neighbouring states and would damage the international "state-building" projects in Bosnia-Herzegovina and FYROM. Second, the atrocities of the war have rendered it impossible to re-integrate Kosovo into the state framework of FRY since, in addition to the unanimous refusal of the Kosovo Albanian elites and people, there is no longer any legitimate reason for re-establishing the previous status of Kosovo. Thus, it is crucial for the EU to find and support actors who might postpone their objective of an independent Kosovo and prioritise the task of developing Kosovo economically, politically and socially. These actors can find and need to find a socio-economic basis in the cores of an urban, qualified and young middle class likely to gain from the economic opportunities. As the Kosovo party scene is very much in flux, close observation and flexible adaptation to new developments are required. As the first post-war local elections showed an urban-rural split similar to that in Bosnia-Herzegovina and Serbia, UNMIK should strive for a wide-ranging autonomy of Kosovo towns and cities that would allow the urban winners to deliver their electoral programmes and turn the urban areas – with the economic and technical support of the international community – into modernisation centres. UNMIK should adapt its own structure towards accommodating urban modernisation coalitions. These coalitions should comprise not only political parties and leaders but also economic interest groups and NGOs.

Being charged with the task of economic reconstruction within the UNMIK framework, the EU is in a position to harness its range of instruments in order to help create such modernisation coalitions, which would in turn allow movement forward in the definition, extrapolation and realisation of the substantial autonomy of Kosovo envisaged in Resolution 1244. This actor coalition would be more willing to decouple the implementation of substantial autonomy from progress made in the final status talks. In contrast, a rurally based actor coalition would advocate a nationalist and anti-modernist set of values and demands, which would provide a basis for blocking the economic and political substantiation of Kosovo's current status in an attempt to realise national independence first, perceiving it as the basis of any development not perpetuating Serbian "colonisation" and sacrificing national identity.

After the end of the Kosovo war, *Montenegro* became the target of a Milosevic regime struggling to mobilise Serb nationalism in order to consolidate its power basis. With the end of Milosevic's rule, Montenegrin-Serb relations can be placed in a new political and constitutional framework, but this requires a difficult balancing between the interests and concerns of both republics and their leaders. Mainly US-American diplomatic pressure and intense negotiation activities of DOS leader Zoran Djindjic kept the Montenegrin government from announcing a referendum on independence during the transition struggles in Belgrade. Parts of the governing coalition and the citizens still favour an independent state and insist that Montenegro is, like all other former Yugoslav republics, entitled to opt for independence. In the given volatile situation, such a step would trigger new and strengthen existing independence and separatist movements in Kosovo, Bosnia-Herzegovina and probably also FYROM. The re-establishment of stable federal relations between Montenegro and Serbia therefore constitutes a core strategic concern for the EU in the Western Balkans. This is not only indicated by the disintegrative effects of further dissolution of FRY but also by the model function of a working federal arrangement for the neighbouring quasi-protectorates of Bosnia-Herzegovina and Kosovo, for fragile FYROM and for Serbia proper.

It follows from this strategic importance that the EU should support those actors in the Montenegrin government and in the Serbian opposition that strive to preserve and reorganise the federation on a consensual basis. The EU has the instruments to provide technical expertise, financial assistance and the backing of high-level European politicians for negotiations between the republics and the re-organisation of inter-republican economic and financial relations.

The key to lasting political stability in the Western Balkans is a democratic change in *Serbia*. The electoral defeat of Milosevic on 24 September 2000 constituted an important step towards democratisation, but further steps are required to achieve a consolidation of democracy. These include first of all fair democratic parliamentary and presidential elections in Serbia, where the socialists remained in power, and a clear commitment of political actors representing the old power structures to comply with democratic principles. Reacting to the appointment of Kostunica as the new Yugoslav President, the EU lifted most of the sanctions applied so far. It should now provide quick and visible support to the democratic opposition and warn representatives of the Milosevic regime that an authoritarian backlash would threaten the European perspective of Serbia. The EU should demonstrate a clear preference for maintaining FRY in its current borders including Kosovo, irrespective of the future name and constitution of the state.

At the same time it is necessary to involve the new leadership in an internationally embedded consultation and information process with respect to the reform of state organisation, convincing them of the potential inter-ethnic conflicts implied by a recentralisation along the lines of an integral nation state. Instead, the new leaders of FRY should be encouraged to seek compromises with the various ethnic communities living in FRY that build on the acquired status and rights these groups had in former Yugoslavia, to expand these autonomy regulations and to protect them by ensuring independent judicial review, international monitoring, special representation and veto rights. The EU has to make clear that existing international conventions protecting national minorities, while setting important and necessary standards, by no means constitute a sufficient basis to accommodate the needs and concerns of the non-Serb ethnic communities of FRY. Rigid sets of core beliefs and approaches have to be changed in Serbian political thinking – a process that requires time, external and political stability and a confidence based on shared practice. For this to occur, the EU needs to increase its support of Serbian NGOs, small business and free media and to involve the young, educated groups of Serbian society in all forms of international contacts. Although Serbian politicians and intellectuals currently tend to make categoric differences between Montenegro, Kosovo, Vojvodina and Sandzak, it needs to be pointed out that only a practice of fair, equal and law-based relations with Montenegro and Vojvodina can demonstrate the qualitative change of Serbian political behaviour that is required before Kosovo can be imagined to be part of FRY again. Until then there is no alternative to the external stabilisation function performed by UNMIK and the international forces in Kosovo.

VI Conclusion

The countries and regions of the Western Balkans are at very different stages of their political and economic transition. Despite a common regional legacy, and, for the successor states of the former Socialist Federal Republic of Yugoslavia, a common state experience, specific constellations of actors, resources and institutions have shaped each country's path of transition. The agenda of strategic problems and the given configuration of actors determine the focus of external, and in particular EU, policy support. This support can be orientated towards indirectly shaping an environment conducive to political change or can have a higher political profile, aiming at the direct realisation of crucial political objectives. It can be confined to economic co-operation and assistance, include support to the domestic NGO sphere or comprise a partisan political engagement. This chapter gave a structured survey of the transition, the relations with the EU, the political positions regarding EU interests, and it identified strategic problems and tasks the EU is faced with.

In Albania, the strategic task is to support economic modernisation and encourage the discernible emergence of "Europeanised" political elites. In Bosnia-Herzegovina, the economic, educational and informational opening of society should be supported, attaining a change of elites in the long term. The Western-oriented Croatian government represents a strategic chance to create a success model in particular for FRY and to stabilise Bosnia-Herzegovina. In FYROM, the EU should consolidate consociational-ist governance by strengthening the rule of law and local democracy. The strategic task for Kosovo lies in consolidating the given status and supporting modernising actor coalitions. In Montenegro, cautious advice, economic assistance and security guarantees for the reformist government are the strategic priorities. In Serbia, the EU should provide visible and significant support for Kostunica and DOS, fostering consensual approaches towards issues related to inter-ethnic relations and Serbian/Yugoslav statehood. These diverging configurations pose a genuine foreign policy challenge to the EU as they require the EU to act not only as a rule-bound and accountable "regime", but also in its quality as an "actor" – capable of dynamic interaction, learning and flexible adaptation.

Southeastern Europe and Regional Co-operation

Predrag Simic

I Introduction

In comparison to other parts of Europe that are covered by dense networks of regional organisations, regional co-operation in the Balkan and Danubian Europe is considerably less well developed. The immediate, though not main, cause for this was the Yugoslav crisis that in various ways affected all the countries of the region by disrupting the development of their relations after the end of the Cold War and by hampering regional co-operation in general. The situation somewhat changed in 1995 with the signing of the Dayton Agreement, and quite a number of initiatives in that direction began right away: In July 1996 the third Ministerial Conference of the Balkan Countries took place in Sofia[1], while the first Balkan Summit was held on Crete in November 1997. Proposals for the promotion of regional co-operation in Southeastern Europe were also forthcoming at that time from the European Union, which launched the so-called Royaumont Initiative[2] and the Regional Approach towards countries of the former Yugoslavia[3], as well as from the United States, which launched its Southeastern European Co-operative Initiative (SECI)[4] covering twelve countries of the region. Despite various ini-

---

1 The first Ministerial Conference of the Balkan Countries took place in Belgrade in 1988 and the second in Tirana in 1990.

2 Declaration on the Process of Stability and Good Neighborliness, Royaumont, 13 December 1995.

3 The EU's Regional Approach pertains to all the republics of former Yugoslavia (with the exception of Slovenia) as well as Albania. Refer to: Prospects for the development of regional co-operation for the countries of former Yugoslavia and what the Community can do to foster such co-operation, Report from the Commission to the Council, SEC (96) 252 final, Commission of the European Communities, Brussels, 14 February 1996.

4 SECI concerns Albania, Bosnia-Herzegovina, Bulgaria, Croatia, Greece, Hungary, Macedonia, Moldova, Romania, Slovenia, Turkey and FR Yugoslavia. South-East European Co-operative Initiative, Dept. of State, 5/28/96 SERPMSCE 9525.

tiatives, there are still only regional initiatives in Danubian Europe: the Working Community of the Danube Regions, established at the beginning of the 1990s, follows the model of the Working Community Alps-Adria. The outbreak of the war in Kosovo and Metohia presented new security threats not only to the region but to the entire continent. It also gave a new impetus to the initiatives for regional co-operation and association with the EU: "Regional co-operation in Southeastern Europe is of even greater importance today, in the aftermath of the conflict in Kosovo, than a few years ago. Despite various initiatives aimed at stimulating regional co-operation in the region in the 1990s, no significant results have been actualised. On the contrary, peace and stability in Southeastern Europe have been seriously undermined precisely by the *lack* of regional co-operation, which has clearly contributed to several armed conflicts in the region, including the most recent war in Kosovo/FR Yugoslavia in March-June 1999. Not surprisingly, the latest initiative of the international community – the Stability Pact for Southeastern Europe adopted in Cologne on 10 June 1999 – rests again on regional co-operation as one of the most important instruments for bringing lasting peace and stability in this part of Europe."[5]

The fact that regional co-operation in Southeastern Europe is lagging in comparison with Western, Central and Eastern Europe, the Baltic and even the Black Sea Region is actually only partly due to the war in former Yugoslavia. Deeper causes may be found in the historical differences and relative backwardness of these countries, in the incompatibility of their economies and, particularly, in their political marginalization during the 1990s. Regional co-operation in Central Europe enjoyed strong support from the United States and the European Union (particularly from a united Germany), while Denmark and the other Scandinavian countries took the lead in the Baltic region, and Turkey, with US support, initiated in the development of Black Sea co-operation (BSEC). In the first half of the 1990s such initiatives were missing in Southeastern Europe. The EU's Regional Approach had lost its momentum soon after the end of the Italian presidency in the EU, whereas the American SECI is a self-assistance programme and can hardly bring significant results without substantial funds from abroad. For that reason some of the Southeast European countries adopted a bilateral approach towards European integration, and this further contributed not merely to the disintegration of former Yugoslavia[6], but also to the deepening of political differences among the Balkan and Danubian countries.

---

5   M. Uvalic: Regional Co-operation in Southeast Europe, Halki Southeast European Network on Economic Reconstruction, mimeo, University of Perugia, 22 January 2000, p. 1.

6   P. Simic: Dynamics of the Yugoslav Crisis, Security Dialogue, Vol. 26, N02/95, pp. 153–172.

The wish to "escape from the Balkans" was the reason for Slovenia's and Croatia's reluctance about the Regional Approach of the EU and American SECI. Furthermore, Croatia was not ready to join any multilateral arrangement with the Balkan countries[7] until the end of the Tudjman regime early in 2000, while quite a number of Balkan countries preferred (and continue) to see themselves as a Central European rather than a Southeastern European country. Southeastern Europe today presents a particularly serious challenge for the European Union. The revolutions of 1989 lifted the Iron Curtain that divided Western and Eastern Europe for several decades, but eventually created a "Golden Curtain" dividing the Balkans from the rest of Europe. While in the 1990s the EU strongly supported transition in Central and Eastern Europe, its contribution to the transition of the former socialist countries of Southeastern Europe was largely limited to ad hoc crisis management that significantly contributed to the spread of ethnic wars, social and economic dislocation and fragmentation of this region. At the beginning of the 1990s there were six countries in this area while today there are ten, including two areas under the international protectorate (Bosnia-Herzegovina, Kosovo and Metohia) and a few countries whose survival in the present form is by no means certain. Until the Kosovo and Metohia war the response of the EU was by no means unified and consistent and thus failed at the first test of its Common Foreign and Security Policy. Thus the new EU Commission established that Southeastern Europe may be among the most important challenges for the Union's CFSP, but also for the final rounds of EU enlargement.

Regional co-operation is, nevertheless, a major condition for most of the countries of Southeastern Europe with respect to their development, their international position and security, and, above all, their accession to European and Euro-Atlantic organisations. The declaration of the Ministerial Conference of Countries of Southeastern Europe held at Thessaloniki in July 1997 therefore stated: "The European orientation of the states of the region is an integral part of their political, economic and social development. The countries of Southeastern Europe look forward to actively taking part in the shaping future developments both in the region and in Europe as a whole. European integration can not be complete without their participation based on the same European principles that helped to establish and develop what is today the European Union."[8]

Among the Southeast European countries, only Greece is fully integrated in NATO and the EU. Turkey is a member of NATO and an associated member of the EU (without the prospect of becoming a full member in the near future), whereas the status of all

7 In January 1998, Croatia passed constitutional amendments prohibiting return to any kind of Yugoslav community.
8 Thessaloniki Declaration on Good-Neighborly Relations, Stability, Security and Co-operation in the Balkans, Eurobalkans, No. 26–27/97, p. 36.

the other countries varies, with only one qualifying for the first round of NATO[9] and two for EU enlargement (Hungary and Slovenia). Slovenia, Romania and Bulgaria have prospects of entering NATO in a second round of expansion (if there is one), whereas the prospects of the remaining countries are uncertain. The enlargement and reform of NATO and the EU will have major consequences on all the Southeastern European countries; so regional co-operation might possibly be the only option – at least until they become eligible for full membership in the Union and NATO. Most of these countries lack the economic resources and strong internal markets to support development of their national economies and to make them attractive for foreign investments. Moreover, with the disappearance of bipolarism and the disintegration of former Yugoslavia, many countries in the region have found themselves in a "security vacuum" and have been forced to deal with social and political problems requiring multilateral action, as was witnessed by the recent crisis in Kosovo and Metohia. They are directed in the same course by the European and Euro-Atlantic organisations requesting a guarantee of peaceful and stable neighbourly relations from the accession candidates, as well as the guarantee of the resolution of existing ethnic and territorial disputes.

II What is Southeastern Europe?

There are immediate questions pertaining to every possible initiative aimed at regional co-operation that must be answered: "What is the region?" and "Do possibilities for economic, political and other forms of co-operation exist in the region?" While the Balkans and the Danube Basin are undoubtedly geographic regions, a broader definition of Southeastern Europe (for instance, the countries included in the Stability Pact), is more complex. It is even more difficult to answer the question of whether these geographic regions are or could become regions in the economic and political sense, considering the historical and current differences among the nations and states of the region.

Of all the initiatives that have been mentioned, the initial Regional Approach of the EU with regard to Croatia, Bosnia-Herzegovina, FRY, Macedonia and Albania was the narrowest. With the exception of Albania, it covered the republics of former Yugoslavia which had constituted a single economic and political region in the seven preceding decades. The disintegration of their common state and the war that has ended only recently, in addition to the desire of the western republics of former Yugoslavia to "escape from the Balkans", were major obstacles to the reconstruction of their former

---

9 Hungary was admitted to NATO in the first round of its enlargement in March 1999, together with Poland and the Czech Republic.

economic ties. Balkan co-operation covers a rather different region. There are consider-able economic and political differences among these countries, however, with regard to the level of their development as well as their economic structure, political orientation etc. A member of NATO and the EU, Greece is more of a Western European country than a Balkan country. Turkey is a member of NATO and an associate member of the EU, but has considerable interests and links with the Black Sea region, the Middle East and Central Asia. Romania and Bulgaria had been members of the Warsaw Pact and COMECON, Albania was the most isolated country in Europe, whereas the republics of former Yugoslavia had developed in particular circumstances. Economic co-operation among these countries was hampered by many obstacles, starting with the different levels of development, the incompatibility of their economies and the relatively small amount of trade between them, the undeveloped common infrastructure and trade barriers – which raises the question of to what extent they really form or could form an economic region.

Table 1: Population and per capita income of Southeast European countries, 1996[10]

Country	Population	Territory (km²)	Per-capita income (US-$)
Albania	3,413,904	28,750	713
Bosnia-Herzegovina	4,383,000	51,233	n/a
Bulgaria	8,350,000	110,912	1,620
Croatia	4,665,821	56,538	3,650
Greece	10,550,000	131,990	10,645
Macedonia	2,160,000	25,333	1,919
Romania	23,198,330	273,500	1,355
Slovenia	1,989,477	20,256	8,400
Turkey	63,535,000	779,360	2,685
FR Yugoslavia	11,101,833	102,350	1,531

The problem was still more apparent with SECI, since it incorporated Slovenia and Croatia as well (two of the former Yugoslav republics which were sceptical about the multilateralism in the Balkans), Hungary (which is part of Central Europe, a member of NATO and a candidate for EU membership) and Moldova (which had been part of the USSR). Other than bordering on what is to be an enlarged NATO in Southeastern Europe, there was little that linked all these countries and it was hard to imagine that

10 L. Adamovic: Ekonomska reintegracija jugoisto~ne Evrope [Economic Reintegration of Southeastern Europe], Melunarodna politika, 1055/97, p. 7.

such an area could ever acquire the characteristics of an economic and political region without considerable inputs from outside. In the Danube region, the problem is rather different. Contrary to the narrow "neo-Habsburg" definition which incorporated only the countries of the upper Danube, the region undoubtedly covers all the (sub-state) regions and countries through which the Danube flows and which have a common interest in the development of transport, industry, tourism, environment protection, cultural co-operation and other activities connected with this waterway. The Danube Commission has the longest tradition in this regard though its jurisdiction is very narrow, whereas the Working Group of Danubian Regions is limited only to the riparian regions of this river. There is the idea that has emerged from Germany and some of the other countries during past few years that Danube co-operation should encompass not only the regions within the states but the states as well, and that it should be a functional co-operation, i.e., concerned with broader problems than simply those directly related to the river's exploitation. Contrary to the riparian approach of the Working Group of Danubian Regions, the objective of such an intergovernmental organisation should be to ensure the political presence of the countries of the Danube in the decision-making centres of the EU.

Thus, there are at least two major types of obstacle on the road to the development of regional co-operation in Southeastern Europe: 1.) those that have been inherited from the turbulent past of this region, and 2.) those that emanate from contemporary developments.

1. In their long historical existence, the Balkans and the Danube region have been the frontiers and battlefields of different empires, great powers and military alliances, all of which is still having its repercussions on relations between the nations inhabiting these areas. From the Roman *limes*, to the Habsburg *Militärgrenze* and the Ottoman military districts in Bosnia-Herzegovina (Krajina), the Balkan nations have often fought each other as guardians of the frontiers of various empires, religions and cultures. Even now, many Croats like to see themselves in the role of *antemurale christianitatis*, or, in more modern terms, as being the front-line state of a future NATO, while the Serbs often see themselves as the western bulwark of Orthodoxy[11], whereas many Bosnian Moslems speak of Bosnia as an Islamic stronghold in a Christian Europe. National revolutions in the Balkans in the nineteenth century launched the idea of "the Balkans to the Balkan peoples", but, at the same time, they confronted the national ambitions of all Balkan nations and incited conflicts that have marked their recent history exposing them to external influences. This is what has brought the Balkans the reputation of being a

---

11 The popularity of the idea that Serbia (or FR Yugoslavia) should join the Russian-Belorussian Confederation was proven by the formal decision of the FRY federal parliament in the spring of 1999.

"European powder keg" and has characterised it in history under the term of "Balkanisation".[12] Just as in the rest of Europe, the Cold War had frozen the old ethnic and territorial disputes in the Balkans, so that they became revitalised once the bipolar order and bloc discipline in Europe collapsed and the fear of local conflicts leading to a European or global war were dispelled. "Decompression" of the bipolar international order had grievous consequences in Yugoslavia, divided by the old demarcation line between Eastern and Western Europe, which many authors of the time considered to be the eastern frontier of European integration. In short, the renaissance of Central Europe[13], the idea that "the Balkans are not part of Europe" and the notion that Orthodox countries have no prospect of being integrated into Europe[14] were strong motives for the western republics of former Yugoslavia to leave their common state and try to "escape" from the Balkans into Central Europe. This is the reason why Slovenia and Croatia and some other countries of the region were reluctant about initiatives like the EU's Regional Approach or SECI or rejected them outright.[15] Their attitude, however, has changed since the Union, under German presidency, launched the Stability Pact as an initiative for regional co-operation that is not contrary to the expectation of stabilisation and association of the Southeast European countries with the EU.

Table 2: Ethnic composition of Southeast European countries[16]

Country	Majority nation	(%)	Largest minority	(%)
Albania	Albanians	98.0	Greeks	1.8
B&H	Three nations			
Bulgaria	Bulgarians	85.7	Turks	9.4
Croatia	Croats	78.1	Serbs	12.2
Greece	Greeks	100.0		
Macedonia	Macedonians	66.4	Albanians	23.1

12 Seven wars have taken place in the Balkans in the twentieth century: the First and Second Balkan Wars, the First and Second World Wars, the Greco-Turkish War, as well as the civil wars in Greece and FR Yugoslavia.

13 C. Cviic: Remaking the Balkans, Pinter for RIIA, London 1990; M. Todorova: Imagining the Balkans, Oxford University Press, New York-Oxford 1977.

14 W. Klaas: President of the Council of Ministers of the European Community of the time, had stated: "Southeast European countries belong, in the cultural sense, to the Byzantine empire that once existed. They have no democratic traditions or the traditions of respecting national minorities. For this reason it would be correct to limit the community's expansion to the 'cultural circle' of Western countries. The Community's extension should be limited to the Protestant and Catholic cultural circles in European countries." Quoted after the Greek newspaper Katimerini, 16 October 1993, p. 9.

15 On the other hand, most of these countries joined the Central European Initiative (CEI) and the Central European Free Trade Association (CEFTA).

16 G. Brunner: National Problems and Ethnic Conflicts in Eastern Europe, Bertelsmann Foundation Publishers, Gütersloh 1996.

Romania	Rumanians	89.4	Hungarians	7.1
Slovenia	Slovenians	87.6	Croats	2.7
Turkey	Turks	83.0	Kurds	14.0
FR Yugoslavia	Serbs	62.6	Albanians	16.5

Aversion to Balkan co-operation may also, to a certain extent, be ascribed to economic motives. Whereas the majority of countries in transition have liberalised their economies, the Balkan region still abounds in obstacles and limitations, some of which have been imposed from abroad. Others are self-imposed while some are inherited. An analysis of trade among the Balkan countries (Table 5) shows that in most instances it was negligible[17] and that the main trading partners of all Balkan countries are Germany, Italy and Russia (Table 3). These considerations suggest that the level of regional integration as reflected in the trade flows is very low even though one has to take into account the considerable illegal trade that is not included in statistical data. Intra-regional trade flows are low and most trade is done with the non-Balkan countries. The region neither creates nor diverts trade from other regions to intra-regional trade. Indeed, it tends to induce trade aversion both in the sense of keeping the overall trade level low and in the sense of diverting trade out of the region through constant policy shocks that induce a high level of uncertainty and thus volatility.[18] Despite geographic proximity, trade with the EU is much more significant for most of the Balkan countries than trade with other Balkan countries. The data being presented must, of course, be taken with some caution as they relate to intra-Balkan trade after the war in Bosnia-Herzegovina had just ended and the UN Security Council trade sanctions against FR Yugoslavia were lifted. One should not lose sight of the fact that a considerable amount of trade in the Balkans is carried on through illegal channels and that a large shadow economy, smuggling and organised crime are among the main problems of the region today.

17 "Regarding more specifically trade links in SEE region, there was relatively little trade among SEE countries in 1989. In the case of Bulgaria, 13.4 per cent of its exports went to and 6.5 per cent of its imports came from two other major SEE countries, Romania and FR Yugoslavia. For the other SEE countries, regional trade at the time was even less important. The share of the three SEE countries in Romania's exports and imports in 1989 amounted to only 3.2 per cent and 4.4 per cent respectively, and in FR Yugoslavia even less (2.1 per cent of exports and 2.2 per cent of imports). These very low shares of mutual trade among SEE countries clearly show that, despite geographical proximity, the SEE region in 1989 was not at all economically integrated, *except* for economic links within former Yugoslavia. The SEE region at that time actually consisted of two subregions, the first, relatively integrated, encompassing economies of the six republics of former Yugoslavia; and the second, characterized by very weak mutual trade links, consisting of the other three SEE countries. Trade flows between the two SEE subregions were negligible." M. Uvalic: Regional Co-operation in Southeast Europe, Halki Southeast European Network on Economic Reconstruction, mimeo, University of Perugia, 22 January 2000, p. 2.

18 On this point: V. Gligorov: Yugoslavia, Macedonia and Albania between Anarchy, Autarky and Integration, WIIW preliminary report, Vienna 1996.

Table 3: Trade of the Balkan Countries with Germany, Italy and Russia, 1996[19]
Exports and imports, per cent shares in 1996 (%)

	Germany		Italy		Russia	
	Export	Import	Export	Import	Export	Import
Slovenia	30	21	13	16	3	2
Croatia	18	20	21	18	2	2
B&H	15	12	26	12	0	1
Yugoslavia	7	12	9	10	8	5
Albania	6	4	51	37	0	0
Macedonia	18	14	4	8	3	7
Romania	18	17	17	15	2	12
Bulgaria	9	10	9	5	9	37
Greece	18	14	14	19	1	0
Turkey	22	18	7	10	5	4

Recent wars and various trade embargoes further disrupted economic links in South-eastern Europe. There has been a substantial growth of illegal economic activities, smuggling (especially across some of the "soft" borders) and the black market. A considerable part of the trade among some of the countries in the region is illegal, sometimes taking barter form, which is in no way registered. "Major disruptions in trade among those countries have taken place in 1999, as a consequence of the war in FR Yugoslavia that has affected all neighbouring countries. Through destruction or damage of infrastructure, transport and communication lines in FR Yugoslavia, the NATO bombardiers further divided Southeastern Europe, creating trade, ecological, and transportation disturbances in the whole region. However, precisely because of these region-wide consequences of the 1999 military conflict, there is major interdependence among Southeast European countries today. At the same time, further disintegration has taken place in FR Yugoslavia, as since the end of the 1999 military conflict it has practically lost territorial control over Kosovo. Furthermore, Montenegro appears to be steadily moving towards full independence, especially after its November 1999 decision to introduce the German mark as a parallel currency."[20] Today, Southeastern Europe is even less integrated than a decade ago due not only to historical legacies, but also to the consequences of the dissolution of former Yugoslavia, decade-long wars and policies of

19   V. Gligorov: Trade in the Balkans, Paper presented at the conference "Southeast Europe after NATO and EU enlargement: Towards Inclusive Security Structures?", WEU Institute for Security Studies, Paris 1997, p 3.
20   M. Uvalic: op. cit., p. 5.

trade embargoes and isolation adopted by the international community.[21] Isolated by the West, FRY and Serbia in particular diverted their trade flows to Russia, China and other Eastern countries. This has had far-reaching economic and political consequences, such as talk of the political initiative to enter into the Russian-Belorussian Confederation.

The end of the bipolar world order, as well as the Yugoslav crisis, marked the political scene of Southeastern Europe during the 1990s. And, while the end of the bipolar order opened the door to regional co-operation, the Yugoslav crisis had the opposite effect. An outcome of the disintegration of former Yugoslavia has been the formation of two sub-regions in the Balkans – the western and southern – which differ very much from one another.

The Western Balkans[22] were the theatre of three armed conflicts between 1991 and 1995, resulting first in the secession of Slovenia, then Croatia and, finally, Bosnia-Herzegovina which was soon divided along ethnic borders between the Serbs, Croats and Moslems. The war for Yugoslavia's heritage among these three nations defined the so-called Western or "Dayton" triangle of the Yugoslav conflict which ended with the signing of the Dayton Peace Agreement. The military aspects of the Agreement – separation of the warring sides, control of armaments, etc. – were quickly fulfilled by the peacekeeping forces under NATO command, whereas the civilian objectives – economic reconstruction and the establishment of political institutions above all – will require the more persistent engagement of the international community to ensure its implementation. However, the Dayton Accords will be the long-term foundation of relations within Bosnia-Herzegovina and with Croatia and FRY, as well as of the international community's overall policy in the Western Balkans. The fact that the international community has assumed major commitments with regard to the economic reconstruction of Bosnia-Herzegovina is of particular significance and will have a lasting effect also with regard to FRY and Croatia. This effect will likewise be felt with respect to the promotion of their mutual trade and economic co-operation. This gives grounds for assuming that, in time, the region will acquire certain specific economic and political features, as well as aspects of security that will set it apart from the regions that border it.

The Southern Balkans are in many ways different from the Western Balkans. Fear that the war in FR Yugoslavia would spill over to Kosovo and Macedonia and provoke Albania, Greece, Turkey and Bulgaria to enter into it, causing a collapse of NATO's

---

21 On this point: J. Minic: Reconstruction and development programme for South Eastern Europe, in: J. Minic (ed.): South Eastern Europe 2000 – A View from Serbia, Stubovi kulture, Beograd 2000, pp. 7–24.

22 Contrary to the EU use of the term "Western Balkans" that encompass all republics of former Yugoslavia, for the purpose of this paper Western Balkans is defined as the Western part of former Yugoslavia.

southern tier, caused the Security Council deploy limited contingents of peacekeeping forces in Macedonia for preventive purposes and the US to send their soldiers there before they joined the IFOR mission in Bosnia. However, the long-expected Serbian-Albanian war started in February 1998, escalating in the spring of the following year into the limited war between NATO and FRY that ended in June by UN Security Council Resolution 1244 and the so-called Military-Technical Agreement signed in Kumanovo (FYROM). Even though there were some similarities between the Dayton Peace Agreement and that at Kumanovo (both being written by the same person), there are substantial differences between the two documents and the character of the international settlements of these two crises. While the Dayton Peace Agreement tends to be a comprehensive international settlement for the war in Bosnia-Herzegovina, the second one is just a temporary military and technical agreement that facilitated the deployment of the international peacekeepers. While the Dayton settlement created "unfinished peace" in Bosnia-Herzegovina, Resolution 1244 and the Kumanovo agreement are often seen as an "unfinished war" that can trigger a chain-reaction of ethnic and territorial disputes in the Southern Balkans.[23] First among these is without doubt the "Albanian question", festering in Kosovo and Metohia, western Macedonia and Albania, and, possibly, southern Epirus (*Chameria* in Albanian). The next issue is the "Macedonian question" which, apart from the Macedonian-Albanian ethnic dispute, involves a whole chain of unresolved problems in relation to this former Yugoslav republic with Greece, Bulgaria, FRY and other Balkan countries.[24] In short, Macedonia is a kind of "strategic buffer" in the Southern Balkans, like Bosnia-Herzegovina is in the Western Balkans. Another problem in this area is presented by ethnic and territorial disputes between Greece and Turkey in Cyprus, the Aegean and Western Thrace, while the Bulgarian-Turkish ethnic dispute has appeared to be easing in recent years. Bearing in mind the strategic importance of the Southern Balkans, especially for NATO and Russia, instability in this region will be a matter of ongoing international involvement (as was proven by the political consequences of the NATO military intervention against Serbia). However, it will be different in substance from the Western Balkans considering that there is no international arrangement or binding international legal basis for it such as is outlined in the Dayton Agreement.[25]

23 On this point: P. Simic: Put u Rambuje: kosovska kriza 1995–2000 (The Road to Rambouillet: Kosovo Crisis 1995–2000), NEA, Beograd 2000.

24 R. Stefanova: Preventing Violent Conflict in Europe – The Case of Macedonia, Paper presented at the conference "Preventing Violent Conflict in Europe", Instituto Affari Internazionali, Rome, 10/11 December 1997.

25 B. R. Rubin (ed.): Toward Comprehensive Peace in Southeast Europe, Conflict Prevention in the South Balkans, The Twentieth Century Fund Press, New York 1996.

The Federal Republic of Yugoslavia, i.e., Serbia and Montenegro, is part of both the conflict "triangles" in Southeastern Europe. As signatories of the Dayton Peace Accords, Serbia and Montenegro carry their part of the responsibilities for its implementation. Moreover, they have assumed commitments in relation to the Serbian entity of Bosnia-Herzegovina under an agreement on special parallel relations with the Republica Srpska. Serbia and FRY likewise have an interest in the settlement of questions that still remain open with Croatia, above all those concerning the return of Serbian refugees from Krajina, and protection of the Serbian minority in this republic of the former Yugoslavia[26], in addition to settling of the territorial dispute over the Prevlaka Peninsula in the Adriatic. Furthermore, FRY is linked with the "southern triangle" by the Serb-Albanian ethnic conflict in Kosovo, parallel interests with Macedonia[27], Greece and Bulgaria, as well as by the interest in transit corridors towards the Aegean and Black Seas. As was already mentioned, the development of economic exchange in this region for FRY might be some kind of compensation for the lost markets of the western republics of former Yugoslavia. The connection with these two main crisis "triangles" in the Balkans makes FRY's international position quite sensitive, but also vital for the preservation of the overall stability in the region as it has been one of the main features of her foreign policy in the last few years. Not only because of her geographic location, the importance of transit corridors passing through her territory, her relative size and economic resources, FRY is also an inevitable factor of every possible form of regional co-operation in Southeastern Europe. Therefore, the exclusion of FRY from the Stability Pact tends to downgrade this initiative on regional co-operation to the level of the *cordon sanitaire* that would harm not only Serbia but also most of its neighbours.

III Initiatives for regional co-operation

Political trends in the Balkans after the Cold War increased fragmentation of this region and brought new divisions. Without strong impetus from the outside, regional co-operation in Southeastern Europe could hardly attain a level that would be similar to that of Western and Central Europe or the Baltics. First initiatives, like the project "Euro-

---

26 About 600,000 Serbs making up 12.5 per cent of the population lived in Croatia before the war. As the result of "ethnic cleansing", the number of Serbs in Croatia has dropped to less than 5 per cent of the total population, while around 300,000 of the refugees of Krajina are presently living in Serbia.

27 FR Yugoslavia, Macedonia and (to a certain extent) Greece, are linked by the common fear of Albanian irredentism which threatens all three countries. The main land corridor of Greece and Macedonia towards western Europe passes through Serbia, whereas FR Yugoslavia's main transport corridor to the Aegean Sea and the eastern Mediterranean passes through Macedonia and Greece.

slavia" of the Italian geopolitical magazine *Limes*[28], came as the conflict in Bosnia-Herzegovina was nearing its end, recommending the way for the post-war reconstruction and the region's integration into Europe. The Dayton Peace Agreement facilitated projects such as the Royaumont Initiative and the EU's Regional Approach, or SECI, the primary purpose of which was to explore the possibilities for regional co-operation in Southeastern Europe and the prospects for its integration into the EU (in the first instance) or NATO (in the second). These projects, however, were neither supported by any significant funds nor given adequate political backing and thus could not produce any significant results. As a result, Southeastern Europe will in all likelihood grow to be a real challenge for the EU and NATO once the first round of expansion is realised and boundaries near the borders of this region augment the differences between the countries that are "within" and those remaining "outside". Slovenia found herself among the five countries to begin negotiations with the EU for membership in the middle of 1998, and it is likely that Slovenia, Romania and Bulgaria will find themselves in the second stage of NATO enlargement (should it ensue). Most probably, the question of the status of the other countries of the region in the EU and NATO will be dealt with in the third or some subsequent round. In the meantime, these countries will be obliged to satisfy themselves with regional co-operation in the Southeastern European region and the Stabilisation and Association Agreements enabling "virtual membership" in the EU, i.e., by partial admission into some EU structures.

The Regional Approach of the EU towards the republics of former Yugoslavia and Albania proceeded from the assumption that it is impossible to reach stability in this region until its infrastructure is renewed and an open market economy is successfully installed. Like the "Euroslavia" project, the EU's Regional Approach also seems to proceed from the supposition that their economies had been integrated and had been compatible in the former Yugoslavia, so that economic logic ordains that they should revive their earlier ties.

---

28 L. Caracciollo and M. Corinman, authors of this project, explained its goals in the following way: "The US is in the process of manufacturing a state of non-war (in Bosnia – P.S.). The model which is being used in Bosnia is analogous to the one already applied to Lebanon, with Serbs and Croats taking the place of the Israelis and the Syrians. But American efforts in the former Yugoslavia cannot be expected to continue indefinitely. (...) It is basically up to us here in Europe to go about the work of building a peace. It is this conviction that has given rise to the idea of Euroslavia. What we mean by this is a proposal for pacification and development in the post-Yugoslav states and in Southeastern Europe, based on a sort of geopolitical exchange: the gradual reintegration of the southern Slavs and other peoples of the region, while continuing to respect the established national borders, as a necessary precondition to their integration within Europe." Quoted after: The Euroslavia Project, Eurobalkans, No 24/1996.

Table 4: Trade by destination of Yugoslav Republics in 1987 (in per cent of GDP)[29]

Republics of Deliveries	Deliveries to the SFR Yugoslavia local market (Exports)	Deliveries to markets of other republics	Deliveries to markets abroad
Bosnia-Herz.	56.1	24.2	19.8
Croatia	67.0	18.7	14.3
Macedonia	60.8	21.4	17.8
Montenegro	57.5	25.0	17.5
Serbia with K&V	69.0	13.4	17.6
Serbia proper	62.3	17.4	20.3
Kosovo & Metohia	64.6	24.0	11.4
Vojvodina	58.1	28.8	13.1
Slovenia	57.5	20.3	22.2

In order to promote economic co-operation in the area of former Yugoslavia, the EU has two channels of influence. The first consists of contractual relations between the EU and individual countries of the region and, as the EU is by far their largest trading partner and point of attraction, such contractual relations constitute a powerful instrument of EU influence on all of them. The other channel of influence has to do with the programmes of financial support and financial co-operation by which intra-and inter-regional co-operation will be boosted directly. Apart from having an interest in stabilising peace, preventing new conflicts and new waves of refugees and bolstering post-war reconstruction in the republics of the former Yugoslavia, the EU is likewise interested in this region since two of its members (Italy and Greece), two future members (Hungary and Slovenia) and three associated members (Romania, Bulgaria and Turkey) border it. The decision of the pan-European ministerial conferences on transport held on the Isle of Crete and in Helsinki supporting the development of so-called European Corridor 10 (Salzburg-Ljubljana-Zagreb-Belgrade-Nis-Skopje-Veles-Thessaloniki with branches in the direction of Budapest-Novi Sad and Nis-Sofia), and Waterway Corridor VII (the Danube) which goes through this region, indicates such interest. In the spring of 1997, the EU passed a document conditioning its ties with these countries with a series of political and other requirements; a reconstruction programme for the area of former Yugoslavia (OBNOVA) was adopted, FRY was approved autonomous trade preferentials and so on, but by the end of the year the EU again lost initiative. One should, nevertheless, emphasise that some EU members – Italy and Greece, for instance – did display interest in the region's development: Italy provided funds within the framework

29 M. Uvalic: op. cit., p. 3.

of a special programme of co-operation with the Balkan countries. This co-operation is decentralised, and while northern Italy is developing ties with Slovenia and Croatia, southern Italy (Puglia in particular) is cultivating ties with Albania, Greece and FRY (Montenegro, above all).[30] Greek investors are active in Bulgaria, Romania and Albania, and more recently in Macedonia, FRY and the Bosnian Serb Republic as well, increasing Greek economic presence in this region considerably.

The other project – SECI – was an American initiative that has provoked controversy in Slovenia, Croatia and Hungary, which were hardly keen about responding to the US invitation for co-operation within Southeastern Europe. This controversy also involved FRY, which had not been invited on account of its internal political situation, and the EU and Russia, which did not show much enthusiasm for America's unilateral approach. The differences between the EU and the United States were soon dispelled and a separate document stipulated that the SECI would be complementary to the EU's initiatives (its regional approach, the Royaumont initiative, the pre-accession strategy, etc.).[31] Despite the question of whether this group of twelve geographically close but in all other aspects different countries could become an economic or political region, the American initiative had its own logic in the broader scope of contemporary changes in Europe.[32] With the incorporation of Poland, the Czech Republic and Hungary in the spring of 1999, NATO's boundaries stretched one thousand kilometres eastward, necessitating corresponding changes on its northern and southern flanks. And, while complex regional structures are being constructed in the north, i.e. in the Baltic, there is nothing of the kind in the south, so the American initiative is probably aimed at filling this gap. SECI is, however, a self-assistance programme which is primarily designed to provide know-how in the field of infrastructure and environment management. For example, the first among 16 projects under the programme is an attempt at facilitating border crossing not only to augment their physical capacities (border crossings, equipment), but to remove administrative obstacles hampering the circulation of persons and commodities.[33] In other words, the US initiative is an attempt to develop the economic capabilities of the region so that it would become more attractive for the investment of foreign capital.

---

30   L. Adamovic: Ekonomska reintegracija jugoistocne Evrope, Melunarodna politika, No. 1055/97, pp. 6–14.

31   South-East European Co-operative Initiative (SECI) – Final Points of Common EU-US Understanding, Brussels 1996.

32   The fact that around 150 million people inhabit the 12 countries covered by SECI has much to say about the potential of the Southeastern European market.

33   Projects launched under the SECI and their results are elaborated in: V. M. Budway: SECI – An Impetus for Stability in South-East Europe, mimeo, Vienna, October 1996.

*Table 5: Intra-Balkan trade (1996)[34] – exports and imports per cent in total**

		Slovenia	Croatia	B&H	Yugoslavia	Albania	Macedonia	Romania	Bulgaria	Greece	Turkey
Slovenia	Export		10.34	3.17	–	–	2.06	–	–	–	–
	Import		6.18	–	–	–	0.75	–	–	–	–
Croatia	Export	13.55		12.16	–	–	1.31	–	–	–	–
	Import	9.88		–	–	–	–	–	–	–	–
B&H	Export	–	–		9.90	–	–	–	–	–	–
	Import	15.00	31.20		68.50	–	–	–	–	–	–
Yugoslavia	Export	–	–	20.60		–	11.50	–	–	5.40	–
	Import	–	–	5.60		–	5.20	–	–	3.20	–
Albania	Export	–	–	–	–		4.00	–	0.10	9.90	6.20
	Import	–	–	–	–		3.50	–	8.20	26.60	4.10
Macedonia	Export	7.10	–	–	21.40	2.80		0.30	3.30	8.90	1.60
	Import	8.30	2.70	–	10.80	0.30		0.70	6.60	4.70	2.70
Romania	Export	–	–	–	–	–	–		–	2.19	4.82
	Import	–	–	–	–	–	–		–	1.62	1.91
Bulgaria	Export	–	–	–	4.33	0.86	3.01	1.50		7.03	8.17
	Import	–	–	–	–	–	0.58	1.49		3.40	1.98
Greece	Export	–	–	–	1.30	–	0.80	1.86	1.75		1.00
	Import	–	–	–	0.40	2.00	0.40	0.80	1.50		2.00
Turkey	Export	–	–	–	–	–	–	1.20	0.60	1.10	
	Import	–	–	–	–	–	–	0.90	0.80	0.90	

* "–" relates to trade considerably below 1 per cent.

34 V. Gligorov: Trade in the Balkans, Paper presented at the conference "South-East Europe after NATO and EU Enlargement: Towards Inclusive Security Structures?", WEU Institute for Security Studies, Paris, December 1997, p. 3.

The objectives of the third initiative – co-operation among the Balkan countries – are far broader, including: (1) stability and good neighbourliness, (2) confidence building and security, (3) a common European orientation (integration in the EU and NATO, (4) democratisation and (5) implementation of the Dayton Accords.[35] Balkan ministerial conferences, held in 1996 and 1997, initiated bilateral, multilateral and regional co-operation among these countries in the field of trade and investment, cross-border co-operation, transport, telecommunication and power line infrastructure improvements, joint environment protection programmes, the promotion of humanitarian, social and cultural co-operation, co-operation in the juridical field, combating organised crime, the eradication of terrorism and combating illicit drugs and arms trafficking. The correlation of Balkan co-operation with the Royaumont Initiative and SECI, the BSEC and the Central European Initiative was specifically deliberated at the Balkan ministerial conference at Thessaloniki in July 1997. Various initiatives for co-operation in the region, none of them supported with adequate finances, call to mind the early 1990s debate in Europe of whether the multitude of European organisations are "interlocking" or "interblocking". The ministerial conferences and summits of the Southeastern European countries, have, however, provided a useful forum for regional leaders to meet and discuss open issues. The First Summit held on the Isle of Crete, for instance, had neither a fixed agenda nor ended with the passing of any imposing declarations, but instead served as a stage for meetings that were otherwise difficult to convene, such as that of the Greek Prime Minister, Costas Simitis, and Turkey's Prime Minister, Mesud Jilmaz, with Macedonia's President, Kiro Gligorov, and that of the Yugoslav President, Slobodan Milosevic, with the Albanian Prime Minister, Fatos Nano, the latter being the first in fifty years.

Regional co-operation in the Danubian region has no tradition (except for the Danube Commission), but developments in Central and Southeastern Europe in the course of the 1990s indicate that this region could soon take on a completely different form. The Danube is, in the first place, Europe's longest river (2,850 km) and is navigable for 2,414 kilometres of its course. Completion of the Rhine-Main-Danube Canal in 1994 opened up the longest waterway in Europe (3,505 km), enabling river transport between Rotterdam and Sulina, that is, between the North Sea and the Black Sea. Compared with the Rhine-Main, traffic on the Danube is, however, considerably more modest; less than 50 per cent of its hydropower potential is being utilised; and co-operation among the countries of the Danube remains undeveloped. As in the case of Balkan co-operation, the bipolar division of Europe over the five previous decades had not provided any space for different forms of regional co-operation, with the exception

35 Thessaloniki Declaration: op. cit., p. 36.

of the Danube Commission. As late as 1991 the regional authorities of Lower Austria came up with an initiative for the formation of a Working Group of the Danubian Regions. The war that broke out in former Yugoslavia and, above all, the UN Security Council's sanctions, quickly renewed obstacles to Danubian co-operation. Indeed, the Western European Union dispatched a fleet of six patrol boats to Romania and Bulgaria to oversee the implementation of the trade embargo against FRY on the Danube, practically stopping traffic on the river. Interest for co-operation among the countries on the Danube is wide: from the development of river transport, power generation, and tourism to environmental protection. The Danube is navigable for its entire course through Serbia (592 kilometres); it is navigable even for river and sea going vessels with a tonnage of up to 5,000 tons as far as Belgrade, which means that there is a possibility for various cargoes to be shipped from Belgrade to the Black Sea and via the Volga and River Don waterways to the Caspian Sea. At its junction in Belgrade, the Danube links with other transport corridors that pass through FRY, which geographically, at least, could establish this city as one of the principal traffic and commercial centres in Southeastern Europe. Most of these initiatives are, however, still only possibilities, their realization remains a matter for the future.

IV European Union and Southeastern Europe

"So far, the most comprehensive initiatives of the European Union towards Southeastern Europe are the Stability Pact and Stabilisation and Association Agreements that were launched as a direct response to the war in Kosovo and Metohia. Since the major responsibility for implementing these initiatives rests with the EU, it is important to look closer into EU policies of recent years. The EU initially underestimated political problems in the heart of the Southeast European region (in former Yugoslavia) while later, constrained by other priorities and problems, it took action only 'the day after', once it was too late to prevent the development of a new crisis situation. The absence of a global strategy for the Balkans has meant in practice that the EU had to apply various *ad hoc* policies, by which most successor states of former Yugoslavia have been particularly disadvantaged."[36] Vladimir Gligorov has pointed out that "diversity and bilateralism have been the name of the game"[37]. The awareness that something must be done on a regional basis came only after the end of the war in Bosnia-Herzegovina, which result-

---

36 M. Uvalic: op. cit., p. 7.

37 V. Gligorov, M. Kaldor and L. Tsoukalis: Economic Reconstruction and European Integration, Paper presented at the "LSE – WIIW Conference, Reconstruction and Integration in Southeastern Europe – Economic Aspects", Vienna, November 1999.

ed in the development of the EU's Regional Approach in 1996 for the five countries of the so-called "Western Balkans" (Albania, Bosnia-Herzegovina, Croatia, FYR of Macedonia and FRY). "The EU Regional Approach strongly encouraged closer economic and political ties among these countries, but it came rather late (only after four years of military conflicts); it remained rather vague (not proposing and elaborating concrete programmes of regional co-operation); it was backed by limited financial resources; and perhaps most importantly, it offered no incentives whatsoever for these countries to carry forward its main objectives."[38]

Therefore, the latest phase of EU policies towards Southeastern Europe is very important. For the first time in ten years, the Stability Pact provides prospects for future EU membership also for five Southeastern European non-candidate countries. A new type of agreement has also been offered – Stabilisation and Association Agreements – for this group of countries, as a part of the Stabilisation and Association Process, as the linchpin of the Stability Pact.[39] The Stability Pact integrated most of the previous initiatives on regional co-operation (Royaumont process, SECI and the like), attempting to mobilise funds both for the long term projects and so-called Quick Start Packages. The results, however, were mixed: even thought the Funding Conference in March 2000 raised considerable funds, most of them are not fresh money but previously committed funds for various projects in the region. Even the first major project that was accepted – the bridge between Varna (Bulgaria) and Kalafat (Romania) – raised some doubts that its purpose is to by-pass transit corridors through Serbia rather than link the industrial regions of the two countries in the lower part of the Danube. Effective reconstruction of the Southeastern European region, in terms of sustainable development rather than just the physical reconstruction of housing, bridges and roads, must have as one key component the creation of new forms of regional economic ties, as was the case in post-war Western Europe. The Marshall Plan was designed to foster regional integration and was backed by the creation of new European regional institutions which were designed to facilitate intra-regional trade (OECD or European Payments Union). Regional structures are therefore needed that are specifically designed to facilitate and promote the expansion of trade and other economic links among the Southeastern European countries. A multilateral credit mechanism ought to be created for extending credit facilities specifically for such purposes, backed by some credible financial organisation, such as the EBRD. "Alternatively, as suggested in 1996 by the former governor of the National

38 M. Uvalic: op. cit., p. 7.
39 On this point: H. Kretschmer: EU-Strategies towards Southeastern Europe: Trouble spot Balkans – Implications for EU policy, Paper presented at the ELIAMEP Seminar at Halki, September 1999.

90

Bank of Yugoslavia, Dragoslav Avramovic, a common regional fund could be created, whose initial capital would consist of the still undivided foreign exchange reserves of former Yugoslavia, which would serve as collateral to attract additional capital on international financial markets."[40]

40   M. Uvalic: op. cit., p. 9.

Issue Reports

Security and Stability: EU and NATO Strategies

Kostas Ifantis

I Introduction

In the aftermath of the Kosovo conflict, Southeastern Europe is at a crossroad. More than ever, today's challenge is to speed up the consolidation of security and stability in a region that has known little of either in the last decade. It is paramount that Southeastern Europe should not become a permanent black hole in the critical part of the wider Eastern European region.

Countries of Southeastern Europe have, for the last decade, enjoyed a great deal of support from the international community in general and the European Union in particular. Despite this, they have continued to suffer from inter-ethnic tensions and conflicts. There has been a lack of substantial political or economic development. Despite major efforts to stabilise individual countries and the region as a whole, the progress made has been fragile. This is clear from the degree to which it has been jeopardised by the conflict in Kosovo. The region is now at a turning point. A new approach to peace and stability, involving both the countries of the wider region and the European Union, is urgently needed. At a time of upheaval and uncertainty in the region, the EU has a responsibility to contribute both to the resolution of the immediate instability and, in the longer term, to the general stabilisation and development of the region. This responsibility has been recognised, but fulfilling it will necessitate decisions on considerable amounts of further assistance, as well as on appropriate implementation mechanisms and legal bases.[1]

The European Union faces an ever greater challenge. In almost every respect, the region has the ability to challenge the security and stability of the EU, as well as to undermine its credibility and potential as a global player. The EU needs to play an impor-

---

1 Commission Communication to the Council and European Parliament, COM(99)235 of 26 May 1999.

tant proactive role in the region. Structural problems and unresolved issues in South-eastern Europe are concentrated mainly, but not exclusively, in the partner states of the EU Regional Approach. The region is heterogeneous in every respect – ethnically, culturally, religiously, linguistically, economically and politically – and some potential causes of conflict are shared by almost all countries, including unresolved territorial and minority questions, economic backwardness and high levels of economic distortion, unstable and often undemocratic political systems, reluctance to resort to peaceful conflict settlement mechanisms and to confidence-building measures and underdeveloped regional co-operation structures.

EU interests in the region include: the containment of violent ethnic conflict as a prerequisite for lasting stability all over Europe; the reduction of migration caused by poverty, war, persecution and civil strife; the establishment of market economy structures with stable economic growth to close the prosperity gap in Europe; and economic interests (growing markets, investment possibilities, etc.). In short, the EU has a real and vital interest in the European perspective for the whole of Southeastern Europe, and should aim at counteracting trends towards destabilisation and marginalisation.[2]

This chapter consists of four parts:

1. The next section traces the impact of the war in Kosovo on the EU's strategy in the region, focusing on the new instruments devised by the EU in order to strengthen its ties with regional players and promote stability and prosperity in the Balkans.

2. Then, the reactions of the Southeastern European states to the Western strategies – especially the Kosovo intervention – are examined.

3. After that, the discussion provides a critical assessment of the EU relations with the Balkans with reference to both the economic and political aspects of the EU strategy in the region. Several themes are examined, including the effectiveness of the EUs "carrot and stick" strategy in the region; the consistency with which the EU's conditionality principle was applied in the Balkans; the effectiveness of such a principle in promoting reform in the region and its compatibility with the main features of the Balkan crisis; and the willingness of the EU member states to sub-ordinate their national agendas under the EU strategy in the region and provide the necessary financial resources in order to substantiate it.

4. The concluding section highlights the pre-conditions for the development and successful implementation of a working regional approach to the problems in the Balkans. In this context, a strategy of linking crisis management with economic assistance is imperative and thus underlined.

---

2   F. Cameron: The European Union's Policy Towards South East Europe, in: The Southeast European Yearbook 1998–99, ELIAMEP, 1999, p. 32.

II The post-Cold War EU strategy

Following the signing of the EC-Comecon Joint Declaration and, in particular, following the fall of the Berlin Wall, the EU[3] sought to devise a strategy towards all East
European countries that was based on three fundamental principles:

- *Conditionality*: Closer relations with the EU being conditional to economic and
  political reforms in the East European country in question.[4]
- *Differentiation*: Whilst the basic format of EU contractual relations with the East
  European countries would remain the same, the specific provisions of each individual
  agreement would vary and would have to be negotiated bilaterally between the EU
  and the East European country in question.[5]
- *Compartmentalisation*: The principle of compartmentalisation was never publicly
  acknowledged as the official EU policy in Eastern Europe. It was, nevertheless, the
  logical conclusion of the previous two principles. Since the EU refused to negotiate
  with the East European countries on a "block to block" basis (i.e., with all the Central and East European countries at the same time) then these countries would have
  to be "grouped" into different "waves" (using the conditionality principle) and then
  be invited to negotiate with the EU one after the other.[6]

Relations between the EU and the Balkans have not remained unaffected by these
principles. The timing of the collapse of communist regimes in the region, their diverse
economic and political starting points, the speed (and quality) of their reform process
and, of course, the war in Yugoslavia enormously affected the performance of Southeast
European countries in the framework of their contractual relations with the EU. Indeed,
the opening of association negotiations with Bulgaria and Romania was not possible
until after the signing of the Visegrád Association Agreements in December 1991. Hence,
the Romanian and Bulgarian Association Agreements were concluded in November and
December 1992 respectively.[7]

---

3   Although not always historically accurate, the term EU is used throughout the text.

4   It is worth noting that the conditionality principle can also be found in the "Accession Partnerships" between the
    EU and the Central and East European Countries who have applied for EU membership (Memo/98/21 of 27 March
    1998) as well as in "Stabilisation and Association Process" for the Balkan region (COM(99)235 of 26 May 1999).

5   The differentiation principle was most clearly expressed in the Commission's proposals for the Association
    agreements with the Central and East European Countries in August 1990. For more details COM(90)398 final of
    27 August 1990, p. 4.

6   On the effects of compartmentalisation on the process of EU enlargement: D. Papadimitriou: The European
    Community and the Negotiation of the Association Agreements with the Countries of Central and Eastern Europe:
    A Study of Bargaining in Iterated Games, 1990–1992, unpublished PhD Thesis, University of Bradford, Bradford
    1999, chapters 7–8.

7   Agence Europe of 18 November 1992 and Agence Europe of 23 December 1992.

In subsequent years, Bulgaria's and Romania's position as second-wave applicants was undermined by poor economic performance and prolonged political uncertainty in the two countries. In addition, despite the hopes created by the electoral victories of Emil Constantinescu in Romania and Petar Stoyanov in Bulgaria, both in late 1996, the two countries' further relegation was confirmed by the Commission's opinions on the East European membership applicants published (alongside Agenda 2000) in July 1997.[8] The Commission's proposals provided for the inclusion of both Bulgaria and Romania (alongside Latvia, Lithuania and Slovakia) into the second, slower lane of enlargement negotiations.

In Albania, it was only after the first multi-party elections in March 1991 that the country was invited to enter into contractual relations with the EU. The country joined the Phare programme in December 1991,[9] whilst a Trade and Co-operation Agreement (TCA) was concluded with the EU in February 1992.[10] However, the desolate economic conditions in the country, coupled with frequent spells of political instability, have prevented Albania from strengthening its ties with the EU. Hence, the country has neither signed an Association Agreement nor yet applied for full EU membership. Instead, in early 1996, Albania (alongside the republics of the former Yugoslavia except Slovenia) became part of the EU's Regional Approach in the Balkans and also participated in Political Dialogue meetings which focused on humanitarian operations and actions to help ensure the economic and political stabilisation of the country[11] following the collapse of public order in 1996 and the frequent outbreaks of violence ever since.

Amongst the former republics of Yugoslavia, Slovenia has clearly been the best performer. Since the 1991 war, Slovenia has enjoyed a sustained period of economic growth and a stable and democratic political system. The country's relations with the EU also developed at a very fast pace, leading to a formal application for membership on 10 June 1996. With the publication of the Commission's positive avis in July 1997, the country further disassociated itself from the rest of the region's poor status. Indeed, the Slovenians prefer not to think of themselves as part of the Balkans at all.

The Former Yugoslav Republic of Macedonia (FYROM), on the other hand, despite

---

8   COM(97), vols. I, II, III of 15 July 1997.

9   Council Regulation (EEC) No. 3800/91 of 23 December 1991. Some (mainly humanitarian) funds had been made available to the country since mid-1991.

10 Following the Commission's request (COM(91)309), Council approval for the opening of negotiations with Albania was given on 23 September 1991 (Bull. EC 9–1991). Following its conclusion on 17 February 1992, the Albanian Trade and Co-operation Agreement was signed by the Council on 11 May 1992 (Bull. EC 5–1992) and came into force on 1 December 1992. For the text of the agreement COM(92)178 final.

11 See, for example, the EU's Joint Actions for the establishment of a viable police force in Albania (Decision 1999/189/CFSP, OJ L 63, 12 March 1999) and the destruction of weapons in the country (Decision 1999/320/CFSP, OJ L 123, 13 May 1999).

its poor economic performance since its independence from Yugoslavia in 1992, came to be recognised as a stabilising factor in the region. The moderate policies pursued by President Kiro Gligorov (1992–1999) managed to preserve FYROM's fragile internal balance, thus safeguarding – so far – its integrity which was threatened by the destructive tensions in Bosnia and Kosovo. Moreover, the gradual improvement of relations with Greece paved the way for strengthening the country's ties with the EU. Hence, FYROM established full diplomatic relations with the EU in December 1995, and since the beginning of 1996 it has been a participant in the EU's Regional Approach and in the Political Dialogue meetings. On 29 April 1997 the country signed a Trade and Co-operation agreement.

For the remaining republics of the former Yugoslavia (Bosnia, Croatia and FRY), relations with the EU were structured around the Regional Approach for the Balkans as agreed by the General Affairs Council on 26–27 February 1996. The Regional Approach was initiated by the EU in an attempt to supplement the Dayton Agreement and OSCE efforts in the former Yugoslavia. It envisaged facilitating the successful implementation of the peace plan by supporting the former Yugoslav republics (excluding FRY) politically as well as economically with a whole set of EU instruments, including financial assistance under the Phare and OBNOVA programmes, autonomous trade preferences, and the offer of Co-operation and Association Agreements. Clearly, the process was designed to provide a framework which would assist in strengthening stability, good-neighbourliness and economic recovery in Southeastern Europe. Meetings between the political leadership of these countries and EU leaders were also scheduled under the Political Dialogue. Within this context, the five eligible countries (Albania, Bosnia, Croatia, FRY, FYROM) were divided into *two groups with different frameworks for the development of relations* with the EU (see also Table 5):[12]

– *the former Yugoslav Republic of Macedonia and Albania, which were not involved in the Bosnian war, and were, therefore, eligible to conclude Trade and Co-operation Agreements with the EU.*

– *Bosnia, Croatia and FRY, which were involved in the Dayton Peace Agreement, would need to comply with the EU's conditionality principle before being allowed to enter into any contractual relations with the EU.*[13]

The General Affairs Council on 29 April 1997 clarified the concept of political and economic conditionality with specific reference to each of the countries of Southeastern

---

12 D. Papadimitriou: The European Union's Strategy in the Post-Communist Balkans: On Carrots, Sticks and Indecisiveness, in: New Frontiers: A Journal of Southeast European and Black Sea Studies, 2000, pp. 5–6.

13 P. Simic calls the former the Dayton/western triangle and the latter the Kosovo/southern triangle of the "(Western) Balkans", P. Simic: Put u Rambuje: Kosovska Kriza 1995–2000 (The Road to Rambouillet: Kosovo Crisis 1995–2000), NEA, Beograd 2000.

Europe (Bosnia, Croatia, FRY).[14] It was also agreed that, depending on the degree of compliance with these preconditions, the three Balkan countries would be eligible for trade concessions through specific trade preferences, financial and economic assistance through the OBNOVA (aid for the republics of former Yugoslavia) and Phare programmes, and eventual establishment of contractual relations (i.e., Trade and Co-operation Agreements). During the same meeting, the General Affairs Council also agreed to grant autonomous trade preferences to Bosnia, which was also deemed suitable to continue benefiting from Phare funding.[15]

Since then, compliance with the EU's conditionality principle has continued to be closely monitored by the Commission and the Council. Thus, the General Affairs Council decided on 9 November 1998[16] to continue granting autonomous trade preferences and Phare operations in Bosnia, but dismissed the country's request for opening negotiations for the conclusion of a Trade and Co-operation Agreement with the EU. Autonomous trade preferences also continued for Croatia, which was excluded, nevertheless, from Phare funding and from opening negotiations for a Trade and Co-operation Agreement. Finally, given the continuation of human rights abuses in FRY and the deterioration of the situation in Kosovo throughout 1998, autonomous trade preferences were suspended and the country's relations with the EU remained virtually frozen.

At the end of 1998, the EU-Southeastern Europe pattern was as diverse as it could be, consisting a full EU member (Greece), a member of the first wave of enlargement applicants (Slovenia), two members of the second wave of enlargement applicants (Bulgaria and Romania – also participating in the European Conference), a membership applicant, whose eligibility for negotiating entry was denied by the EU (Turkey – not participating in the European Conference), two members of the Regional Approach with a Trade and Co-operation Agreement with the EU (Albania and FYROM), a member of the Regional Approach eligible for Phare funding, but without a Trade and Co-operation Agreement with the EU (Bosnia), a member of the Regional Approach with neither Phare eligibility nor a Trade and Co-operation Agreement with the EU (Croatia), and a country without any official contacts with the EU (FRY).[17]

---

14   PRES/97/129 of the 2003rd Council Meeting – General Affairs – Luxembourg, 29/30 April 1997.
15   PRES/96/16 of the 1902nd Council meeting – General Affairs – Brussels, 30 January 1996.
16   PRES/98/369 of the 2129th Council Meeting – General Affairs – Brussels, 9 November 1998.
17   D. Papadimitriou: op. cit., 2000, p. 7.

III Post-Kosovo war strategies

The breakdown of the Rambouillet talks over Kosovo and the subsequent NATO bombing of FRY (March 1999–June 1999) marked a turning point in the EU's and NATO's relations with the wider Balkan region. For NATO, the campaign has been hailed as a decisive turn-around in Western policy. At the same time, the outbreak of war demonstrated that the EU's "civilian" efforts, including its economic strategy, to stabilise the region were not working. In December 1998 the Vienna European Council had already recognised the difficulties of existing EU policies in the region and had called for a broader and more integrated approach based on a "Common Strategy on the Western Balkans".[18] The Kosovo war clearly accelerated this process and affected the EU's relations with the countries of the region. The launch of the Stability Pact on 10 June 1999 was the first example of the EU's changing strategy.[19] Since then the EU has opened a long-term accession perspective for the countries of Southeastern Europe and it has become common wisdom that the eventual inclusion of the region in the EU enlargement process is the most promising and cost-effective way of promoting and consolidating security, stability and prosperity, both for the region and for Europe as a whole.[20]

The Stability Pact for Southeastern Europe

It is important that the Stability Pact marked a fundamental policy shift in Europe's approach to the region, eventually learning the overdue lessons of history. From the clearly reactive crisis management policies that the international community pursued throughout the 1990s in former Yugoslavia, the Stability Pact seems to have most of the elements needed for a coherent, long-term conflict prevention policy that aims at addressing the looming security problems of the region well before they erupt. At least in theory, the Stability Pact is the "missing integrative, long-term policy that is moving away from the country-limited focus of the recent past, and, instead, perceives the

---

18 Conclusions of the Vienna European Council, Doc/98/12 of 11/12 December 1998.

19 The establishment of the Stability Pact was originally envisaged by the General Affairs Councils on 8–26 April 1999 (PRES/99/94 of the Special Council Meeting – General Affairs – Luxembourg, 8 April 1999 and 2173 and PRES/99/118 of the Council Meeting – General Affairs – Luxembourg, 26 April 1999). The plan was then approved by the Council on 17 May 1999 (PRES/99/146 of the 2177th Council Meeting – General Affairs – Brussels, 17 May 1999) and was officially launched by the Cologne special international meeting on 10 June 1999.

20 Bertelsmann Foundation (ed.): The Balkans and New European Responsibilities, Strategy paper presented to the special meeting of "The Club of Three and the Balkans", Brussels, 29/30 June 2000, p. 14.

region as a whole",[21] taking full account of the regional and structural nature of the impediments to political democratisation and market-reform. Moreover, contrary to almost all past initiatives (the European Royaumont process and the American Southeast European Co-operative Initiative), in this case there is a considerable consensus among all the participants on the main features and goals of the project. Bringing together a very large number of countries and organisations (including the EU, the US, Russia, the IMF, the UN, the OSCE and others, including numerous international NGOs), the Stability Pact seems to be the expression of a serious determination to create a framework for the coordination of military and economic efforts to stabilise the region and to contribute to the consolidation of lasting peace, democracy and economic prosperity. In this respect, the Stability Pact has been a strategic decision of high political value for the region and for Europe as a whole.

As for NATO and especially for the membership prospects of the Southeast European countries, things were quite different. In the "Statement on Kosovo" and in the final communiqué of the Washington Summit of 24 April 1999, it became clear that the time for a decision was not yet ripe. The confirmation of the Alliance's "open door" policy and the offering of a new "Membership Action Plan" was carefully crafted so as not to raise any additional expectations on further enlargement rounds.[22]

However, NATO forcefully "declared" its distinct interest in getting involved with the Stability Pact. Following a US drive, NATO announced its "Southeastern Europe Initiative" (SEEI) and arranged a "19+7" meeting at the Washington Summit. By declaring its own interest, the Alliance strongly endorsed the Stability Pact and offered to set up a "consultation forum for security issues". Moreover, "the appeal of this body is that NATO has designed a distinct, tailor-made forum (...) going beyond the Euro-Atlantic Partnership Council and the Partnership for Peace, thus strengthening its voice and gaining stronger leverage in the region."[23]

Although NATO demanded to have a major say at the "Regional Table", as well as at the third "Working Table" on security issues, its role was watered down due to mainly French and Russian reservations[24]. In such a "high politics" context, it remains to be seen whether SEEI will become merely a discussion forum or whether it will become an

21 R. Biermann: The Stability Pact for Southeastern Europe – Potentials, Problems and Perspectives, ZEI Discussion Paper C 56, 1999, pp. 5–7.

22 It has to be noted, however, that during the crisis, NATO offered temporary security guarantees for Montenegro and FYROM.

23 R. Biermann: op. cit., p. 24.

24 The role of NATO in the Third Table is remarkably small. Even in the sub-table on Security and Defence Affairs, only three projects were NATO-sponsored. W. van Meurs: Think Tanks Around the Third Table, Conference on Research Co-operation on Security Issues in Southeastern Europe, Bertelsmann Foundation and Office of the Special Co-ordinator of the Stability Pact, Brussels, 29/30 May 2000.

important and effective process of interregional institutionalisation that can stabilise the expectations of the Southeast European countries and essentially advance regional co-operation on security issues. And it also remains to be seen whether SEEI will be closely co-ordinated within the Stability Pact or whether bypassing NATO will cause the Alliance to pursue its initiative de facto separately.[25] In any case, "the relation with NATO is crucial for the Third Table in order not to end up with the question, who is duplicating whom?"[26]

Above all, however, progress and success ultimately depend on the full engagement of all the actors in the process, especially of the Southeast European countries. "The Stability Pact as a comprehensive long-term structural project is under tremendous pressure of time and expectations (from donors and recipients) to produce accountable, sustainable results in the short term."[27] The Stability Pact is doomed to fail if there is no strong determination by the countries in the region to shoulder the primary responsibility themselves, thus creating the pre-conditions for further democratisation, building civil societies, establishing favourable conditions for investment and trade, good neighbourly relations and regional co-operation.[28] That clearly implies that the regional actors cannot afford to "remain de facto objects of the process, torn between the multiple international actors with their own agendas and priorities".[29] And this is an enormous challenge for a region with a poor record of intra-regional co-operation.

The Stabilisation and Association Process

Within the wider context of the Stability Pact, the EU launched a new type of relationship with the countries of the region in June 1999: the Stabilisation and Association Process.[30] The Stabilisation and Association Agreements were made available to five countries – Albania, Bosnia, Croatia, Macedonia and FRY – provided they comply with the EU conditionality principle as it was elaborated within the context of the Regional Approach in April 1997. For the first time, the Stabilisation and Association Process has offered these five countries a prospect of EU integration, based on a progressive approach

25 R. Biermann: op. cit., p. 25.
26 W. van Meurs: op. cit.
27 Bertelsmann Foundation (ed.): op. cit., p. 17.
28 F. Cameron: op. cit., pp. 40–44.
29 R. Biermann: op. cit., p. 32.
30 These new types of agreements were proposed by the Commission on 26 May 1999 (COM(99)235 of 26 May 1999). The agreements were approved, in principle, by the Cologne European Council (Conclusions of the German Presidency, 4 June 1999) on 4 June 1999 and by the General Affairs Council in Luxembourg on 21/22 June 1999 (provisional conclusions of the 2192nd General Affairs Council meeting, 21/22 June, 1999).

adapted to the situation of the specific countries. This prospect is a historic turning point in the relations of the five countries with the European Union.

The Stabilisation and Association Process is a major step forward in Western policy insofar as it offers stronger incentives to these five countries, but it also places more demanding political and economic conditions on them. The basic principle of the Stabilisation and Association Agreements is conditionality, although regional co-operation is one of the main conditions. Indeed, the need for regional co-operation is stressed particularly strongly. In order to develop a closer relationship with the EU, these countries will have to gear their political, economic and institutional development to the values and models underpinning the European Union: democracy, respect for human and minority rights, a market economy, inviolability of borders and good-neighbourly relations. The European Union will support and assist them in introducing the reforms necessary to progress in these areas.

The Stabilisation and Association Agreements constituted a step further from the Trade and Co-operation Agreements (first generation) and resembled the Association (or Europe) Agreements, but with a greater emphasis on regional co-operation, democratisation, the development of civil society and institution building. The agreements will also include provisions for trade liberalisation, financial assistance, co-operation in a wide range of policies (including judicial and domestic policies) as well as the strengthening of the process of Political Dialogue.[31] In order to give a signal of determination, FYROM was the first country to be selected by the Commission to begin Stabilisation and Association Agreement negotiations with the EU,[32] on 16 June 1999. In the eyes of the Commission, FYROM has made the most significant progress in democratisation, economic transformation and good neighbourly relations. Albania and Croatia (following the results of the presidential election on 7 February)[33] are likely to follow in the near future. Meanwhile, trade relations with the countries concerned would continue to be regulated by the Trade and Co-operation Agreements (for FYROM and Albania) and by the autonomous trade preferences (for Bosnia, Croatia).[34]

The stabilising potential of the Stabilisation and Association Process is yet to be seen. There is room for scepticism. Firstly, this new political instrument was proposed at the

31 COM(99)235 of 26 May 1999.

32 COM(99)300 of 16 June 1999. The Commission's proposals were accepted by the Council on 19 July 1999 and on 8 September 1999 the Commission submitted a request for the granting of negotiating directives.

33 Statement of the Council on the elections in Croatia, Pesc/00/9, 8 February 2000. On 9 March 2000, EU Foreign Relations Commissioner Chris Patten said in Zagreb that Croatia was fit to be considered for an Association and Stabilisation Agreement. RFE/RL Newsline, 10 March 2000.

34 The autonomous trade preferences for both countries were renewed and improved on 5 January 2000 (Regulation (EC) No. 6/2000), OJ L 2, 5 January 2000 (for Bosnia) and Regulation (EC) No. 7/2000, OJ L 2, 5 January 2000 (for Croatia).

Council meeting when the Commission was obviously trying to ward off more ambitious proposals on EU enlargement to Southeastern Europe. The Stabilisation and Association Agreement primarily serve these countries that have not concluded Co-operation Agreements with the EU up to now. For FYROM and Albania, the prospect of negotiating an Association Agreement has simply been replaced by the Stabilisation and Association Agreement perspective.[35] Secondly, the Commission has stressed that the Regional Approach remains basically valid. Thus, the conditions for upgrading EU relations with those specific countries and extending financial aid will not be tempered.

Thirdly, this new contractual perspective does not affect Bulgaria and Romania, who already signed "Europe Agreements" years ago and were invited to begin accession negotiations. The aftermath of the Kosovo crisis saw a substantial improvement in their relations with the EU. The two countries' crucial support of NATO's bombing of Yugoslavia (against a not very enthusiastic domestic audience) did not go without reward. Soon after its appointment, the new EU Commission came out in favour of an all-inclusive enlargement process. The Progress Reports on enlargement, published on 13 October 1999,[36] argued for the inclusion of Bulgaria, Latvia, Lithuania, Romania and Slovakia into the "fast lane" of accession negotiations. The Commission's proposals were agreed to by the Helsinki European Council in December 1999[37] and the formal opening of accession negotiations of the former second wave applicants took place on 28 March 2000.

IV Regional reactions to Western strategies

The Kosovo conflict has deeply affected the domestic politics, national economy, foreign policy and national security of the region's countries. High expectations have been created regarding future economic assistance, defence ties, political relationships, and their prospective integration into the Euro-Atlantic community. By focusing on the state reactions to the NATO air campaign against FRY, the conflict and its aftermath is placed in the broader perspective needed for constructing policies aimed at establishing security and stability in Southeastern Europe.

For *Bulgaria*, the war came as a blow. The economic consequences have been great, with destruction of almost all bridges over the Danube and the loss of transit routes through Serbia. This gravely affected Bulgarian exports (mainly agricultural products)

35 R. Biermann: op. cit., pp. 19–20.
36 For an overview of the Progress Reports, IP/99/751, 13 October 1999.
37 Presidency Conclusions of the Helsinki European Council, Doc 99/16, 10/11 December 1999.

and any remaining industrial competitiveness (including tourism). Foreign investment was severely curtailed, and unemployment shot up. The costs caused by the war are moderately estimated to be around US-$ 1 billion. Two years of hard won promising economic improvements have been threatened.[38] Politically, the crisis also changed the political fabric of the country. Supporting NATO's *Operation Allied Force* was hardly a popular policy. It gave a major opening to the opposition parties to undermine the Stoyanov reform government's domestic political support. Nevertheless, the Bulgarian government granted permission for air rights (though not ground transit), improved relations with FYROM,[39] abided by NATO's wish that it turn down a Russian request for use of Bulgarian airspace to fly troops to Prishtina. It adhered to the oil embargo against FRY, and firmly denounced the ethnic cleansing policies of Milosevic. Since then, it has made Bulgarian forces available to KFOR.

Having clearly cast its lot with the West, in the aftermath of the crisis Bulgaria has considerable expectations regarding the future. They include compensation for losses, financial assistance for the rebuilding of bridges and infrastructure measures (such as improvements in the electricity and telecommunication systems and augmented transportation routes), aid for the restructuring of foreign debt, and the provision of foreign direct investment.

Above all, however, the Bulgarian government seeks early entry into both NATO and the EU. An active programme of military reform is already underway, with armed forces being substantially reduced, reorganised, and trained to provide rapid-reaction and peacekeeping capabilities. It should not be surprising that the Ministry of Defence has given the highest priority to the implementation of NATO's Membership Action Plan (MAP). Public support for joining NATO remains strong even though the conflict seems to have been counterproductive in this respect.[40]

The situation in *Romania* has many similarities to that of Bulgaria, although there are clearly some important differences. The war created a heavy economic burden for the country. Lost trade with FRY was costly as was adherence to the oil embargo. The estimated financial toll of US-$ 900 million of the Kosovo conflict came as a blow to a Romanian economy, which was already under severe economic stress and deterioration due to a decrease of the 1998 GDP of over eight per cent, the worsening of an already large current account deficit and a far from stable banking system.

At the political front, the government gave its full support to the NATO policies against a very critical opposition and in the framework of a very unfavourable public

38 A. J. Pierre: De-Balkanizing the Balkans: Security and Stability in Southeastern Europe, United States Institute of Peace, Washington 1999, p. 4.

39 Sofia negotiated a conclusion to the language dispute and gave away to Skopje tanks and defence artillery.

40 A. J. Pierre: op. cit., p. 5.

opinion. Air transit rights were accorded when requested, the potential basing of NATO forces in the country was never ruled out, and Russia was not granted overflight permission in its decision to augment forces at the Prishtina airfield.[41] It was a strategy strongly reflecting the government's paramount political aim of integrating the country into the western institutional web. As is the case with Bulgaria, the Romanian Ministry of Defence is already implementing an impressive reform programme in accordance with MAP, while at the same time remaining a very active participant in the Partnership for Peace and contributing to the peacekeeping operations in Bosnia.

Overall, Romania responded to the Kosovo crisis by further promoting a co-ordinated regional strategy that gives priority to integration with the wider European structures. The approach has been shaped by a strong focus on regional infrastructure projects such as transportation and energy, incentives for foreign investment and economic growth. Moreover, all these are seen as directly contributing to the critical aim of advancing regional integration by creating conditions of confidence, trust and stable expectations.

The greatest problem for *FYROM* – a country with multi-ethnic composition, predominantly ethnic Slav but approximately one-third ethnic Albanian – during the Kosovo war was that the manifold and severe pressures created would undermine the coalition government (encompassing both groups) and derail the pursued policies of economic reform and western orientation, thus destabilising a state, which was in any case fragile. As was expected, the crisis resulted in a deep division. The Albanians of FYROM fully supported the NATO operation as well as the KLA drive for an independent Kosovo. At the same time, however, they also took care – at least in public – to restrict KLA recruitment and activity in FYROM itself in an attempt to safeguard the delicate domestic balance. The Macedonian Slavs, on the other hand, were unsupportive if not directly opposed to the air strikes. Not only did they have economic reasons (business and trade have traditionally been through Serbia) but there were also fears that the Belgrade regime would attempt to spread the crisis to FYROM given the stationing of NATO forces there. Multiethnic communities experienced an ethnic anxiety and a dangerously tense social environment, which still persists itself today and can at some point lead to a major breakdown.[42]

Economically, the war had a devastating impact. Commerce with FRY, traditionally the largest trading partner, as well as agricultural exports ground to a halt. Unemployment rose to 40 per cent and the country spent far more on the construction and maintenance of the nine refugee camps than it received from the international community for

41   A. J. Pierre: op. cit., p. 6.
42   A. J. Pierre: op. cit., p. 9.

this purpose. The total estimated cost of the Kosovo conflict for a country of 2.1 million people has been over a US-$ 1.5 billion. Despite this shock, the government responded by accelerating the opening of the country to the western community. The OSCE monitors, who had to leave Kosovo, were based in Skopje as was the related NATO "extraction" force that was to guarantee their safety.[43]

Albania, being the poorest European country with an annual GDP per capita of only US-$ 800 and an extremely high unemployment rate, especially in the rural areas, has been experiencing a political situation which can only be found in the developing world. The economy, already devastated by the 1997 pyramid investment scheme crisis, was further crippled by the Kosovo conflict, which led to an increase in the budget deficit. The obstacles to economic development are manifold: widespread lawlessness in most areas outside of Tirana, massive corruption in government agencies, a weak judicial system with limited prosecution of criminal activities, poor infrastructure with badly needed transportation and telecommunications projects tied up by bribery and bureaucracy, and an extremely slow moving privatisation programme. This problematic state of affairs is hardly conducive to attracting desperately needed foreign investment.

In such a failing situation, the conflict brought almost 20,000 NATO troops with their equipment into the country. NATO helped construct refugee camps for some 400,000 Kosovar Albanians and assisted the humanitarian workers in distributing humanitarian aid. On an operational level, the Alliance established a planning cell and was preparing to use the country as its prime basing area should it become necessary to undertake ground action against FRY. In every way, Albania put itself at NATO's disposal.[44]

For the Albanian government, NATO presence has translated into the much needed stabilising domestic factor; it thus sought to extend it as much as possible. The desire for a continuing international presence is, in part, a reflection of the deep mistrust that exists among the population and between their political actors. It is widely believed that the country cannot survive in its present status without the active engagement of the international community. In this context, the government is also seeking major economic development assistance. It has been developing a multi-million dollar list of infrastructure and energy projects to be financed by the West. Whether the existing bureaucracy and habits are capable of handling massive projects without falling prey to the criminal misuse of funds is, however, an open question.

Nevertheless, this is a critical moment for Albania. The situation continues to be a

---

43 Approximately 15,000 NATO troops were placed in FYROM during the conflict, making the country a most valuable logistics support area, providing lines of supplies and communications for KFOR and other NATO forces. A. J. Pierre: op. cit., p. 9.

44 A. J. Pierre: op. cit., p. 11.

potential source of major political instability for neighbouring countries and a factor for exacerbating crime and related social problems in the region as a whole. The atavistic dream – shared by some – of a "Greater Albania" can hardly be said to have disappeared and needs to be handled with determination for the interests of both the country and the international community.

The foregoing analysis reveals that Southeastern Europe, without any doubt, is at a critical juncture for its future development. No less importantly, the Euro-Atlantic community is at a watershed in its approach to the region. The discussion of the responses of the regional actors makes it clear that their reaction to the Kosovo conflict was and is to enhance their efforts and commitment to gaining a place in the European integration map. They have incurred considerable economic costs, undergone social dislocation and accepted political risks, all with the desire of advancing and consolidating their integration prospects. The importance of the EU to a prosperous and benign future for the region cannot be underestimated. The EU is the major pole of attraction and the most effective stabiliser to which the Southeast European states are drawn and look upon. Their desire to join, no matter how far away accession may be, should create the momentum for helping to successfully implement the necessary political and economic reforms. The EU's strategy has been discussed earlier. The next section focuses on its limitations and shortcomings.

V The elusive balance of the EU strategy

As we have seen, the EU has tried to act as a stabilising factor in the region, employing a mixture of threats and promises. The EU's arsenal for the delivery of such a "carrot and stick" strategy included a variety of "weapons": trade measures available through the Common Commercial Policy (CCP), aid and financial assistance available through the G-24 and the EU's own budget, and, of course, instruments available though the newly created CFSP. In retrospect, it is arguable that neither the "carrot" nor the "stick" ends of the EU's Balkan strategy has been employed successfully. The "carrot" was often absent; when present, it was late and presented in an uncoordinated fashion.[45] For the first half of the 1990s, the EU lacked an integrated approach to the region's problems. Instead, its relations with the Balkan countries were regulated by a variety of frameworks (i.e., Trade and Co-operation Agreements, Association Agreements) which, nevertheless, linked each country bilaterally to the EU and did not provide for a coherent solution to the region's problems. For those countries (Bulgaria and Romania)

---

45   D. Papadimitriou: op. cit., p. 10.

with relatively advanced forms of relations with the EU, the strengthening of co-operation with the region's less developed countries was seen as a distraction from the ultimate goal of EU membership as well as an admission of their separation from the Visegrád group. For those countries with weaker (e.g., Albania) or no (e.g., FRY) contractual relations with the EU, the "carrot" was far too small to make a difference. The initial linking of the G-24 assistance (in particular the Phare programme) to foreign investment activities also undermined its effectiveness as a "carrot" strategy in the Balkans.[46] In a region plagued by war and a slow pace of economic reform (hardly a paradise for foreign investors) the rules governing the G-24 financial aid programme led to the paradoxical situation of Eastern Europe's poorest countries receiving (per capita) only a fraction of the assistance distributed to the Visegrád group.

The introduction of the Regional Approach in 1996 sought to rectify some of the mistakes of the EU's early Balkan strategy. However, from the outset its success was undermined by the lack of sufficient financial resources[47] and, more importantly, by the fact that it was far less "regional" than its title indicated. Bulgaria, Romania and Slovenia (already linked to the EU by Association Agreements) did not have any meaningful association with it. Moreover, the strengthening of the conditionality principle inevitably affected the coherence of the Regional Approach. Of its five participants (Albania, Bosnia, Croatia, FYROM and FRY), three had no contractual relations with the EU (Bosnia, Croatia, and FRY), two (Croatia and FRY) did not qualify for Phare funding, while soon after its initiation FRY was excluded from the process all together. Against such a background of fragmentation, the launch of a "regional" programme was, no doubt, destined to fail. The same can also be argued for the Stabilisation and Association Process. The EU and the region face the same fundamental dilemma the conditionality principle entails: "Preconditions for reform assistance and enhanced relations favour countries that have already managed to fulfil minimum conditions of stability and reform on their own, while the countries with the largest stabilisation deficits would fail to qualify for the conditional EU offers."[48] Despite the inclusion of

---

46 Before the changes introduced by the Copenhagen European Council (June 1993) to the Phare operations, "development of the private sector" accounted for more than 25 per cent of the total Phare funding to Eastern Europe. Since 1993 this trend was reversed and much more emphasis was put on infrastructure projects. However, for the period 1990–1996 "private sector development" accounted for more than 18 per cent of the total Phare funding in Eastern Europe, second only to "infrastructure projects" which accounted for 22.1 per cent of the total.

47 On earlier manifestations of the EU's inability to provide sufficient financial resources and trade concessions to the Central and East European Countries in accordance with its rhetorical commitment to the transition process, U. Sedelmeier: The European Union's Association Policy towards Central and Eastern Europe: Political and Economic Rationales of Conflict, SEI Working Paper, No. 7, Sussex European Institute, Falmer 1994.

48 Bertelsmann Foundation (ed.): op. cit., p. 22.

positive proposals such as the eventual granting of associated status to the region's best performers, the Stabilisation and Association Process does not depart from the fundamental principles of the Regional Approach such as the differentiated levels of contractual relations with the region's countries based on their compliance to the conditionality principle. Here, too, the level of adequate financial resources is the decisive factor for substantially enhancing (or undermining) the ability of the plan to generate economic development and political stability, bearing in mind the destructive effects of the Kosovo conflict.

VI Reconciling Western strategies with regional realities

Conditionality has been a fundamental feature of the EU strategy in Eastern Europe ever since the 1988 EC-Comecon Joint Declaration. Together with the principle of differentiation, the application of conditionality has led to the de facto creation of a multi-tier Eastern Europe with different Central and East European Countries negotiating the different rungs of the EU's ladder of contractual relations at different speeds and times. However, the compartmentalisation of the Central and East European Countries into different waves was neither meant to be permanent nor was it supposed to reflect "fixed preferences" favouring certain Central and East European Countries over others. Instead, the grouping of the East European applicants into different waves was meant to be based on an objective assessment of their political and economic performance. The door for "promotion" was, thus, left open provided that economic and political progress in a particular country justified it. This strategy, it was hoped, could provide two-fold benefits: on the one hand, inclusion into the first wave would "reward" those Central and East European Countries committed to democratic values and the market economy, whilst exclusion from it would provide the more poorly performing Central and East European Countries with an incentive to engage in serious economic and political reforms.

Whilst the need for an ethical dimension to the EU's Balkan strategy can hardly be disputed, the effectiveness of compartmentalisation, as a reform-boosting mechanism in the Balkan countries, is debatable. Even for some of the region's best performers (like Bulgaria and Romania, which are currently negotiating entry into the EU) conditionality/compartmentalisation did little to reduce the electoral strength of reactionary political forces or to deter frequent plunges into political instability. The dominance of the Iliescu regime (1990–1996) in Romania and the disastrous Videnov government in Bulgaria (1995–1997) were clear manifestations of this. The same can also be said for the resilience of the Mafia-linked Berisha regime in Albania (1992–1997) and the consolidation of war-lords in power in Bosnia, Croatia and FRY.[49] Even when dubious regimes were finally removed from office, this was more often associated with domestic popular uprisings (e.g., Bulgaria) or the physical disappearance of those embodying the regime (e.g., Croatia) than with direct EU pressure.

Arguably, the inability of reform-oriented forces within the Balkan countries to play the EU card successfully in initiating or carrying out reforms has been impeded by the fact that compartmentalisation and exclusion from the first wave has encouraged the consolidation of an "underdog culture"[50] which has been so evident in the region for centuries. There are already convincing arguments[51] on how such a culture plays into the hand of populist/extremist forces which thrive under conditions of prolonged crisis and effectively block the process of the region's Europeanisation. Moreover, this inability has resulted in fortifying Southeast European borders – "bringing tariffs, smuggling, bribery, organised crime and mutual suspicion instead of trade and investment flows."[52] If in practice, Europeanisation means, among other things, extending the cross-border monetary, trade and investment arrangements that already operate within the EU across Europe's southeastern periphery, such a process is profoundly hampered by the economic side effects of exclusion from fast-track integration into the EU, as well as local insecurity and political reaction. Whilst the substantiation of a firm cause-effect relationship is difficult, there is evidence that even the best-performing economies in the Balkans have consistently under-performed compared to those Central and East European Countries with fast-track relations with the EU (the Visegrád group) both in terms of macroeconomic stabilisation and foreign investment.[53] Comparison between the Visegrád countries and the Balkan countries whose economies have been directly affected by the Yugoslav wars (Albania, Bosnia, Croatia, FRY and Macedonia) reveals even greater disparities. Moreover, the application of conditionality to the EU's and G-24's aid programmes (combined with the fact that these programmes were initially linked to entrepreneurial activities in the region) in Eastern Europe has led to the strikingly

---

49 For the evolution of East European politics since the fall of the Berlin Wall, S. White, J. Batt, P. Lewis (eds.): Developments in East Europeans Politics, London 1993.

50 N. Diamantouros: Cultural Dualism and Political Change in Post-Authoritarian Greece, in: Centro de Estudios Avanzados en Ciencias Sociales: Estudios Working Papers, Madrid 1994.

51 M. Glenny: The Fall of Yugoslavia: the Third Balkan War, 3rd edition, New York 1996.

52 B. Steil, S. L. Woodward: A European 'New Deal' for the Balkans, Foreign Affairs, November/December 1999, Vol. 78, No. 6, pp. 97–98.

53 According to data provided by the EBRD, (1997) foreign investment in Bulgaria and Romania for the period between 1989–1996 reached just US-$ 58 per capita in comparison to US-$ 686 for the Visegrád group. Average GDP growth in Bulgaria and Romania for the period 1991–1999 was –3.2 per cent as compared with –1.2 per cent in Poland, Hungary and the Czech republic. For more details on recent economic performances in Eastern Europe European Commission, European Economy: Supplement C. Economic Reform Monitor, No. 3, October 1999.

unequal distribution of aid, with the Balkan countries receiving per capita less than half the amount of aid available to the Visegrád group.[54]

The adverse effects of conditionality on the economies of the Balkan countries and the ever growing gap between Central and South East Europe would clearly have been easier to justify had conditionality been applied consistently by the EU. A closer look at the development of the EU's contractual relations with the region reveals some interesting patterns:[55]

In August 1990, the Commission excluded Bulgaria and Romania from entering into association negotiations with the EC on the basis that the two countries did not fulfil the conditionality requirements on economic and political reform.[56] However, in September 1991 the Commission revised its position and, against a sceptical European Parliament (particularly in relation to Romania), proposed the opening of association negotiations with the two countries. In fact, within this period the pace of reform in the two countries changed little, as the National Salvation Front (NSF) in Romania and the Socialist Party (BSP) in Bulgaria continued to resist a far-reaching reform process. In fact, as the Commission[57] and later the Presidency[58] acknowledged, the decision to allow the opening of association negotiations with Bulgaria and Romania (as well as of speeding up the process of opening negotiations with Albania and the Baltics) was dictated by the events in the former USSR (the August coup in Moscow and the clear prospect of the country's disintegration) as well as the escalation of the war in Krajina (former Yugoslavia) during the summer of that year.

In subsequent years, the deepening of the crisis in the Balkans also led to fundamental changes in the EU's strategy in Eastern Europe. Back in 1990–1992, for example, the EU repeatedly refused to incorporate a clear reference to eventual full EU membership for East European applicants into the Association Agreements.[59] However, almost six months after the conclusion of the Bulgarian and Romanian Association Agreements, the EU's position was to change in the Copenhagen European Council (June 1993), where full EU membership for the Central and East European countries became a mutual objective. Building on the Copenhagen commitment, the Essen European

---

54 For example, during the period 1990–1995, the total G-24 assistance (including grants, foreign debt relief, export credits and emergency/humanitarian aid) to the Balkan countries (Albania, Bosnia, Bulgaria, Croatia, FYROM, Romania, Slovenia and FRY) was ECU 388 per capita, less than half of the amount distributed to the Visegrád group (Poland, Hungary, and the Czech Republic) ECU 882.

55 D. Papadimitriou: op. cit., 2000, pp. 14–16.

56 COM(90)398 final of 27 August 1990.

57 Agence Europe of 5 and 7 September 1991, p. 7.

58 Debates of the European Parliament, 11 November 1991, pp. 153–154.

59 On the negotiations of the Association Agreements between the EU and the Central and East European Countries, D. Papadimitriou: op. cit., 1999.

Council in December 1994 agreed on a pre-accession strategy for the Central and East European countries aiming to pave the way for their fast accession into the EU.[60] Here too, the radical changes in the EU's *Ostpolitik* seem to correlate more with important turning points in the Bosnian war (such as the collapse of the Vance/Owen peace plan in May 1993 or the Sarajevo market square bomb in February 1994 and the subsequent NATO ultimatum to the Bosnian Serbs), rather than a spectacular advance in the reform process in Eastern Europe.

Perhaps the most striking example of how "high politics" overshadowed conditionality in shaping the EU's strategy in the Balkans can be seen in the aftermath of the Kosovo war. In July 1997, the Commission excluded Bulgaria and Romania[61] from fast-track accession negotiations on the basis that neither country complied fully with economic and/or political conditionality. In October 1999, however, the Commission's policy of multi-speed enlargement negotiations changed, with the new enlargement Commissioner Günter Verheugen opting for an all-inclusive process. The Kosovo war made the Commission rethink its priorities. It is true that "the EU demonstrated enhanced awareness of the strategic and political dimension to enlargement".[62] It is equally true, however, that once again the change of policy had little to do with the process of internal reform in the two Balkan countries. The reform-oriented presidents Stoyanov and Constantinescu were in office in Bulgaria and Romania at the time of the 1997 exclusion. By the end of 1999, however, the geopolitical situation in the Balkans was radically different and the two countries were to be rewarded for their support of NATO's bombing of FRY.

Strategy adaptation in accordance with a rapidly changing international (and regional) setting is both legitimate and advisable. Nevertheless, frequent changes (or inconsistent use) of the principles on which such strategies are based is far more problematic. Against this background, the inconsistency with which the EU has applied conditionality in the Balkans raises two important questions. The first pertains to credibility. How can the EU pursue an effective "carrot and stick" strategy when the principles behind it remain blurred? How can the EU deliver the message clearly enough that reform, not crisis, will lead to the carrot? Reversing the argument, how can the EU convince those at the end of the stick that they are penalised because reform is not sufficient and not because of pre-determined discrimination against the region, a concept so closely associated with the Balkan "underdog culture"? The second question arising from the fre-

---

60   The Essen European Council also agreed to align the Bulgarian and Romanian trade liberalisation timetables (granted under their Association Agreements) with those of the Visegrád countries. Similar requests by the Romanian and Bulgarian governments have been rejected by the EC on previous occasions.
61   Slovakia, Latvia and Lithuania were also excluded.
62   Bertelsmann Foundation (ed.): op. cit., p. 23.

quent changes of the EU's *Ostpolitik* relates to the more general theme of enlargement. Over the last decade, EU relations with the Central and East European countries have developed astonishingly fast. But what does this tell us about the EU's ability to control the pace of rapprochement with Eastern Europe? Does such pace mirror the member states' determination to end Europe's division swiftly and decisively, or is it indicative of how an unprepared Union has reacted spasmodically to the economic and political vacuum in Eastern Europe? The failure of Amsterdam to resolve the question of institutional reform and the bitter disagreements over the reform of the EU's policies in view of enlargement revealed some alarming divisions. Without doubt, the outcome of the new IGC will be critical in allowing a more comprehensive assessment.

VII Conclusions and recommendations

The best way forward for the stabilisation of the Balkans continues to be an issue that generates much heated debate. There is little doubt that whatever strategies the EU chooses to pursue in the region, sceptics will always be able to present powerful counter-arguments. This is indicative of the region's complex and rapidly changing security environment that the EU strategy aims to address. Whilst the debate over the content and execution of EU strategy continues, the Kosovo crisis has produced broad consensus over the ends that such a strategy should serve. Today very few, inside and outside the region, dispute the fact that Southeastern Europe will either recover collectively or will not recover at all,[63] and this "truth" should signpost EU strategy.

An essential precondition for achieving collective recovery – on a regional scale – in the Balkans is that the (new) status quo is not disputed by the regional (and extra-regional) actors. In this respect, "the Serbian question" must be addressed immediately. Time matters, and the continuing isolation of Serbia makes the process of political change and economic reform far more difficult and prolonged.[64] An isolated Serbia will, no doubt, be in a position to threaten regional stability on many fronts including Vojvodina, Montenegro, Bosnia and, of course, Kosovo. With this in mind and taking into consideration that so far Serbia's isolation has not weakened Milosevic's repressive regime, a formula that would allow large parts of Serbia's population to participate in this process is essential. Economic recovery and relative normalisation of domestic politics in Serbia are likely to be the most effective weapons against a regime which seems to prosper by exploiting the culture of victimisation that international isolation

---

63   D. Papadimitriou: op. cit., 2000, p. 16.
64   B. Steil, S. L. Woodward: op. cit., p. 103.

breeds. The economic and political implications of a complete and long term isolation both for Serbia and the overall success of the region-wide reconstruction efforts have been understood. The EU's February 2000 decision (followed by the United States) to relax sanctions against Serbia is a case in point.[65]

Albanian nationalism may also present a major threat to the recovery efforts. The Western policy of maintaining an autonomous Kosovo within Yugoslavia seems to have failed, which has further bred Albanian revisionism. A year after the end of the war in Kosovo, KFOR finds it hard to contain the exportation of Albanian nationalism to neighbouring countries. Western governments, particularly in the US and Britain, who had sided with the armed representatives of Albanian nationalism in their efforts to win the war in Kosovo, are keeping their distance now, warning against the dangers of violent borders changes in the region.[66] Whilst today's status quo in Kosovo is becoming increasingly unsustainable, the future settlement of territorial disputes (if any) remains unclear. Against this background, predictions of whether Albania will emerge as a challenger of the (new) status quo are also difficult to make – the future of a Greater Albania remains uncertain.[67]

At the same time, there are developments that allow for much needed optimism. Both the recent Greek-Turkish rapprochement that led to the signing of a series of "low politics" agreements between the two countries and the reaffirmation of Turkey's European orientation after Helsinki have paved the way for the elaboration of a more consistent EU strategy in the Balkans. Nevertheless, neither of the two developments are irreversible. In this respect, the encouragement of the Greek-Turkish rapprochement must be placed high on the agenda and should be seen as inextricably linked to any Western strategy for stabilising the region.

In the more specific and absolutely critical case of Kosovo, wisdom is not always perceived as common. The state of affairs in Bosnia-Herzegovina today, more than four years after Dayton, shows that initial optimism for early peace consolidation was not very well-founded. The country has been unified only in name and could fall apart if left alone. Moreover, reconstruction has moved at a very slow pace, no sign of a self-sustainable development dynamic is in sight. As a result, the international community has not managed to scale down its involvement considerably, as it initially intended to do within a short period of time.

Lessons must be learned, and in practical terms they should include: the inadvisabil-

---

65   On the sanctions issue, see the chapter by Brusis and Galer.
66   Cf., for example, the US Secretary of State Madeleine Albright's speech in the Albanian Parliament. Press release by the Office of the Spokesman of the U.S. Department of State, 19 February 2000. Also BBC Report, Kosovo: What happened to peace? of 28 February 2000.
67   D. Papadimitriou: op. cit., 2000, p. 17.

ity of separating the civilian and military aspects of peace implementation, the problems in coordination, efficiency and effectiveness caused by the involvement of numerous international actors among which the various tasks are divided on political grounds, the great difficulties in returning all refugees to areas dominated by a different ethnic group, and the need for more substantive reconstruction and development assistance, targeted where really needed and guarded from Mafia-linked fraud, etc.[68]

To date, Southeastern Europe has been the exception to the tide of integration, but the EU (and the United States) should not overlook the region in the future. There was – and in some parts still is – concern at the prospect that unrest in Southeastern Europe could spill over into bordering regions, derailing progress that has been made within the Euro-Atlantic area over the past decade. So far, the Euro-Atlantic response to these events has been fragmented, but now the fundamentals for a more comprehensive strategy seem to be at hand. Kosovo underscores the need for such a strategy. First, the security of Europe as a whole is indivisible from the security of Southeastern Europe because of the potential of instability to spread. Secondly, the recipe for success has been well-tested in other parts of Europe, and it clearly works. Thirdly, the Balkans are not fundamentally different from other regions of Europe, their complex and sometimes horrific history notwithstanding. Hence, integration can work in Southeastern Europe and is the only solution in the long run. In the short term, integration could proceed on the basis of the differentiation model already dominant in the case of the Eastern enlargement as well as within the EU itself. A functionally differentiated integration road map "would assist and commit individual Southeast European states (without member or candidate status) in their preparation for EU candidacy, grouping other initiatives and forms of regional co-operation around the Stabilisation and Association Agreements."[69] Such a policy operated and directed by a Common Strategy for Southeastern Europe "could take full account of the fact that Southeastern Europe involves many institutionalised policy domains in Brussels: External Relations, the Stability Pact, CFSP, Enlargement, Development, Trade and Humanitarian Aid", thus producing "a solid and consistent policy framework for the co-operation with international organisations, among EU institutions and for the decision-makers in the region."[70]

---

68 Nea Democratia, A Stability and Reconstruction Plan for Southeast Europe, International Relations and European Union Secretariat, Submitted to the European People's Party Summit Meeting, Bonn, 2 June 1999, pp. 3–4.

69 Bertelsmann Foundation (ed.): op. cit., pp. 24–25.

70 Bertelsmann Foundation (ed.): op. cit., p. 27.

Security Risks and Instabilities in Southeastern Europe

Plamen Pantev

I Introduction

The chain of events and developments in Southeastern Europe during the 1990s provoked increasingly sophisticated political reactions, political approaches and longer-term strategies towards the region on part of the EU. The requirement of ethnic tolerance and respect of human rights constitutes one end of the range of EU positions concerning Southeastern Europe. The gradual beginning of the process of integration of some countries from the region into the Union constitutes the other end. At the end of the 1990s, these positions gravitated towards two principles – regionality and conditionality. These principles are partly overlapping and mutually reinforcing, but to some extent also contradictory.[1] The institutional arrangements of these two principles by the EU are identified with the Stability Pact (July 1999) for the principle of regionality on the one hand, and with the accession negotiations and the Stabilisation and Association Process for the principle of conditionality, on the other hand.

The history of the Southeast European region has no better example of a "benign" external engagement than these two dialectically interacting EU principles. However, the experience of the four wars during the last decade in the Southeastern part of Europe – a plethora of continuing risks, instabilities, but also opportunities – calls for re-thinking and improving the strategic principles and instruments of the EU for Southeastern Europe. Counting on both the regionality and the conditionality principle, the EU has the chance of developing a consistent and encompassing strategy for Southeast-

---

1 For more details on this issue, cf. the contribution by K. Ifantis in this volume.

118

ern Europe. This strategy should exploit as much as possible the potential of the two strategic principles and their institutional expressions, while improving the management of a sustainable process of change from predominantly regional stabilisation and conflict prevention towards the integration of Southeastern Europe into the EU. Depending on individual national cases, the contents of this management process (including the management of expectations) will be defined by the terms of "differentiated pre-accession".[2] In line with the dialectics of regionality and conditionality, some countries in the region may qualify for a pioneering role and act as regional generators of stability.

II Structural instabilities and general requirements for strategic approaches

In Europe, the process of integration in the EU context is the dominating and most powerful tendency of the 1990s and the beginning of the next century. The need for adequate EU strategies in meeting the challenges of the Southeast European region stems from two major, closely interrelated factors: the existence of security risks and instabilities in that part of the continent, and the necessity of differentiated pre-accession of Southeastern Europe by the EU.

Greater and more dangerous instabilities in international relations are typical of transitional periods between the old and the new structure of the international system at its different levels. In these circumstances even the smallest changes may cause strong reactions to the transformation of the initial conditions. In the case of Southeastern Europe, instabilities are driven by the following structural causes:

- The transition from a bipolar to an as yet undefined structure of the international system has led to the interim outcome of a tendency towards unilateralism and of turning the area into one of the global knots of conflicting interests and states. A national aspect of this process in the region is the decision of the individual countries to gravitate towards one or another centre of global power. The EU with its Euro-Atlantic dimension is certainly one of these centres of global power. Another consequence is the age-old possibility of "Balkanisation", the fragmentation of the regional state relations and the subsequent polarisation of Balkan international relations around external poles of power. In the post-Cold War situation in the Balkans, the EU, the United States and the other developed nations generate and stimulate the European integration of the Balkans, while Russia is hesitant – oscillating between a role as the broker of new balances of power and dependencies for the Balkan coun-

---

2   Bertelsmann Foundation (ed.): The Balkans and New European Responsibilities, Strategy paper presented to the special meeting of "The Club of Three and the Balkans", Brussels, 29/30 June, 2000, pp. 24–28.

tries and a constructive role as a world leader of a 21st-century type, stimulating region-building tendencies as an organisational expression of globalisation.

- The painful shift of the region from the state of a non-existent common economic and trading area to a more co-operative regional economic space. This includes all the real and potential divergence of the economic interests of the individual local (and external) actors in that process of the evolution of new opportunities for prosperity.

- The internal systemic transitions of the individual countries of Southeastern Europe and the varying national attitudes to the regional social, economic, political and strategic homogeneity and different orientations to the presently emerging global centres of power – for principle or conjuncture reasons.

- The varying patterns, rates and levels of adaptation of the individual countries of the region to the eastward expansion of the democratic civic state are based on the principle of the "security community" and the market economy space – a process triggered by the collapse of socialism in its Soviet and Yugoslav versions.

- The predominantly destructive disintegration of the Yugoslav Federation, the four wars that followed and the (re-)appearance of state-building issues in Southeastern Europe.

- The prevention of the slowing-down or eventual halt of the pace of the European integration process calls for coping with the security risks and instabilities, with their structural causes. Furthermore, the provision of adequate strategic instruments for carrying out this task before and during the projected differentiated pre-accession of the region has started to progress. The strategic approaches of the EU to the region in the process of differentiated pre-accession in the coming years with the objective of successfully coping with these issues should meet certain general requirements:

  1. The system of EU strategies needs to reflect how it will deal with structural instabilities, with the multitude of resulting current instabilities and risks and their variation from country to country, as well as how to utilise or neutralise the strategic potential of the national attitudes of the Southeast European countries. Hence, adequate and comprehensive EU-specific strategies for *individual* countries of Southeastern Europe are needed and have significant practical consequences for the outcome of the differentiated pre-accession of the region.

  2. A general requirement of EU strategies is sufficient readiness to act in combination with the framework requirement to keep costs as low as possible. This means that the EU must be in possession of an adequate mechanism for deciding what its priorities are and where the emphasis must be in the particular period and situation.

  3. The strategies of the EU must reflect possible and probable contingencies realisti-

cally. They should also be backed up by adequate personnel, financial and material capacity and resources. Effectiveness of performance is a "must" for any EU strategy applied to Southeastern Europe.

4. An adequate analytic and decision-making mechanism should assess the sequence of evolving events and determine the timing of the use of respective strategies in terms of early-warning time, the rate of mobilising the means for application and the length of the availability of the applicable tools.

5. A no less important requirement for the EU system of strategies is the mobilisation of European public opinion – on a national and Union level. A supportive EU public may decide on success or failure of the Union's strategy of dealing with the risks and instabilities in Southeastern Europe in the process of differentiated pre-accession of the region. Respective EU strategies for the management of knowledge, information and perceptions are required.

6. EU strategies should include effective interlocking and coordination with other international institutions or individual governments. Preventing the duplication of efforts and the waste of resources reinforces the capacities of the different organisations, fora and mechanisms and should therefore be an integral component of EU strategies for Southeastern Europe.

A significant aspect of this last requirement is the solution of the "Russian factor" – how bring and keep Russia within a benign external involvement in Southeastern Europe without damaging the Euro-Atlantic integration process of the region. The Southeast European terrain provides political, economic and strategic opportunities for Russia to join the regional and Euro-Atlantic integration processes as a "welcome" power. Obstructing or "spoiling the integration game" would have more negative consequences for Russia than acting as a constructive or even neutral player in the processes of the Euro-Atlantic integration of Southeastern Europe. Russia's positive image would be guaranteed if this world power does not hinder EU and NATO integration of the Southeast European countries should they opt for accession. EU-Russian relations should, therefore, include this aspect of the EU strategy in Southeastern Europe.

III EU strategies for systemic instabilities in Southeastern Europe

The systemic nature of the main security risks and instabilities, stemming from the structural causes, legacies of the past, the ethnic and religious diversity of the area, its heterogeneous social contents and specific individual countries' policies and political cultures, requires a complex system of interrelated and interacting EU strategies with sophisticated management of their implementation.

Security risks and instabilities

Even a brief survey of systemic factors constituting security risks and instabilities pertaining to both Southeastern Europe and Europe as a whole includes the following elements:

Firstly, the economic, technological and infrastructural deficits of Southeastern Europe coupled with continuous internal national economic, social and political crises. There are various historical antecedents of the belated economic, technological and infrastructural modernisation of Southeastern Europe. It suffices to mention only the Cold War period with the three types of states and blocs that existed at that time: NATO, the Warsaw Pact and those who were non-aligned. The infrastructure – transport, communications, economic relations, etc. – reflected polarised Cold War thinking and acting. The outcome was the separation of the countries, and because they were unlinked, a further distancing of the region from the other parts of the world that were adapting to the growing requirements of economic, information, humanitarian globalisation. The broader picture was additionally darkened by the hardships of the transition societies (all except Greece and Turkey) that experienced the shift from state-owned property and a central-planned economy to private ownership and a market economy. Poor management of the transformation processes, including adventurous political and economic behaviour in some countries, repeated cases of criminal privatisation – all these instabilities generated a whole spectrum of security risks, occasionally threatening the continuation of state authority in individual countries (Albania, Romania and Bulgaria).

Secondly, ethnic and religious antagonisms, augmented by conceptual, perceptual, cognitive and emotional deficiencies and multiplied by the purposeful activism of political careerists. This is the most discussed source of conflicts in Southeastern Europe in the last decade – a source of lasting instabilities, national and regional threats and risks to security. The ethnic mobilisation of the Serbs has focused the attention of observers and participants in the conflicts in Southeastern Europe. Croats, Hungarians and Bulgarians traditionally and justly complain of violations of their individual and collective minority rights by the Serbian authorities. The children of Serbia are still being brought up and educated in hatred towards neighbouring nations as "eternal enemies". This negative ethnic stereotyping in Serbia is an overt educational goal with negative messages for the sake of internal Serbian consolidation on a destructive nationalist basis. However, there is only one example of inter-ethnic relations that might be more or less classified within the conceptual frameworks of the "clash of civilisations" – the relations between Serbs and Albanians. All the other ethnic and religious differences and conflicts are definitely within the realm of political management and legal regulation. Their escalation or resolution depends on political will, resources and strategies.

Thirdly, state-building challenges, turning into security risks and major instabilities for the whole region. The catastrophic disruption of the former federal state of Yugoslavia, the appearance and the assumption of political meaning of the "Albanian Question" and of the "Serbian Question" as well as the difficult process of transition from totalitarian, authoritarian and centrally planned systems to pluralist democracy and market economy are the three determinants of this source of security risks and instabilities in Southeastern Europe, also known as the "triple transition".[3]

Unlike the Czechoslovak Republic and even the Soviet Union, the Yugoslav Federation, driven by political careerists and ethnocentric leaders in the dominant republic of the former federal state, Serbia, ended its obviously no longer needed federalist existence in a most destructive way. The subsequent state-building of the constituent republics of the former federation was additionally burdened by assertive and aggressive Serbian political behaviour: the wars of Serbia against Slovenia, Croatia and Bosnia-Herzegovina; the continuing destabilising activity, driven by Belgrade, of the Serbian political and intelligence agents in Macedonia (FYROM); the obstructions created by Serbia for a democratic social and political organisation of the constituent republic of Montenegro in the new Yugoslav Federation; the inadequate treatment of the complex issues of the Kosovo region of Serbia by the political leadership in Belgrade that led to the rise of even more complicated ethnic and constitutional problems.

The two national questions, with their irredentist political advocates, bear a troubling promise for the future: the consolidation and continuation of the irreconcilable Albanian and Serbian Questions. The stability of the states in Southeastern Europe – borders, population, intentions for the future – may become dramatically contingent upon the ethnocentric plans of Serbian and Albanian political leaders and on unresolved inter-ethnic hatreds and mistrust. The irredentist inclinations and political platforms increase the fragility of the newly independent states, bordering territories with Serbian and Albanian populations. The potential instrumentalisation of ethno-demographic pressure for destructive purposes was already purposefully used by the dictatorial regime in Belgrade in 1999, provoking the near-collapse of Albania, FYROM, Bosnia-Herzegovina and Montenegro. The notion of "Greater Albania" and corresponding political behaviour creates similar problems for neighbouring Serbia, Greece and FYROM.

State-building problems are worsened by the transitional economic, social and political issues that most of the former Yugoslav republics and now sovereign states experience. The transition from "real-existing socialism" to functioning consolidated democracies caused major problems of institutional stability even in such well-established

3   Berg/Van Meurs, Vol. I.

states as Bulgaria and Romania throughout the 1990s. The problems in Albania, FYROM, Bosnia-Herzegovina were even worse.

Fourthly, FRY and the persistent hard-security risk of war. There is frequent aggressive behaviour by the regime in Belgrade either as a last resort to save itself from internal popular pressure or because of Kosovo and Bosnia-Herzegovina or, alternatively, low and medium intensity conflict with Albanian irredentists. Therefore, as long as the need for stability in Kosovo exists, KFOR/UNMIK and its UN, NATO and EU dimensions continue to be a valid hard-security need with no apparent compromise to be seen. The hard-security threats originate in Kosovo itself, but the Serbian military's claims that the Yugoslav Army has the constitutional right to return to the province – as a sovereign territory of Serbia and FRY – clearly demonstrate the pending danger of serious military clashes. The situation in Bosnia-Herzegovina is similar, though at a lower level of risk. The SFOR contingent will be needed until all the provisions of the Dayton Agreement have been implemented and stability is guaranteed.

Albanian irredentism is no less of a security threat and source of longer instabilities in Southeastern Europe. Its potential for low-to-medium intensity fighting requires adequate international deterrence and battle forces. The international forces in Kosovo, Bosnia-Herzegovina and FYROM should continue to serve this additional security need.

Fifthly, soft security risks. It is no surprise that analysts and politicians believe the fight against criminality and the risks and threats originating from it have become a priority integrative factor in Europe. Southeastern Europe is full of organised crime, terrorism, clandestine immigration, smuggling and drug trafficking, corruption, money laundering and proliferation of small weapons (and reportedly even radioactive materials).

Crime has specific national, social, economic, cultural and psychological roots. The peculiarity of the situation of the plethora of soft security risks and instabilities in Southeastern Europe is favoured by the belated modernisation of the region in terms of economic, technological, social and political development and management. Also important are the fragility of the state institutions in the newly independent states of former Yugoslavia, linked with the difficulties of state-building; the situation of failed states (Albania); delayed transition processes (in Romania and Bulgaria); the long years of wars and the potential hard security risks; economic sanctions; opportunities for crime created by the ethnic and religious divisions; and, last but not least, criminal methods of implementing the transformation processes in the post-communist countries of the region with the participation of pervasively corrupt administrations.

The EU's strategic approaches in treating this awesome set of security risks and instabilities should not be misled by the expectation of an automatic shift from hard to soft security risks in Southeastern Europe. The soft security risks will definitely be reduced with the containment of the hard security risks. The uncertainties inherent in the current situation in FRY and the irredentist Albanian factor do not provide much perspective as to how and when this shift would take place. However, once the influence of hard security risks decreases in Southeastern Europe, continuing attention will need to be devoted to the interaction between other factors fostering soft security risks and the realisation of the risks themselves.

Sixthly, the tensions between the two parts of Southeastern Europe, the Western Balkans and the EU accession states: information and perception influence knowledge, decisions and activities. That is why perceptions of the Balkans should become more sophisticated and reflect the complexity and plurality of factors determining the regional social, political and security developments. This is crucial in preventing information delivery or perception attacks from transforming into miscalculations about strategy, concrete decisions or into an incorrect cognition. Situational awareness, experienced by the people engaged with the Balkans, necessitates a comprehensive and encompassing picture rather than certain outlines. In the last decade, moreover, Southeastern Europe was by and large identified with former Yugoslavia.

The term "Western Balkans" correctly differentiates the zone with security problems from the rest of the region, dominated by region-building issues. The challenge for the observer and for those engaged in the region is to sense the post-conflict reconstruction developments in the Western Balkans and the ensuing security risks for the other parts of the peninsula, while reflecting Southeastern Europe in its entirety.

The present tension between the two parts of Southeastern Europe will inevitably transform and probably increase when the more advanced stages of the process of differentiated pre-accession of the region to the EU are implemented. A compensatory mechanism will have to be implemented to preserve stability in order to not let disparities in institutional memberships transform into higher tensions and security risks. The prospect of membership for all countries of Southeastern Europe in the EU, made explicit at the Feira European Council,[4] is to be the corner stone of such a mechanism.

Seventhly, the ecological security risks and a long neglect of environmental degradation. The consequences of the over-industrialised, centrally planned socialist economies in combination with cross-border pollution has created a fundamentally unsatisfactory environmental situation in the last two decades. The cases of polluted rivers, including the Danube, and the continuing degradation of the Black Sea environment from the biggest rivers in Europe remind us of the immense tasks facing the people of Southeastern Europe in upgrading the ecological situation of the region. The pollution caused by the NATO strike against FRY, especially through the fires in the oil refineries, further

---

4   Feira European Council (19/20 June 2000): Presidency conclusions [*http://europa.eu.int/council/off/conclu/june2000/june2000_en.pdf*].

worsened the ecological situation. Thus, Southeastern Europe assumed the features of a permanent humanitarian and ecological "disaster zone" with the risk of turning the Black Sea into a "dead sea".

Eighthly, risks stemming from the wider regional neighbourhood of Southeastern Europe. The CIS, the Black Sea–Caspian Sea area, the Eastern Mediterranean and the Middle East are no less unstable direct neighbourhoods of Southeastern Europe. In fact, its only stable and stabilising neighbourhoods are the EU member and first-round accession states to the north and south. All three other neighbouring regions have the potential for and actively bear conflicts, security risks and longer-term instabilities. The risk of proliferating some of the tensions and instabilities to Southeastern Europe in the short or medium term is mostly in the realm of soft security.

EU strategies to cope with these risks and instabilities should utilise the existing opportunities for a constructive evolution of the three listed neighbouring regions, as well as the potential for stability in the other parts of Southeastern Europe that directly border the CIS, the Black Sea–Caspian Sea area, the Eastern Mediterranean and the Middle East.

The system of recommended EU strategies for Southeastern Europe

Despite the predominance of risks, some positive factors and strategic instruments of the EU currently at work may also be listed as a counterpoise:
- Greek membership in the EU
- Accession negotiations with Bulgaria, Romania and Slovenia, adding to the implementation of the Europe Agreements with these countries from the mid-90s. A specific aspect of this evolving relationship in the security and defence area is the projected inclusion in the appropriate forms of the gradually emerging Common European Security and Defence Policy (CESDP) of the EU. The specific Southeast European aspects of the CESDP in combination with the various forms of NATO involvement in the region may produce the most effective net result.
- The upcoming talks for concluding a Stabilisation and Association Agreement with Croatia and FYROM, adding to the Phare Programme instrument; the perspective of an eventual launch of Stabilisation and Association talks with Bosnia-Herzegovina and Albania; and other EU aid programmes. The motivating, mobilising and organising effect is real in the two pairs of countries, pointing towards more stability and co-operation even at this stage of the evolving process.
- The "candidate for EU membership" status for Turkey, in addition to its membership in the Customs Union of the EU

126

- The Stability Pact for Southeastern Europe (July 1999)[5]
- The projected regional organisation for free trade and economic co-operation[6]
- The coordination of present EU efforts in Southeastern Europe with other regional initiatives such as the Southeast European Co-operative Initiative (SECI), the Organisation for Black Sea Economic Co-operation (BSEC), etc.

The Pact of Stability, and, to some extent, the accession negotiations with Slovenia, Bulgaria and Romania, as well as the Stabilisation and Association Process applied by the EU to Southeastern Europe, accentuate the necessity of "region-building", conflict prevention, conflict management, post-conflict reconstruction and resolution of the causes of the conflicts.[7] The "regionality" principle of the EU reflects the bottom-up tendency of regionalism, stability, co-operation and integration in the EU and the top-down policies of support of the positive developments in Southeastern Europe. On the other hand, it also reflects the common need of the majority of countries from Southeastern Europe and the EU for security and stability on a democratic basis. "Region-building" is directly linked to strategies of conflict prevention, post-conflict rehabilitation and conflict resolution.

The accession negotiations and the Stabilisation and Association Process of the EU with countries from Southeastern Europe are the institutional reflections of the "conditionality" principle. The latter also reflects the fundamental structural disparities of the individual countries, as well as the territory divisions within the Southeast European region: the Eastern Balkans – generating stability with a record of integration and region-building activities – and the Western Balkans, which are characterised mainly by wars, disintegration, various conflicts, hatred and instability.

However, the Western Balkans are also in a step-by-step process of getting ready for the kind of relations dominating the Eastern Balkans – a logical reaction to the continuous social degradation and to the positive example of the alternative presented by Bulgaria, Romania, Slovenia and recently by Croatia. This is why the recommended improvements of current EU strategies are expected to stimulate positive developments in the Western Balkans, contribute to the neutralisation of the negative ones, and provide for the boosting of the Eastern part that would solidify the EU vision and practices for stability and prosperity in Southeastern Europe. The special border role of the Eastern Balkans relating to other EU neighbourhoods – the CIS, Black Sea–Caspian Sea area, the Eastern Mediterranean and the Middle East – adds substance to that strategic approach.

---

5   Bertelsmann Foundation (ed.): op. cit.

6   Composite Paper Regular Report from the Commission on Progress towards Accession by each of the candidate countries 13 October, 1999 [*http://europa.eu.int/comm/enlargement/report_10_99/composite/50.htm*].

7   S. Clément, P. Pantev: South-Eastern Europe, in: R. Dwan (ed.) Building Security in Europe's New Borderlands: Subregional Co-operation in the Wider Europe, New York, London, 1999, pp. 69–116.

The following suggestions are therefore perceived as useful elements of a comprehensive strategy or even a common strategy that will utilise to the fullest the potential of the regionality and the conditionality principles within a more dominant and decisive EU policy towards Southeastern Europe.[8]

Firstly it is necessary to radically deal with the still existent but obsolete Cold-War type of relations in economic, energy, transport and communications infrastructure. Southeastern Europe needs to become a compatible component of the all-European transport and communications infrastructure. EU policy should be aimed at overcoming the fragility of the transition processes in Bulgaria and Romania and turning the two countries, alongside Slovenia and Croatia, into net contributors of EU economic potential. For this reason, the EU should concentrate on the issues of capital investment, management of foreign financial aid, unemployment, the conditions of living of the younger generation and retired people. This would help the countries in transition overcome the clientelist loyalties and networks such as the environment of organised crime and corruption, stimulate the rise of a middle class and change the trend towards the establishment of a few extremely rich people with a life-style of western luxury, in contrast to a very poor majority of more than 80 per cent of the population.

Special attention should be devoted to the reorganisation of agriculture in the countries of Southeastern Europe – a major source of economic productivity of the people of the region. A longer-term strategy of adaptation and compatibility with the agricultural sector of the EU would prevent future conflicts of interest. Dealing seriously with this issue by the EU would most probably lead to a diminishing influence of conservative political elites in certain countries of Southeastern Europe geared towards isolationism and protectionism. A significant aspect of this strategic approach of the EU is its support for bilateral, trilateral, multilateral and regional projects by countries from Southeastern Europe and by external actors in the Stability Pact framework. Self-help in upgrading the economy and infrastructure of the region is a realistic, sustainable solution that deserves substantial backing and stimulation, but without overestimating its potential.[9] Regional economic co-operation may positively add to the EU integration of Southeastern Europe.

Secondly, focus on Serbian assertive nationalism and Albanian irredentism and develop comprehensive programmes and plans for treating the two issues. A special emphasis should be placed on breaking the vicious cycle of Serbian-Albanian relations: "conflict – hostile perception – threatening behaviour – more hatred – acts of cruelty –

---

8   Bertelsmann Foundation (ed.): op. cit.
9   Bertelsmann Foundation (ed.): op. cit.

acts of revenge – a more intense, even violent conflict".[10] The key question is how to switch from threatening to more conciliatory behaviour. Two factors are of key importance in that respect: the improvement of the cognitive element of perceptions about Southeastern Europe on which longer-term psychological inclinations are based on the one hand and the achievement of decisive progress in the countries of Southeastern Europe that symbolise the EU integration future of the region (Bulgaria, Romania and Slovenia) on the other hand. It is predominantly the positive, developed and progressive direct environment of the most repulsive and dangerous ethnic antagonisms that would dilute the ethnic tension and steer the way of the opposing sides to normal, European routes of social and political behaviour. Our concept is that the change of behaviour from a threatening type to a conciliatory one is linked to presenting and proving there are more options for the two sides – not in the field of conflicting attitudes, but in the area of constructive efforts and higher living standards. At the same time, full implementation of the Dayton Agreement, UN Security Council Resolution 1244 and the Military-Technical Agreement for Kosovo[11] must be guaranteed as well as bringing all war criminals who committed genocide and crimes against humanity to international justice.

All of the other security risks and instabilities that stem from ethnic and religious differences are directly manageable politically. Each potential or real ethnic issue in Southeastern Europe should be mapped and monitored so that adequate political and legal instruments are applied in time to prevent escalation. There are also modest efforts by players in the region to act as mediators in complex and tense conflicting relations between Serbs and Albanians. Bulgaria, for example, has initiated such efforts for the Kosovo Serbs and Albanians, with some positive results. These and similar activities in the field of building-up a negotiating culture for dealing with conflicts deserve the support of the EU.

Thirdly, stabilising state borders and state institutions in Southeastern Europe. An international conference, recently initiated by the French EU Presidency, may lead to support for particular countries in Southeastern Europe and further isolation of the regime of Milosevic as well as confirmation of the democratic principles of state-building in the region. The inviolability of state borders is a major principle for the stability of the individual states and a corresponding international conference reiterating this fundamental international legal principle.

---

10 Balkan Regional Profile: the Security Situation and the Region-Building Evolution of Southeastern Europe, Background Issue, March–April 1999, at: *http://www.isn.ethz.ch/isis*.

11 General Framework Agreement for Peace in Bosnia-Herzegovina, 21 November 1995, Paris; UNSC Resolution 1244/10 June 1999; Military-Technical Agreement for Kosovo between General Jackson and Yugoslav Authorities, 9 June 1999.

Another source of strengthening state-building in Southeastern Europe is the improvement of the social and economic situation in the countries of the region, the assimilation and internalisation by the political and social elites of the principles of democracy as well as religious freedom and ethnic tolerance.

Yet another, extremely significant component of the strategy of the EU in this field is the insistence on the involvement of ethnic minorities in the activity of the state institutions. In parallel, friendly relations with the neighbouring country where the majority of the population is of the same ethnic origin as the ethnic minority of the respective state can also contribute to the stability of the state institutions. Denial of ethnic separatism is of paramount significance for the stability of the state borders and state institutions.

The regional process of co-operation and security from Sofia 1996 and its continuation after the end of the Kosovo war – this time without the participation of FRY – underlines this aspect of regional stability. The EU may continue to monitor and support the regional activism aimed at improving the security situation and the climate of co-operation. A pending return of FRY to the process contingent on the state of democracy in this country is another incentive for the opposition against the regime of Milosevic.

Fourthly, preserve a vibrant strategy of countering hard security risks and instabilities. It would be premature for at least the next decade to pull out the international forces from Kosovo, Bosnia-Herzegovina and FYROM. The need to maintain a deterring fighting potential on the ground of these ex-Yugoslav territories would also serve as a guarantee for the progress of the differentiated pre-accession of Southeastern Europe by the EU.

The EU should utilise to the maximum the positive effect of regional multinational military co-operation and force-building. The Rapid Reaction Force of Southeastern Europe (MPFSEE), as well as the accession negotiations of Bulgaria, Romania and Slovenia, are appropriate opportunities to adapt the regional component of the evolving CESDP. It may effectively interact with the extensive NATO networks in the region. In terms of eventual missions of the Southeast European component of the CESDP of the EU, peacekeeping, search and rescue missions, humanitarian, peace enforcement and emergency planning are tasks and operations that have been experienced since 1994 by those regional states contending for EU support in co-operation with Partnership for Peace (PfP) countries from Southeastern Europe. Participation in IFOR/SFOR and in KFOR missions provided the best lessons in co-operative security and the evolution of the regional strategic culture of the European and Euro-Atlantic type – a fundamental prerequisite for improved homogeneity of the states in the region.

Another direction in the hard security and defence area that the EU may utilise is the stimulation of transparency, confidence-building and the establishment of combined military units of countries from Southeastern Europe. Transparent, accountable and responsible armed forces, military budgets and a democratically controlled military are strategic goals of priority importance, with a multiplying positive effect for the stability and peace of the whole region.

The EU should also provide the necessary conditions and include differentiated programmes for the defence industry of the regional actors and their military-production complexes. The already institutionalised co-operation of the Ministers of Defence of the countries of Southeastern Europe (the South Eastern European Defence Ministers group, or SEDM) provides an opportunity to be involved in some way in the activity of the newly shaped military institutions of the EU – the Military Committee and the Military Staff of the Council of the EU. Certainly this would require also a higher level of institutionalised co-operation of the Union and the North Atlantic Alliance.

Fifthly, counter soft-security risks by the economic and social development of the region, by resolving the ethnic conflicts and by ending the wars and the economic sanctions regime.

However, the EU should also implement a direct fight against soft-security risks and instabilities by insisting on the harmonisation of legal codes in Southeastern European countries with the Union laws. This should be reflected in the legislative activity, the judicial reform and the interior ministries' co-operation in the region. Furthermore, the existing network of bilateral, trilateral and multilateral police co-operation should be placed in an interactive relation with EU police co-operation on issues of common interest.

Sixthly, overcome the tension between the militant Western part of Southeastern Europe and the region-building and stable Eastern part by the following strategic approaches. Provide clear criteria for membership, pre-accession and differentiated pre-accession to all countries of Southeastern Europe, and promise the perspective of getting on the EU integration train (and the faster integration train when conditions for that get ripe), while applying interim programmes that would accelerate the individual national processes of progress and adaptation to the EU membership criteria. The key to the Union's strategy in this field is a well balanced and individualised application of the Accession Negotiations, the stabilisation and association talks and the Stability Pact instruments in combination with the various forms of NATO involvement in the region, including its enlargement policy.

Seventhly, meet the ecological security risks of Southeastern Europe by characterising this issue as an all-European problem, introducing EU environmental programmes in the region and catalysing national mobilisation and regional co-operation of the countries from the Balkans to improve the environmental situation.

Co-operation on environmental issues in Southeastern Europe has the potential of a positive spill-over to other areas of relations. This is why the EU strategy should target enhancing co-operation on cross-border and regional ecological issues.

Eighthly, dealing with the risks stemming from the neighbourhoods of Southeastern Europe – the CIS, the Black Sea–Caspian Sea zone, and the Eastern Mediterranean and the Middle East requires a three-fold EU strategy:

- Implement and develop the existing instruments of relations of the EU with these neighbourhoods: EU-Russia and EU-Ukraine structured relations, extension of more EU programmes and projects to Georgia, Azerbaijan, Armenia and other states;
- Join forces with NATO in countering the risks and instabilities in the region; and
- Assign a special "border" role to the countries of Southern, Southeastern and Eastern Balkans parallel to the "connecting economic and infrastructure" role relative to the three neighbouring areas.

IV The "Arc of Stability" and the "Locomotive Strategy"

The EU "country strategies" in Southeastern Europe should be tailored according to the ability of the individual states in the region of "self-correction" of national attitudes in the process of the EU differentiated pre-accession. From this perspective, a leading element of the EU "country strategies" is the encouragement of national initiative and efforts to build democracy, market economy, respect for human and minority rights in line with international standards and the rule of law. The EU should augment the national potential of dealing with all these tasks. A necessary protective measure in implementing this strategic approach is a careful analysis and judgement of the participation of groupings of organised crime in positions of power that traditionally belong to state authorities or of the links that might exist between the governments or individual ministers and criminal or Mafia structures.

Another general requirement of the EU "country strategies" is preventing interested and adventurous local regional actors in a conflict from playing external powerful states or institutions against each other. The experience of Milosevic in playing that game should be a good lesson to responsible powerful states attempting to bear global responsibilities.

An additional component is utilisation of the so-called "locomotive strategy" – rendering encompassing support for countries that drive the train of regional stability in the interest of the individual states, Southeastern Europe and in the direction of EU integration. This strategy corresponds to the "arc of stability" in Southeastern Europe: Slovenia–Hungary–Romania–Bulgaria–Greece–Turkey. What matters most for this strategy is its multiple effect: It gives a potential solution for the tension between regionality and conditionality principles, defines the particular priorities of the differentiated pre-accession to the EU of Southeastern Europe, mobilises the capacity and the responsibility of countries from the region towards individual and regional integration in the Union and provides an opportunity of "burden-sharing" on the way to EU integration.

Keeping these general requirements for the country strategies in mind, the EU should draft individual "country strategies" with the intention that each of these individual strategies would interact with the first two levels of strategies suggested at the two higher levels of abstraction and aimed at guaranteeing the success of the differentiated pre-accession of Southeastern Europe. Here are some ideas that might be helpful and add to the drafting of the individual "country strategies" of the EU towards Southeastern Europe, depending on the specific security risks and instabilities that need to be dealt with:

The Federal Republic of Yugoslavia

The main security risks and instabilities stem from the undemocratic regime in Belgrade, from its destructive potential, including a war-making one, and the persisting organisational incapacity of the Serbian opposition to effectively present a political alternative to its people. It is probable that this organisational inefficiency of the opposition is a function of the generally repressive character of the regime and the planned infiltration of that very opposition by the security services of the Milosevic government.

Another major problem is the conceptual grounds of the eventual future leadership in Belgrade, i.e., how far the new leaders of FRY will have drifted away from the assertive nationalistic Serbian mindset – essentially a trouble-maker for the region of Southeastern Europe and for its own people in the last ten years. In practical terms, the dominant thinking in Serbia continues to rely on the notion that a nation is a biological and not a historical category. There is not much promise that present and future decisions will not be based on 500–600-year old premises. The tendency to grab a spontaneous democratic movement of young people and place it under the banner of "Greater Serbia" thought is a long-term destabilising factor in Southeastern Europe. Its repercussions are a return to a new version of division of Europe into opposing blocs. It is only on the basis of disintegration that Serbia would be in a position to eventually play the role of a regional hegemonic power, or at least the balancer of power in Southeastern Europe. The acceptance by Russia of the "observer" status of FRY in the "Russian-Belorussian Union" is a logical component in the mosaic of an eventual "divided Southeastern Europe in a divided Europe" – never whole and free to enjoy democracy, diversity and liberty.

133

Here are recommended strategies of the EU:

- FRY must be deterred militarily for the mid-to-long term.
- Democratisation of FRY, including an eventual constitutional reform that would reflect the democratic will of the nations and the national minorities of the federation and democratic standards of Europe.
- The option of starting talks with the new authorities in Belgrade for a Stabilisation and Association Agreement should be kept open as an incentive for a positive change of policy, society and its mentality.

Kosovo

Being de jure a province of the sovereign Serbian republic, Kosovo constitutes a special case within the FRY issue. It presents six major security risks:

- A blockage of the post-conflict rehabilitation and reconstruction;
- The lasting and persisting ethnic intolerance, driven by the two main communities – the Albanian and Serbian – with changing roles of initiators of the antagonistic relationship;
- The pending constitutional arrangement of the province;
- The hard security risk of a new military confrontation;
- The risk that Kosovo separatism may trigger separatist behaviour in other regions and countries with Albanian populations – Southern Serbia, FYROM, north-western Greece;
- The risk that the volatile situation in Kosovo is continuously exploited for the purposes of polarising an Islamic extremist movement in Bosnia-Herzegovina, Albania, FYROM, Sandjak as well as for inducing tensions between Turkey and Greece.

Apart from the strategic approaches stemming from the above considerations, the EU should concentrate also on the following options:

First, keep a permanent and active dialogue with the governments of the countries where Albanian brethren live, and contain also by all other existing channels the rise of "Greater Albania" nationalism. The political leaders of FRY, Kosovo, FYROM and Albania as well as the administrative leadership of north-western Greece should preserve their dialogue with the EU and, as much as possible, among themselves.

Secondly, the EU should not stop its co-ordinating effort to encourage international organisations (UN, OSCE, CE, NATO) and regionally important external governments to continue their political pressure on the internal political factors, with a potential to dilute ethnic tensions and guarantee a more tolerant ethnic behaviour. The education of the culture of ethnic tolerance is a long-term issue that the EU should take care of.

Thirdly, continuation of the deterring and restraining presence of the UN-mandated international forces – as long as they are needed for the stability of the province and Southeastern Europe.

Fourthly, prevention of the polarisation of the extremist Islamic movement in the region and its linkage with other "hot" places in the world such as the Caucasus, Central Asia, the Middle East, etc. The stimulation of the Greek-Turkish rapprochement would guarantee the multiplying effect of destroying both the pan-Islamic and the pan-Orthodox axis formation in Southeastern Europe. The policy of Bulgaria on the ethnic and religious issues may be exemplified and encouraged throughout the region.

Bosnia-Herzegovina

Security risks requiring special attention in Bosnia-Herzegovina are:
– The fragility of the post-conflict reconstruction activity;
– The fragility of the state with its unstable central institutions;
– The hard security risk of military confrontation between the ethnically defined entities and with FRY.
The EU strategic approaches should therefore include:

First, the knowledge/information/perception strategic component of gradually erasing the ethnic hatreds and stimulating the perception of the commonality of interests in the present and future for all ethnic groups in a larger European context.

Secondly, preserve the international protectorate as the regulative administrative organ as long as it is needed for the development of the local conditions towards responsible self-rule, stability and integration. This strategic approach should be complemented with a purposeful and keen selection of new, modern, tolerant, internationalist and integrationist leaders and politicians who are in favour of regional stability and co-operation and have closed the pages of ethnic hatred and antagonism. They must demonstrate a willingness to work for the federal authority and not for semi-independent ethnic groups.

The strengthening of central authorities of the, in fact, three-party federation should have its domestic and international dimension. Building trust among the different national parties, involving the central institutions in successful international tasks and projects, bringing the nascent Bosnian armed forces into contact and co-operation with the existing multilateral military networks in Southeastern Europe – these are some of the potential trends for work.

Thirdly, maintain as long as it is needed an effective military force for deterring and effective combat purposes.

Fourthly, bring the issue of strengthening the Croatian component and its contribution to the stabilisation of the federal structure of Bosnia-Herzegovina into the list of requirements for starting the stabilisation and association negotiations with Croatia.

Fifthly, continue the autonomous trade preferences of the EU for Bosnia-Herzegovina as an incentive to increase political predictability and state-institution effectiveness. The implementation of these requirements may prompt the start of stabilisation and association negotiations of Bosnia-Herzegovina with the Union.

The former Yugoslav republic of Macedonia

The security risk and instability list in FYROM includes:
- The hard economic conditions caused by the deprived economic status within the former Yugoslav socialist federation, the difficulties of the transformation of the economy and the devastating effects of the Belgrade-driven ethnic cleansing with expected consequences of creating a new "sick man of the Balkans" issue – the young state of FYROM;
- The ethnic balance and the fragility of the mutual tolerance relationship between the two main ethnic entities;
- The national identity obsession of the political elite, especially of the pro-Serbian political forces, and the dangerous interaction of this issue with the ethnic stability issue;
- A continued dependence on and influence of Belgrade on the pro-Serbian political forces in FYROM. The influential factors on Skopje are nostalgia for the stability of ex-Yugoslavia, the "anti-Bulgarianism" orchestrated by Belgrade, the agents of the intelligence and security services of FRY, and the possession of strong positions in the Social-Democratic Party (former Yugoslav communists) ranks. These three factors interact and produce a destructive critical mass for the young Macedonian statehood; and
- A hard security risk of war with Albania (due to the Albanian irredentist behaviour) or with FRY (because of Serbia's intentions to destabilise the ethnic and state-border situation in Southeastern Europe and preserve the conflicting attitudes in the whole region).

In the light of these risks, the EU strategic approaches should thus consider:

First, the needed support for pro-EU and Euro-Atlantic integration political forces.

Secondly, the need to distance the young state from the destructive nationalistic, anti-European, anti-regional and conflict-driving influences of Serbia and Serbian nationalism in general.

136

Thirdly, the need for economic and financial support, especially after the trauma inflicted by FRY on FYROM with its 1999 ethnic cleansing campaign against the Albanians in Kosovo.

Fourthly, the need to stimulate the young state's nation-building activities in a constructive direction, building on the positive achievements in the post-1992 period and not on the antagonistic pattern of slicing common Balkan history, language and culture. A lesson that needs to be learned by present and future leaders in Skopje is that the commonality of the roots of different nations and states is not necessarily a factor of antagonism and paranoia, as demonstrated by FYROM to Greece and Bulgaria in the 1990s. On the contrary, this is a good reason for developing positive peaceful relations with neighbouring countries, thus serving as the building-block of European integration.

Fifthly, act to block the Albanian irredentist tendencies that may lead to the disruption of the state.

Sixthly, keep an international military force in FYROM for deterring and preventive purposes, and as an additional guarantee of the sovereignty of the state, the nation and all their additional attributes. The participation of FYROM in the various multilateral military networks in Southeastern Europe should be stimulated.

Seventhly, use the negotiations for concluding a Stabilisation and Association Agreement as a guiding instrument to promote the previous six requirements.

Albania

Much of the present perceptions in Europe on organised crime, drug trafficking and illegal immigration are linked to the "Albanian connection". These threats to security are important both for the safety of the EU countries and for the internal stability of Albania and the whole region of Southeastern Europe.

The improvement of the economic, financial and internal political situation is certainly an issue (along with the solution of the aforementioned threats to the stability of the country) that the EU may substantially influence.

The future launching of stabilisation and association negotiations with Albania should be utilised to the maximum for dealing with these issues. So-called "pan-Albanianism" is another area that seems politically manageable in EU-Albanian relations. The incentive of EU and NATO membership is strong enough to help Albanian society and politicians overcome the temptations of polarising the "Albanian issue".

Insisting on developing co-operative neighbourly relations and a benign role in solving the Kosovo constitutional issue should be a part of the EU's country strategy towards Albania too.

V Conclusion and strategy recommendations for the process of differentiated pre-accession

The present strategic instruments of the EU – the Accession Negotiations, the Stabilisation and Association Negotiations and the Stability Pact for Southeastern Europe – should be preserved and developed for a more versatile content and performance, and eventually placed within an encompassing strategic framework.

EU strategic approaches to Southeastern Europe should reflect a vision of overcoming the structural causes of mid- and long-term instabilities and security risks. They should be tested if they meet the requirements enlisted in the second section of this chapter.

However, coping with the needs of more effective strategic approaches concerning Southeastern Europe, as well as with the requirements of a regular decision-making process, would necessitate a more systematic and comprehensive "knowledge basis" that takes account of regional perceptions. It should also include a more vigorous analysis and recommendation support arm, composed of EU and Southeastern Europe experts on the region.

The integration of Southeastern Europe is one of the short-to-mid-term litmus tests of the EU capacity to serve as a world actor by solving major security and other social issues of global significance in its own backyard. Hence, placing Southeastern Europe's integration in the priority short-to-mid-term list of global tasks is of vital importance for the Union as one of the centres of global power.

Since the integration of Southeastern Europe in the EU is – as is European integration in general – an incremental process, regional and country strategies of the Union should in the short-to-mid-term range give way to and stimulate the core group of "willing and able" countries in the region that have started their integration into the EU. Such strategies should thus promote the "locomotive" strategic role these countries play, while preserving the inclusive approach to the integration of all countries from the region in the mid-to-longer-term range. If there are countries that initiate and implement "European" policy in the Balkans, then the EU should also bring itself closer to the local generators of stability and "European-ness". At the same time, the "locomotive strategy" of the EU will bring those countries from the region closer to EU membership who most ardently and effectively work for the closer integration of the Southeast European region in the Union. This kind of evolution in Southeastern Europe would also clearly demonstrate to the Serbian people the benefits of democracy, free markets and European integration.

Minority Issues

Minorities in Southeastern Europe: Legacies of the Past

Lucian Boia

I Introduction: Minorities in East and West

The problem of national minorities can be found everywhere, in East and West alike. But the realities to which the term refers are not always equivalent. In spite of a number of spectacular manifestations and sometimes bloody confrontations (Northern Ireland, the Basque Country, Corsica, etc.), minorities in the West pose problems of an occasional and local character, which do not affect overall cohesion. In the other half of Europe, however, and particularly in Central and Southeastern Europe, the situation is of a *structural* nature. The size of the minorities, their diversity and their specificity are on a quite different scale to what prevails within the present boundaries of the European Union.

The historical inheritance of the two parts of Europe is different. Since the centuries of instability which accompanied and followed the fall of the West Roman Empire, Western Europe has experienced no major historical rupture. The borders between languages and cultures, between the future nations or nation-states of Western Europe were already more or less settled during the Middle Ages. To the east of the Germanic space, on the other hand, linguistic and ethnic frontiers remained fluid until much later (with appreciable modifications again at the end of the Second World War, and even more recently in the Balkan region).

The reasons for this fluidity are the following:

– The "great invasions" continued in the East for several centuries after the end of the phenomenon in the West: the Slavs penetrated the Balkans in the 6th to 7th centuries, the Bulgars arrived in 679, the Hungarians settled in Pannonia in 896, the last great invasion was that of the Tatars in 1241;

- Frontiers were mobile, as territories frequently passed from one master to another (from the Middle Ages to the 20th century).

- Until the age of nation-states, this part of Europe was essentially divided among states of imperial type, which gathered together very different cultures and ethnicities: Hungary, in Central Europe, followed by the Habsburg Empire (Austria and Austria-Hungary) until 1918; the Ottoman Empire, from the 14th century to the First World War, in the Balkans (and for a time, in the 16th and 17th centuries, even in Central Europe, after the fall of the Hungarian kingdom); not to mention Poland and Russia to the north and east of the zone under discussion. These imperial structures favoured the mixing of populations and left the nation-states a complex ethnic inheritance (Hungarians and Germans in the countries of Central Europe, Turks and other Muslims in the Balkan countries).

- The lower demographic and economic density of this space, in comparison with the West, attracted waves of immigrants. German colonists settled all over the zone in successive waves from the 13th to the 19th centuries: in Poland, in the Baltic countries, in Hungary, in Transylvania, in the Banat and Vojvodina, in Russia, in Dobrogea etc. The Jews were also very numerous, in their two branches: Sephardic Jews who fled from Spain to the Ottoman Empire at the end of the 15th century, and the more numerous Ashkenazy Jews, who moved from western Europe, particularly Germany, towards Poland, Hungary, Romania, etc.

The result of these conditions and historical evolutions was an ethnic and cultural mosaic that made a territorial division between nation-states very difficult to create. From this point of view, there is an evident contrast between the West and the East. In the West, the future nation-states were already constituted by the end of the Middle Ages – France, Spain, England, etc. – or at least prefigured by clearly defined cultural spaces – Italy and Germany. Even in multi-ethnic countries like Switzerland and Belgium, there was not a mixing but a juxtaposition of ethnicities and languages. This was not the case in Central and Southeastern Europe. In the beginning, the nation-states of the region gathered together very diverse populations living together in the same territory. Moreover, the differences between one ethnic and cultural group and another were very pronounced. The range of cultures and religions was much larger than in the West: Romanians, Hungarians and Germans in Transylvania; Orthodox, Catholics and Muslims in Bosnia; or Greeks, Turks, Bulgarians and Albanians (to mention only a few out of a much longer list of ethnic groups) in the central Balkans. The variety and the range of multiple and contrasting combinations possible go far beyond the ethnic and cultural diversity of the West. While Western civilisation is unitary, despite ethnic differences, in this region over and above these ethnic differences there is the confrontation between three types of civilisation, in other words between Catholics and Protestants (the advance guard of Western civilisation), Orthodox and Muslims. The zone is thus pulled in three different directions. There is both cohabitation and compartmentalisation, the "Other" being both very close and very different. Consequently, there is an exacerbation of the identity–alterity relationship.

II Concentration of minorities

This diversity is unevenly distributed. The region also has zones which are relatively homogeneous from an ethnic point of view, with "nuclei" around which the present nation-states formed. In the population of the pre-1918 "little" Romania (which united the former principalities of Wallachia and Moldavia), Romanians accounted for a large majority (92 per cent of the population in 1899, almost all of whom were Orthodox). But the Greater Romania created in 1918 attached several other regions to this nucleus, regions with a Romanian majority (absolute or at least relative), but inhabited also by numerous and extraordinarily diverse minorities: Transylvania (taking the term in its broadest sense, as a generic name for all the former Hungarian territories); Bukovina, which had belonged to Austria; Bessarabia, which had been under Russian domination for more than a century; and finally Dobrogea, which had been joined to Romania in 1878 (after belonging to the Ottoman Empire for four and a half centuries). From the point of view of the logic of the nation-state (on which the Europe of today, the Europe of nations, was founded), these regions, with their Romanian majorities, fitted naturally into a Romanian national state. However, the weight of the minorities remained considerable, placing Greater Romania half-way between a national state and a multi-national state.[1]

Table

	Transylvania	Bukovina	Bessarabia	Dobrogea
Romanians	58 %	45 %	56 %	44 %
Hungarians	24 %			
Germans	10 %	9 %		
Ukrainians		28 %	11 %	
Jews		11 %	7 %	
Russians			12 %	
Bulgarians				23 %
Turks				19 %

1   Populatia Romaniei, in: Enciclopedia Romaniei, Vol 1, Bucharest 1938, p. 148.

The little Serbia of 1900 had the same degree of homogeneity as little Romania: 92 per cent Serbs. But the Balkan Wars of 1912–1913 followed by the First World War completely changed the situation. While dominated by the Serbs, Yugoslavia was clearly a multi-ethnic and multi-cultural country. Moreover, it was cut in two by the cultural divide which separates Catholic and Protestant Western Europe from Orthodox Eastern Europe (Croats and Slovenes were Catholic, Serbs Orthodox). In addition to this, there was the third element of the Muslim population. The dismembering of Yugoslavia was in the nature of things: no other European country concentrated so many ethnic, religious and cultural contradictions. But even Serbia itself joined to its homogeneous nucleus two regions which affected the cohesion of the whole: Kosovo, conquered from the Turks in 1913, and Vojvodina, ceded by Hungary after the First World War. In Kosovo, the Serbs were less numerous than the Albanians (whose numerical advantage has continued to grow, so that they now make up over 80 per cent of the population). Vojvodina had a mixed population, in which the Serbs enjoyed at the most a relative majority, the Hungarians and Germans together being more numerous than the "Slavs".

Greece, from the time it was constituted, incorporated a considerable number of Albanians and Turks (most of the latter ended up leaving the country). Bulgaria in its turn inherited a significant Turkish population. The division, following the Balkan Wars of 1912–1913, of the last Turkish territories (Thrace and Macedonia), which were very mixed from an ethnic and confessional point of view (Greeks, Bulgarians, Turks, Macedonian Slavs, Albanians, Vlachs or Macedo-Romanians, and Jews), considerably complicated the problem of minorities, as well as creating tensions between the successor states to the Ottoman Empire.

Minorities and socio-economic divergence

Another characteristic of this region, which has left traces on a social and cultural level, was the identification of certain ethnic groups with well-defined social categories. National antagonisms were thus accompanied and amplified by social antagonisms. Transylvania offers the "ideal" model of such a disposition. Romanians made up the bulk of the peasantry; their aristocracy was almost non-existent (no more than a small rural nobility) and their numbers in the towns were very low. The aristocracy was Hungarian, and the bourgeoisie largely German. Here we have the origin of stereotypes which, without being entirely false, simplify relations which were evidently more complex (for there were certainly also Hungarian peasants and bourgeois or intellectuals among the Romanians): the Hungarian was the oppressor and the Romanian the oppressed, in the national as well as the social sense of the terms. The same model applies in the majority Slav regions of former Hungary, or in the Balkans, where the aristocracy was Turkish or Muslim and the bourgeoisie largely Greek. This situation of superiority–inferiority encouraged and continues to encourage a logic of confrontation, the more so as the roles are now reversed. In Transylvania it is now the Romanians who are on top. It is possible to detect in their attitude the memory of former frustrations, while among the Hungarians nostalgia for a past in which they were the masters only serves to feed similar frustrations. The same type of confrontation and the same reversal of roles is found also in the Balkans between Christians and Muslims (with the latter picking up the bill for centuries of oppression in the past).

The extreme case of this identification of ethnic group with social category is represented by the Roma. In the Romanian lands, their condition was that of slaves until the middle of the nineteenth century. And although the Roma are now divided between several social categories, they continue to be regarded overall with a sort of contempt inspired by their original condition. Where the Roma are concerned, we can even speak of a sort of racism, which manifests itself overtly, without the slightest restraint.

Minorities and the urban-rural divergence

Another typical disposition in Central and Southeastern Europe – which further accentuated disparities at the national level – was the particularly cosmopolitan character of urban life. The differences between town and country concerned not only the specific structures of these two types of habitat, but also their ethnic composition. Sometimes the town presented a quite different ethnic profile to the surrounding countryside. In predominantly Romanian zones of Transylvania, the towns had a clear German and Hungarian majority. But even pre-1918 little Romania, homogeneous as it was at the rural level, included significant minorities in the majority Romanian town population (Jews, Greeks, Armenians, Germans, etc.), who often accounted for the most active economic and commercial elements. Around 1900 half the population of Iassi, the capital of Moldavia, was Jewish; in 1930 the Jews still made up a third of the population of the city. Bucharest had a population of nearly 280,000 in 1899. The census does not specify nationality, but religion and citizenship. 201,000 were Orthodox (71 per cent), 43,000 of Jewish faith (15 per cent), and 37,000 Catholic or Protestant (13 per cent). In terms of citizenship, "ethnic" Romanians must have represented around 70 per cent of the population of the city.[2] A few decades later, in 1930, Bucharest had a

---

2   Bukarest, in: Brockhaus Konversationslexikon, Vol. 2, Leipzig 1901, p. 672.

population of 639,000, of whom 495,000 were Romanian; "non-Romanians" thus accounted for over 22 per cent of the population. In the same year Braila, one of the most important Danube ports, had 68,000 inhabitants, of whom 52,000 were Romanian, 6,600 Jewish, and 4,500 Greek (in total, 25 per cent "non-Romanians").[3]

The situation in the Balkans was the same. Istanbul (the Constantinople of the Christians), was the same type of cosmopolitan city. Around 1900 the population of the Ottoman capital included 557,000 Muslims, 275,000 Greeks, over 100,000 Armenians, 45,000 Jews, 7,000 Bulgarians, and 140,000 foreign residents. Salonica, the capital of a multi-ethnic Macedonia, had the appearance of a great Jewish city; in fact the Jews made up more than half its 120,000 inhabitants, followed by Greeks (25 per cent), Turks (5 per cent), and, in smaller numbers, Bulgarians, Serbs and Macedo-Romanians. In 1887, out of a population of 30,000, Sofia had 5,000 Jews, 2,000 Turks, and 1,000 Roma. Budapest was likewise highly cosmopolitan. Around the middle of the 19th century it had a German majority. In 1900, out of a total population of 732,322, 168,985 were Jewish (23 per cent) and 104,500 German (14 per cent). Altogether, "non-Hungarians" accounted for over 40 per cent of the total.[4]

Integration and assimilation

The creation and strengthening of nation-states has constantly eroded the weight of the minorities. This is not, indeed, a phenomenon limited to this zone of Europe. Almost everywhere the philosophy of the nation-state has been assimilationist. Almost everywhere, if we compare the statistics of 1900 with those of the year 2000, we can see that the majority ethnic groups have consolidated their position (with the evident exception of countries organised on a multi-ethnic basis like Switzerland and Belgium). Even a country like Finland, where Swedish is considered an official language with equal status to Finnish, bears witness to a process of erosion of minorities. Around 1900, Swedes accounted for over 14 per cent of the population; nowadays only 8 per cent speak Swedish. Moreover, a century ago Swedish was the language of the towns and of the elite; now it is spoken only by the Swedish minority, concentrated close to the border with Sweden.

But what is different from one country to another or from one region to another is the scale of the phenomenon and the methods put in operation. In some cases there has

---

3 The figures are taken from: S. Manuila: Recensamantul general al populatiei Romaniei din 29 decembrie 1930, Bucharest: Imprimeria Nationala, 1938.
4 The figures regarding the population of the towns in 1900 are taken from: Budapest, in: Brockhaus Konversationslexikon, Vol. 3, p. 649; Konstantinopol, in: op. cit., Vol. 10, p. 577; Saloniki, in: op. cit., Vol. 14, p. 226; etc.

been a sort of "objective" assimilation by the mechanisms of the nation-state, which have imposed a certain language and a dominant culture, through administration, education, the army, etc. (This is how France has operated for centuries, thus succeeding in almost completely assimilating its minorities.) Emigration, or inversely immigration, or colonisation can modify the balance, in addition to varying demographic growth of the various ethnic groups. On the other hand there are more brutal methods. Emigration may already be an indicator of discontent among a certain ethnic category, or of discriminatory treatment. One step further is ethnic cleansing by expulsion. And further still there is genocide.

All these methods have occurred in this part of Europe. The Armenians were the victims of genocide at the hands of the Turkish authorities starting in 1915; even if the subject remains controversial (planned genocide or deportation with tragic consequences?), the fact remains that a great many Armenians disappeared – between 600,000 and 800,000 according to some estimates. During the Second World War the genocide carried out against the Jews led to the disappearance of over 200,000 people in Romania (almost half of them in Northern Transylvania, which was then occupied by Hungary, the rest mainly Jews from Bessarabia or Bukovina) and of a similar number in Hungary (approximately between a third and a half of all Romanian and Hungarian Jews – it is difficult to reach an exact and indisputable assessment). Most of the Jews in Greece (60,000 out of 74,000) likewise perished, deported to Auschwitz, including the Jewish agglomeration of Salonica. The Roma were also the victims of a genocide project, though it was less systematically followed through than that against the Jews. And finally, the massacres recently perpetrated in Bosnia and Kosovo – with the aim of ethnic cleansing – belong to the same category.

Another method of ethnic cleansing has been the expulsion, or preferably exchange, of populations. This procedure functioned to the full between Greece and Turkey in the wake of the First World War (the Greek-Turkish War of 1920–1923, ended by the Treaty of Lausanne in 1923). A million and a half Greeks left Turkey (before this exodus the coast of Asia Minor was largely Greek), and, in the opposite direction, some 400,000 Turks passed from Greece to Turkey. The Greeks also expelled 250,000 Bulgarian residents of Thrace (replacing them with refugees from Asia Minor). Romanians and Bulgarians likewise carried out an exchange of populations after the return to Bulgaria, in 1940, of the southern part of Dobrogea (the Quadrilateral), which the Romanians had annexed in 1913. Some of the Turks of Dobrogea emigrated to Turkey, but it was Bulgaria that incorporated the largest Turkish minority. The assimilation policy of the communist regime, intensified towards the end of the 1980s, pushed 300,000 Turks to emigrate from Bulgaria (out of a total of over a million – the closing of the border finally prevented what would no doubt have been a larger number from taking the same road). The Germans were also subjected to a similar evacuation process at the end of the Second World War. This was in fact the largest ethnic cleansing ever practised in Europe: twelve million Germans were expelled, mostly from Poland and Czechoslovakia, but also from Yugoslavia (half a million, principally the entire German population of Vojvodina), and to a lesser extent from Hungary and Romania (a few hundred thousand).[5]

New migratory currents were set in motion by the communist regimes, particularly as a result of the precarious economic and social conditions in the respective countries. These conditions indeed affected the population as a whole, but "minority people" sometimes had the "good fortune" to be able to leave more easily than "majority people". (They might be invited and sometimes even bought – as in the case of Ceausescu's Romania – by their co-nationals, in addition some communist regimes were not averse to a sort of "covert" ethnic cleansing.) It is a fact that those Jews who had survived the Second World War almost completely abandoned this part of Europe. Likewise, Germans emigrated to West Germany. The figures for Romania are revealing: there were 452,000 Jews on the present territory of Romania in 1930; 355,000 in 1945; and 8,955 in 1992. The decline of the German minority is also very pronounced: 633,000 Germans in 1930; 385,000 in 1956; and 119,000 in 1992.[6] With its Jews and its Germans gone, Central and Southeastern Europe has also lost a part of its history and its cultural heritage.

Communism also eroded minorities by its forced programme of industrialisation and urbanisation. A massive migratory current was established from villages to towns (and from one region to another within the same country). This movement caused populations to be mixed together, and considerably reduced or even completely annulled the former cosmopolitan profile of the towns, reinforcing the weight of the majority population.

In general, the philosophy of communism promoted uniformity and was hostile to "specific" values. It sought to blur the differences between individuals and groups, submerging them all in a single "socialist nation". Through the promotion of a single system of education and a single culture, minorities inevitably lost ground in relation to majorities. The proclaimed "resolution of the national problem" in fact simply meant the refusal to take it truly into consideration. The sliding of communism towards nationalism – a phenomenon present everywhere in the region – led to an even more accentuated subordination of the minorities to the "unitary national" project.

---

5 For changes and displacements of population, and for the numerical weight of minorities in general: A. Sellier, J. Sellier: Atlas des peuples d'Europe centrale, Paris: La Découverte, 1991.

6 The figures are taken from: Recensamantul populatiei si locuintelor din 7 ianuarie 1992 (volume Structura etnica si confesionala a populatiei), Bukarest 1995.

The result everywhere was a pronounced ebb in the numbers of minorities. This was the consequence partly of an "objective" evolution which can also be found elsewhere, but above all of a certain political and national "philosophy". The member of a minority has long been seen as a sort of "foreigner", who has to accept the law of the majority or, even better, give up his place to the latter. This is in fact the result of the conflictual history of this part of Europe. Moreover, and paradoxically, communism, which had claimed to be able to resolve equitably the problem of nationalities, pushed things even farther in the same direction, by its political project of unification and homogenisation on the one hand, and on the other by its economic failure, which prompted massive emigration.

A few figures will give an idea of the extent of the phenomenon. In 1930 Romanians accounted for 78 per cent of the population of the present territory of Romania; by 1992 this had risen to 90 per cent. In the same interval, the proportion of Hungarians fell from 10 per cent to 7 per cent; Germans from 4.4 per cent to 0.5 per cent; and Jews from 3.2 per cent to almost zero. In Transylvania the proportion of Romanians rose from 58 per cent to 74 per cent, while the proportion of Hungarians fell from 24 per cent to 21 per cent. Dobrogea was a multi-ethnic territory, probably the most heterogeneous in Europe; now it is over 90 per cent Romanian. All the towns, with the exception of those in the two majority Hungarian counties in eastern Transylvania, now have a substantial Romanian majority. To give two examples: Cluj, capital of Transylvania, in 1930: Hungarians – 48 per cent, Romanians – 35 per cent, Jews – 13 per cent; in 1992: Romanians – 76 per cent, Hungarians – 23 per cent; Timisoara, capital of the Banat, in 1930: Germans – 30 per cent, Hungarians – 30 per cent, Romanians – 27 per cent; in 1992: Romanians – 82 per cent, Hungarians – 10 per cent, Germans – 4 per cent. The denominational structure of Transylvania has also been substantially modified. Between the wars, Orthodox Christians accounted for only a third of the population, as part of the Romanian population was Uniate (Greek Catholic). In 1948, the Greek Catholic Church was suppressed by the communist authorities and most of its members returned to Orthodoxy. This ban was lifted in 1990, but the lost ground could only partially be recovered. In 1992, the number of Greek Catholics was 223,000, that is to say, a little less than 1 per cent of the population of the country, although they were 8 per cent in 1930. In Romania as a whole, the Orthodox represented 73 per cent in 1930, while they are now 87 per cent. Without being uniform, Romania is now far more homogeneous than in the inter-war period.

Certain evolutions are even more striking. Greece has become a country almost without minorities – over 98 per cent of the population are Greek and Orthodox (the remainder being about a hundred thousand Turks, 1 per cent of the total, in western Thrace, and a small number of Albanians and Vlachs). This was not the case at the beginning of the formation of modern Greece. The others were either expelled or exchanged (Turks for Greeks), or they were assimilated, effectively or at least officially (thus becoming "invisible").

Bulgaria still has a significant Turkish minority of 8 to 9 per cent of the population. But the weight of this minority was much greater around 1900 – 17 per cent according to the 1893 census. Bulgarians were then 75 per cent of the population (2.5 out of 3.3 million). There were also Romanians (63,000), Greeks (59,000), Roma (52,000) and Jews (28,000). Today the proportion of Bulgarians has risen to 89 per cent, and minorities other than Turks and Roma (2 per cent) are statistically insignificant.

Even the present-day territory of Hungary, that is to say the genuinely Hungarian "nucleus" of pre-1918 Greater Hungary, was not completely ethnically homogenous. According to the census of 1920, there were 8 million inhabitants within the present borders of Hungary. The census classified people by mother tongue. According to this criterion, Hungarians (7.1 million) represented 89 per cent of the population, followed by Germans (551,000, or 6.9 per cent) and Slovaks (142,000, or 1.8 per cent). The Jews should also be taken into consideration. They were Hungarian-speaking, but nevertheless formed a distinct group, as their situation during the War proved. They represented 5.9 per cent of the population (470,000). Nowadays, Germans represent no more than 2 per cent of the population, and the Jews have almost disappeared as a minority.

The most fragmented territory from an ethnic, religious and cultural point of view remains that of the north-western part of the Balkans, more precisely the space of the former Yugoslavia. In Bosnia everyone belongs to a minority (Muslim, Serb or Croat); in Macedonia more than 20 per cent of the population are Albanian; Kosovo belongs to Serbia but the Serbs are a small minority there in relation to the Albanians. On the other hand the Serbs now constitute an absolute majority in Vojvodina, which certainly was not the case when the territory was first annexed (the largest minority there remains Hungarian – the Germans have disappeared).

This process of ethnic homogenisation has two quite divergent effects: on the one hand, there is a strengthening of nation-states and a firmer integration of minorities (who often manifested centrifugal tendencies in the interwar period); on the other, conversely, there is a heightened resistance of some minorities to the phenomenon of assimilation and, in general, diminution of their weight in the population as a whole. A certain "aggressiveness" on the part of the Hungarians of Transylvania can no doubt be explained by the fact that this population is failing to "keep up the pace". They see that their territory is diminished and fragmented. They feel more and more "drowned" in the majority population. Hence we see a tendency to withdraw into themselves and an offensive attitude which compensates to some extent for worries about the future. The moment has come to find a new balance, avoiding both extremes: the assimilatory pull of the majority but also isolation and the "anti-majority" attitude which tempts some ethnic groups.

III Legacies of the past

Another distinctive characteristic of this part of Europe is the ever-present weight of history. The "historical discourse" continues to be heard with a frequency and an impact that it no longer enjoys in the West. It is an attitude closer to the romantic nationalism of the 19th century than to the mentalities associated with the "border-less" technological information world of today. The past is made powerfully present according to contradictory scenarios. It is a conflictual past which sets in relief the combat between one group and another: Christian peoples against the Turks, Romanians against Hungarians, etc. This also justifies a certain unfavourable attitude towards minorities or a hostile attitude of minorities towards the majority. Historical right is very often (too often) invoked as a source of solutions to problems which actually belong to the present, not to the past. The answers are all the more contradictory, in as much as from one period to another the history of the region presents countless modifications on the political, territorial, ethnic or religious levels. There is something there to suit everyone. Each country or nation has known its moments of glory and of distress. History can eventually prove anything.[7]

Above all, origins are valorised and set to work (within the well-known framework of foundation myths). Antiquity (anteriority in relation to the "others") and continuity are key concepts. Modern Greece is seen by the Greeks as the continuation of ancient Greece. (The opposite opinion, that the Greeks of today are a different people from the ancient Greeks, provoked widespread protests among Greek historians). It follows that they have rights, at least theoretically, over a certain space, which is noticeably larger than that of present-day Greece. This historical perspective has fed conflicts between Greece and the Turks (a problem which was finally "solved" by the ethnic cleansing of the coast of Asia Minor), and is nowadays the source of a "terminological" dispute concerning Macedonia. Greece refuses to accept that a country can bear a name which it considers part of its historical heritage (even if it is a history over 2,000 years old!).

The Kosovo conflict was not provoked by history, but contradictory historical dis-

---

7   In the considerations regarding history and the past-present relationship, I have made use of arguments from my own books. See in particular: L. Boia: Istorie si mit in constiinta romaneasca [History and Myth in Romanian Consciousness], Bucharest: Humanitas, 1997, and L. Boia: Doua secole de mitologie nationala [Two Centuries of National Mythology], Bucharest 1999.

courses fed and inflamed it. According to the Serbs, Kosovo was the "cradle" of their nation, and the Albanians only settled there in more recent times. According to the Albanians there is no doubt about their own "anteriority". They are the descendants of the Illyrians and the Thracians and the inhabitants of the zone since antiquity, the Slavs settled much later. The appeal to history sometimes seems to resonate louder than the imperatives of the present and the voice of reason.

Between Romanians and Hungarians there is likewise a thorny problem of continuity. The absence of documents leaves much in doubt concerning the true history of the Romanians during the first centuries of the Middle Ages. For some Austrian historians of the eighteenth and nineteenth centuries and for Hungarian historiography of the present day, the Romanian people originated somewhere in the Balkans (in an ill-defined zone towards the north-west of the region), whence the Romanians migrated towards their present territory from the thirteenth century onwards. In historical terms, Transylvania was thus Hungarian before it became majority Romanian. Romanian historians, on the contrary, uphold the perfect continuity of ancient Dacia and modern Romania, the Romanians being the descendants of Romanised Dacians. This dispute has inflamed both historiographies (and no less so public opinion in the two countries), which take up intransigent and radically opposed stands: absolute continuity or immigration (contradictory theories based on the same sources!). History has thus poisoned relations. It has almost ended up eclipsing the present reality, which is that of a Transylvania with a Romanian majority (regardless of the anteriority of one group or the other), but also an important Hungarian minority, which is a constituent part of the past and present of the province.

IV Current and future risks

Nowadays, risks are not equally distributed. We may consider as a primary risk factor the concentrated presence of powerful minorities, which in certain zones are actually in the majority (while in these same territories the majority population are in the minority). Where these zones are close to the corresponding nation states, the situation can become explosive. Kosovo offers an already classic case – an Albanian "minority", in fact a local majority of 80 to 90 per cent, concentrated in a region bordering on Albania. From this point of view Macedonia presents a similar risk: the Albanian minority here is also concentrated near the Albanian border (where it is in the majority). There are two situations of this type involving Hungarian minorities; the south of Slovakia and the north of Vojvodina are home to Hungarian populations who are minorities overall but locally in the majority, in strips of territory along the Hungarian border.

In Romania there is also a region with a Hungarian majority, made up of two counties, Harghita and Covasna, where, according to the 1992 census, Hungarians are 470,000 in number, four and a half times more numerous than Romanians (103,000). But the geopolitical situation here is different, as this region is right in the centre of Romania, several hundred kilometres from the Hungarian border.

A second risk factor concerns the attitude of "majorities" and the political authorities towards minorities. It is a factor which can combine with the first to aggravate or attenuate its effects. It is evident, for example, that Romanian behaviour in Transylvania is very different from Serbian behaviour in Kosovo. In Kosovo, the combination of the size of the Albanian population, the proximity of Albania and the intransigence of the Yugoslav government provoked a crisis. In Romania, on the other hand, apart from the more fragmented character of the Hungarian population, which is spread across a majority Romanian territory, crisis (which reached the point of bloodshed in Targu Mures in March 1990) has been attenuated by the capacity of the two sides to find a common ground of understanding. The Hungarian party (UDMR: Democratic Union of Magyars of Romania) has participated in the government of the country since 1996. Laws have been passed which give the Hungarian language a better position in teaching, administration and justice. The demand for a Hungarian university remains in suspension, one compromise solution perhaps being that of a multicultural university. The fact is that the atmosphere of Romanian-Hungarian relations is much improved within Romania, as a are relations with neighbouring Hungary. The Franco-German reconciliation is invoked as a model for a new type of relations between the two nations and countries (although there is still some distance to be covered before this level is reached).

The relations of the Romanians with the Roma minority present a quite different aspect. In contrast to the Hungarians, the Roma are dispersed across the entire territory. In their case the issue is not local autonomy, but social and cultural integration. They have long been regarded as a socially and culturally inferior population. Their conditions of life and their degree of integration remain very low. They continue to live in their own way, as a sort of distinct society within Romanian society. Moreover, attitudes towards them are more or less overtly racist. It would be an exaggeration to say that the dysfunctional relationship between Romanians in general and Roma could destabilise Romania. But it does give rise to a state of social unease (with the Roma considered as its potential delinquent), punctuated by sometimes bloody incidents. The integration of the Roma (with respect for their identity and their dignity) remains an objective still to be attained. Their number is open to question; according to the 1992 census, there were 410,000 Roma, that is to say 1.8 per cent of the country's population. But much larger figures have also been advanced: one or two million, or even more (an "inflation" which betrays a certain anxiety on the part of the majority population: the fear of being swamped by a "primitive" people in full demographic expansion). The situation of the Roma of Hungary and Bulgaria is similar. Everywhere we find this type of relation with the majority: non-integration from one side, discriminatory attitude from the other.

An important risk factor in the region is without doubt poverty. Even if it is not poverty that engenders prejudices and ethnic confrontations, it feeds them and amplifies them (the more so when a certain ethnic category finds itself in an inferior situation to the others – the case of the Roma already mentioned). A noticeable improvement in the standard of living would serve to ease contradictions on the ethnic and religious levels. Responsibility must be borne first of all by the nations and governments involved, but also by the "rich" West. Bosnia and Kosovo must be considered an alarm signal. The instability of the region represents a danger for the whole of Europe. The effort must be made in the interests of all, of each country and of Europe in its entirety. No price can be too high, as the cost of a major crisis would undoubtedly be much higher.

V Long-term policies on history and ethnicity

Integration in the European Union may be considered the most certain path towards stability in the region. Steps have already been taken in this direction. Hungary, Slovenia, Romania and Bulgaria have started negotiations for membership. From the point of view of the problem of minorities, the advantage would be twofold. On the one hand, a positive economic evolution would serve to attenuate contradictions, while on the other, the relaxing of frontiers would lead to easier and closer relations between dispersed minorities and their nations of origin (thus the Hungarians of Transylvania, Slovakia and Vojvodina would be brought closer to Hungary, not by modifying borders, but by modifying their significance). In a united Europe, the problem of minorities will cease to exist. There will no longer be a majority nation. Everyone will belong to a "minority". It is an ambitious project, and still a remote one, but it represents a chance, the only chance, for all the nations of Europe.

There is also the issue of a certain pedagogy which ought to be applied with conviction and perseverance. Conflictual states are maintained not only by objective conditions (cultural differences or economic context), but also, and perhaps even more, by a certain image of the Other. For too long we have practised a narrow discourse of identity and conflict. It is time for everyone to understand that in order to be part of Europe we must abandon racist and xenophobic discourses. Indeed history too must be examined in a new light. Why insist so much on conflicts, when this part of Europe offers a remarkable model (valid for the whole of Europe) of the interference of civilisations and their mutual enrichment? History "as it actually happened" was perhaps less conflictual than the history which we have become accustomed to invoke in the age of nations and minorities (in the last two centuries, that is to say). Thus the Romanians have conceived their history as a prolonged conflict against Turks or Hungarians. The fact is that, beyond these conflicts, and in a more essential sense, part of the Romanian people participated for centuries in the history and civilisation of the Southeast European space dominated by the Ottoman Empire, and another part in the history of Central Europe, along with Hungarians and Germans. There is a whole common history here, which, from the perspective of the present, is more significant than the phases of conflict. It would be very useful if the teaching of history were conceived in such a way as to bring peoples together rather than separating them (in Romania there was a very animated controversy in the autumn of 1999 about the new history textbooks, which set out precisely to concentrate on issues of civilisation). The normalisation of inter-ethnic relations must be considered a priority objective, engaging the action of governments, legislation, teaching and the mass media. Nothing can be done without a shift in consciousness.

A co-ordinated programme of evaluation of the history textbooks in use in the countries of the region would be very useful. (Other categories of textbook – geography, civic education etc. – should perhaps be covered too, but history, as I have shown, remains the most sensitive area.) Proposals concerning the improvement and harmonisation of textbooks should give particular attention to the ways in which relations between nations and ethnic groups can be treated in a new spirit, less conflictual and with an emphasis on common or complementary values.

However, there is a need for a larger project on a European scale. European integration began with the economy. Then it was extended into the political sphere. However, the cultural and ethical dimension of the project was neglected. If it does not share a common set of values, Europe runs the risk of failure. The Haider case has recently shown that even the West is not immune to divergent developments. The problem is all the more pressing at a time when the Union is preparing to extend towards Central and Southeastern Europe, into a space which is culturally somewhat out of step with the West. Here the national ideology still has a sort of supremacy over other values, which may be detrimental to the development of democracy and the normalisation of relations between the majority and minorities. Now is the time for Europe to complete its economic and political project with an educational project, which should be placed on the same level of importance. This will seek to explain to people, and especially young people, what it means to be European. The elaboration of a European Charter, defining unequivocally the values which lie at the base of the European construction, and the types of behaviour which can no longer be accepted, would be useful. Multiculturalism and a positive attitude towards minorities need to be inscribed as conditions *sine qua non* of the future of Europe.

In the 19th century people were educated insistently in the spirit of nationalism. The national consciousness did not appear of its own accord, it was the result of an educational process. What we need at present is an equally persevering education in the European spirit, all the more so as we need to attenuate the nationalist reflexes which have been acquired over generations. (This does not, of course, mean rejecting national particularities, but putting aside the barriers and prejudices that divide nations and ethnic groups.) This educational project must nowadays be considered a European priority.

Legal and Political Aspects of Protecting Minorities in Southeastern Europe in the Context of European Enlargement

Kinga Gál

I Introduction

"Enlargement will modify the Union's geopolitical situation and its proximity to critical zones in Eastern and Southeastern Europe. Bilateral disputes involving acceding members, and issues related to national and ethnic minorities, could burden the Union's cohesion and its Common Foreign and Security Policy, and would have to be effectively tackled before accession."[1]

The crises in the Balkan region have created new momentum for the enlargement process and have emphasised the essential contribution of European integration to peace and stability in Europe at the very end of the century. After the Commission recommended that negotiations should be opened in 2000 with all candidate countries who fulfil, among others, the Copenhagen Criteria (democracy, rule of law, human rights and respect for and protection of minorities), two core questions appeared immediately among the conditions of accession: stability and protection of human and minority rights.

In order to understand the stability problems in the region and assess risks for stability in Southeastern Europe, it is necessary to look at the coexistence of the different ethnic groups in these countries and at the structures established for the protection of national and ethnic minorities. To the same extent it is necessary to look at the dynamic in states – minorities – home states, as related issues might create tension with-

---

1 Impact Study, The Effects on the Union's Policies, of Enlargement to the Applicant Countries of Central and Eastern Europe, 15 July, 1997. Cf.: *http://europa.eu.int/comm/enlargement/agenda*2000/impact/21.htm.

in the society and between neighbouring countries, while polarising the parties to a large extent.

From a legal-political perspective, this study will focus on issues of the protection of national minorities in Southeastern Europe. This paper will focus mainly on those countries that have been involved in the accession negotiations by the European Union (Slovenia, Romania and Bulgaria). Nevertheless, in order to give a clear picture of the overall minority protection structures in the region, and because minority protection in these countries is strongly linked with relations to neighbouring states, it will also address ethnic management in Croatia, the Former Yugoslav Republic of Macedonia, as well as Bosnia-Herzegovina. The Federal Republic of Yugoslavia was deliberately left out the scope of this study. This not because it would not be relevant and timely to address the situation in Vojvodina or even more in Kosovo, but due to the fact that in the Federal Republic of Yugoslavia there is an immense gap between written law and dictatorial practice. Although there is an international regime established in Kosovo, the actual situation is exceptional rather than normal. Therefore it is useless to analyse the legal framework or give any structural analysis of the existing or non-existing minority protection system. With regard to the rest of Yugoslavia there is no progress in minority protection – although one has to admit that in the multiethnic Vojvodina[2] the situation is better than in other parts of the country. This study will thus proceed as follows:

1. The opening section of the paper will emphasise the general background and most relevant factors with direct influence on minority situation and protection in the region.

2. Next, the core issues of minority protection will be addressed, with special regard to the requirements established by international standards, as well as expectations of international organisations towards these countries in the field of protecting minorities.

3. Thereafter, national policies will be described. In this context, the actual measures taken and commitments made on the side of respective governments will be analysed. A special emphasis will be put on the implementation of domestic legal and political measures, as well as on the application of the undertakings. Good practices and processes, as well as shortcomings, will be enlisted.

4. Finally, the study will identify the problematic issues that could be considered risks for peaceful coexistence in these multiethnic states and therefore, stability in this region in general.

---

2   Having a long tradition of coexistence of multi-ethnic population, long-established minority schools system and more or less well organised minority associations.

II Minorities and stability: Why are minority issues so problematic in this region?

During the modernisation process taking place in this part of Europe, a civil society has to be built or rebuilt that is able to fulfil the tasks of democratisation and developing an economic structure and that is able to define its own identity without suppressing others. The principles of democracy and the rule of law were useful for the reforms needed and for the international legitimacy of governments but were abstract ideas for the people in Southeastern Europe. These principles were regarded as intangible and were hard to interpret in practice, as the democratic forms of managing public affairs did not have long traditions in this part of Europe.

In addition, due to the rather delayed process of establishing nation-states, as well as due to the suppression or misuse of national feelings by communism, nationalism was sufficiently rooted in society to become the ruling state ideology in some of the countries in Southeastern Europe. In other cases, the nation building process is taking place more smoothly because of democratic forces in government, although even these democratic forces from time to time play the national card when it is seen as useful to remain in power.

Nationalism (both in its negative and positive sense) is a phenomenon which one can find in most countries where different ethnic groups live together, but in former communist countries, which are practically all multiethnic states, nationalism finds particularly fertile soil. On the one hand, the majority population in these countries has seen the transformation process as an opportunity to strengthen nation-state and national feelings. National feelings have appeared very strongly and in an extremely manipulative way especially in the first half of the decade. The leaders, formerly representing the communist regime, saw their only chance of survival after the changes in becoming nationalist in order to legitimise their power.

On the other hand, minorities tried to achieve a more effective protection of national identity and to establish their own institutions, in some cases self-governing. While the majorities in the communist countries were suppressed by the regime in their political and basic human rights, sometimes even in their national feelings, the minorities were oppressed in a double way – as citizens and human beings, but at the same time also as minorities. This way, they hoped for the radical alteration of their situation during the early 1990s. However, the new constitutions and the most important laws adopted mostly in 1991 and 1992 reflected much more the nation-state building tendencies and were less aimed at effective minority protection. Therefore, the minority communities urged for clear legal guarantees, the larger and well-organised minority groups even articulated their claims in a more explicit way, using the terms of collective rights, self-governments and cultural and territorial autonomy.

Basic developments took place during the first years after the changes in the life of minority communities in several countries, especially in Bulgaria and Romania. This period is characterised by the first attempts to correct disadvantages caused by the communist regime. Important steps were taken in legislation, encouraging minorities to build their own associations (parties). NGOs and minority language publications were established. Central governmental bodies were established in charge of issues related to ethnic and national minorities. However, some of these steps were regarded as part of a general "window dressing" policy towards the West, and were perceived by some minorities as recompensing for the deficiencies of previous decades without satisfying their real needs. Tensions escalated especially during the early 1990s, with a clear improvement in inter-ethnic relations after democratic forces came into power during the mid-1990s, although problematic issues still remained.

The strength and popularity of national ideas differed from one state to another depending on the development of the society, the actual stage of nation-state building process and on the strength of the democratic forces, as well as on whether these could or could not become part of the ruling elite. Escalation of ethnic tensions could be avoided where the nation-state building process of the majority did not come into open contradiction with the identity preserving manifestations of the minorities living in the same country. (Fortunately, the inter-ethnic tensions from Targu Mures (Romania) in March 1990 did not end like similar tensions in Yugoslavia, but on the contrary ended in strong co-operation among civic associations and NGOs on both sides, which were able to mobilise the civil society towards improvements.) Where this nationalism became state policy, the whole democratisation system was endangered by its side effects. The nationalistic ideology led to substantial violations of human rights (Yugoslavia).

There was a clear shift in the field of ethnic management during the second half of the decade. Important developments took place with the empowerment of the democratic forces in Romania (after the elections in 1996, when the Democratic Alliance of Hungarians in Romania became part of the coalition government), Bulgaria (the non-communist United Democratic Forces came to power in 1997), Former Yugoslav Republic of Macedonia (the formation of a new democratic coalition with a moratorium sui generis on issues concerning inter-ethnic relations in November 1998), Slovenia (centre-right government formed in February 1997) and Croatia (new democratic government in 2000). Still, especially as the Romanian warnings might show, the democratic institutions and the civil society are far from being strong enough to keep power.[3]

Relations between most of the neighbouring states can be regarded as consolidated

---

3 According to the results of the municipal elections and the polls about the voting preferences for the general elections to be taking place in November 2000 in Romania, the democratic forces will lose the elections.

by the end of the decade, especially in the case of Slovenia, Romania, Bulgaria and FYROM. This is mostly the result of efforts to establish good neighbourly relations with neighbouring states and, in consequence, stabilisation of their geopolitical position in Southeastern Europe as a clear requirement for any step towards Euro-Atlantic integration. The accession negotiations with the European Commission also have a stimulating role in the process of concluding bilateral treaties between the neighbouring countries.[4]

III Core legal and political aspects of minority protection: international standards and EU instruments

The core issues of minority-majority relations and effective protection and promotion of minority identity can be divided into five main areas. These issues appear in the form of standards in the international political and legal documents in the bilateral treaties signed between neighbouring countries in the region. They are also addressed by most of the new constitutions in this region.

1. The less problematic, although basic, provisions deal with the right to non-discrimination and the protection of cultural, linguistic, religious identity of the individuals belonging to such minority communities.

2. More debated and divisive questions are related to linguistic rights, language use in the private and public sectors, in education, media, culture and official contacts. Language rights, which are cultural rights with a collective dimension, can be regarded as the most sensitive issues in minority protection.

3. Strongly linked to linguistic rights are educational rights (to learn the minority language and to be instructed in a minority language on all educational levels), which constitute a key issue for minorities. These educational rights are the ones which states are less generous in promoting.

4. Effective participation and representation in decision-making on different levels of the administration as well as local self-governments are also very important, as the improvement in further basic minority rights is strongly related to the possibility of influencing decision-making or putting pressure on the adoption of basic laws im-

---

4 The most relevant treaties in this regard are the bilateral treaties adopted between Hungary and Ukraine, Slovenia, Croatia, Slovakia and Romania (all signed and ratified between 1991 and 1996), all containing detailed provisions for minority protection; between Romania and Bulgaria (1992, without any special norm regarding the protection of national minorities); Romania and the Federal Republic of Yugoslavia (1996 – general principles and reference to multilateral international norms); Hungary (1996); Ukraine (1997) detailed article (art. 13) on minority protection, as well as Moldova (2000). Croatia has signed bilateral treaties with Hungary and also bilateral agreements on the rights of members of national minorities in 1992 with Italy and 1995 with Hungary. In 1996 the Rep. of Croatia and the Federal Republic of Yugoslavia signed an agreement on the normalisation of relationships.

159

proving their effective protection. This is especially the case in Southeastern Europe where participation in political life and administration is regarded as extremely useful in order to achieve improvements and have decisions implemented.

5. Cross-border co-operation is highly important in the life of minority communities living in border regions. Contacts across the borders in Southeastern Europe are promoted with the help and the influence of European Union and Council of Europe projects.[5]

Four key instruments have played and are continuing to play an important role in promoting the above areas: the European Convention for the Protection of Human Rights and Fundamental Freedoms (1950); the European Charter of Local Self-Governments, the Framework Convention for the Protection of National Minorities (1995),[6] as well as the European Charter for Regional or Minority Languages (1992). In addition to these standards, the Parliamentary Assembly and the Committee of Ministers of the Council of Europe have adopted soft law provisions.[7] At the same time the OSCE has adopted politically strong, but legally non-binding documents (such as the Document of the Copenhagen Meeting of the Conference on the Human Dimension, 1990). Furthermore, the recommendations of the High Commissioner on National Minorities have also become part of monitoring the political criteria that all candidate countries have to consider in order to become part of the enlargement process.

While most of the countries in the region have already ratified the European Convention on Human Rights (ECHR)[8] and the Framework Convention, and a few have even signed (though not necessarily ratified) the Language Charter, adherence to these instruments, which constitute a European "acquis," is an important common target for all countries in the region.

---

5 For example, note the joint project of the European Union and Council of Europe "National Minorities in Europe", started in 1994, or the project in the framework of the Congress of Local and Regional Authorities of the Council of Europe "Local Democracy Embassy", etc.

6 The Framework Convention entered into force on 1 February 1998. This instrument of the Council of Europe became the main legal framework for the development of minority protection in Europe, as it is the first legally binding document in this respect.

7 In the context of minority protection the Committee of Ministers' recommendations (92) 10; (97) 10 on the protection of minorities and recommendation R (2000) on the education of Roma children in Europe, as well as the Parliamentary Assembly recommendations 1134 (1990); 1177 (1992), 1201 (1993); 1300 (1996) played a particularly important role.

8 The following states in the region have signed and ratified the European Convention for the Protection of Human Rights and Fundamental Freedoms: Albania, Bulgaria, Croatia, Greece, Hungary, Moldova, Romania, Slovenia, "the former Yugoslav Republic of Macedonia"; the Framework Convention for the Protection of National Minorities: Albania, Bosnia-Herzegovina, Bulgaria, Croatia, Hungary, Moldova, Romania, Slovenia, "the former Yugoslav Republic of Macedonia". Greece just signed the Convention, but did not ratify it; the European Charter for Regional or Minority Languages: Croatia, Hungary, while Romania, Slovenia and "the former Yugoslav Republic of Macedonia" have just signed without ratifying it.

The European Commission started to play a leading role in monitoring achievements in this respect in the candidate countries. The regular reports of the Commission (three reports for each country: 1997, 1998 and the "key" report of 13 October 1999) stressed the need for efforts to protect minority rights,[9] particularly those of the Roma population in many of the candidate countries, especially in Romania, Bulgaria and Slovenia.

The provisions dealing with minority rights in the bilateral treaties strongly bear the imprint of these international and regional instruments on minority issues. One can find in these treaties provisions quoted almost word for word from several documents on the rights of national minorities, such as the UN Declaration on Minorities (1992),[10] the CSCE Copenhagen Document (1990), as well as the Council of Europe's Framework Convention or its Parliamentary Assembly Recommendation 1201 (1993).[11] The bilateral treaties give legal force to these documents through their incorporation into the agreements.

IV National policies and commitments

Domestic legislation

Legal provisions existing in these countries governing minority protection were adopted during the early 1990s and have a common approach. They are based on the principle of non-discrimination with provisions of positive support and protection of individual rights of persons belonging to national minorities, based on OSCE and Council of Europe standards and recommendations.

The constitution plays a role in positioning minority issues in the given state. Most of the new constitutions of the states in Southeastern Europe declare the primacy of international undertakings over national laws. This is an important principle when looking at the status of the national minorities and their protection system in the different states of the region. All these constitutions deal with the status of minorities, mostly referring

---

9   "The treatment of minorities demands continued attention in all of the candidate countries. (...) Prejudice in many of the candidate countries continues to result in discrimination against the Roma in social and economic life", Regular Reports from the Commission on Progress towards Accession by each of the candidate countries, 13 October 1999, cf.: *http://europa.eu.int/comm/enlargement/report_10_99/intro/index.htm*.

10 United Nations Declaration on the Rights of Persons Belonging to National or Ethnic, Religious and Linguistic Minorities, adopted by General Assembly resolution 47/135 of 18 December 1992.

11 Parliamentary Assembly of the Council of Europe Recommendation 1201 (1993) on an additional protocol on the rights of national minorities to the European Convention on Human Rights, Assembly debate on 1 February 1993 (22nd Sitting).

to the basic rights of non-discrimination and identity protection of the minorities living in the country[12], while further special measures are transmitted to normal legislation (educational rights, linguistic rights, rights in the field of political participation[13], and freedom of religion).

More problematic is the constitutional definition of the titular nation and state, as well as of the description of the status of co-existing national and ethnic minorities. The acknowledgement of minorities and the right to preserve their special identity in the constitution may positively influence the general legal framework and openness of the society for affirmative action in favour of minorities. In contrast, if the constitution stipulates the idea of one nation – one state, it is difficult to find any justification for differentiation in favour of minority groups and to adopt special laws in this regard. In conformity with the unitary and national character of the state, in all these countries only one official language is accepted: that of the majority. Therefore, the constitutional concept of the nation-state determines the position of the minority languages within the overall legislation and in everyday use.

For example, according to the Romanian constitution (art. 1.1), "Romania is a sovereign, independent, unitary and indivisible National State"; the "State foundation is laid on the unity of the Romanian people" (art. 4.1). The "ethnic sense" of nation is highlighted in Romania also by doctrinaire writings of those who were involved in drafting the Constitution: According to their approach, nation is defined as "a community of ethnic origin". The Romanian Helsinki Committee recommended in its shadow report on the implementation of the Framework Convention that a declaration made by the Romanian Constitutional Court would be welcome that explicitly defines the civic character of the term "national" in order to eliminate various interpretations and requirements from minorities to declare loyalty to the state.

The Macedonian constitution mentions the minorities living in the country in its preamble, while according to its constitutional concept, the Republic of Macedonia is a unitary state, in which sovereignty derives from the citizens and belongs to them. The concept is based on the principle of individualisation of rights. This way, it does not establish collective rights for national or ethnic minorities. Therefore, the Macedonian

---

12   Constitutions of Bulgaria, Croatia, Romania, Slovenia and of the former Yugoslav Republic of Macedonia.

13   The *Bulgarian Constitution* and the Law on Political Parties (Art. 11 par. 4 of the Bulgarian Constitution of 13 July 1991 and art. 3. par. 3 of the Law on Political Parties) prohibits for example the foundation of political parties on an ethnic, racial or religious basis. The Bulgarian Constitutional Court, however, interpreted these provisions as constituting only a formal but not substantial prohibition (Judgement no. 4 of 21 April 1992, in: Drumeva, ZAOeRV 1993, p. 112.) Contrary to this approach, the *Constitution of Slovenia* adopted an approach, which provides a constitutional guarantee of freedom of association to national minorities to comprehensively protect minorities against discrimination in the exercise of the right of political participation. (Art. 64. par. 1 of the Slovenian Constitution of 23 December 1991.)

constitution does not envisage any separate institutional solutions inherent to consensual (con-societal) democracy. In fact, the Macedonian case represents a country strongly divided among ethnic lines.

The constitution of the Republic of Croatia ("Historical Foundation", par. 3) declares the Croatian state as a unitary, "national state of the Croatian nation and the state of members of autochthonous national minorities: Serbs, Czechs, Slovaks, Italians, Hungarians, Jews, Germans, Austrians, Ukrainians and Ruthenians and the others who are its citizens, and who are guaranteed equality with citizens of Croatian nationality and the realisation of national rights".

Deriving from the constitutional framework, national legislation strongly reflects the spirit of the constitution. Therefore, the status of ethnic and national minorities described by the constitution influences to a large extent the whole legal system in this field, and even more, it has a strong impact on the attitude of the administration towards the application and implementation of the legislative acts in this regard.

Two different systems exist in addressing minority rights. The first one handles minority rights through a general law on minorities, the second one addresses minority questions through specific acts, such as language law, education law or law on local self-government.

First, *laws on national minorities* reinforce generally accepted international minority rights while adapting them to the particular needs of minorities living in the respective country. These laws mostly establish a special regime of minority protection in the form of a certain type of minority self-government.

Croatia has passed a constitutional law on human rights and freedoms and on the rights of ethnic and national communities and minorities in the Republic of Croatia (1992), based on the promotion of collective minority rights and providing cultural autonomy for "ethnic and national communities or minorities" (art. 5), but also a constitutional law on the non-application of the former (1995). According to the first law, a special status allowing for a far reaching cultural autonomy was attached to districts in which more than 50 per cent of the population belongs to a minority. However, this provision has been suspended since 1995, as well as all those provisions that relate to special rights and protection of those ethnic and national communities or minorities that comprise more than 8 per cent of the overall population of Croatia according to the census of 1991, until the results of the first census of the population of the Republic of Croatia are published. Such a census has not been taken yet, it is being prepared for 2001.[14] However, in May 2000 the 1995 amendments of the constitutional law were

---

14 Data from September 1999, Report on the Implementation of the Framework Convention, Croatian Helsinki Committee.

revoked through a whole set of legislative acts passed by the Croatian Sabor.[15] These improve the legal situation of minorities by providing a more precise and more generous regulation of minority language use and teaching. However, the territorial autonomy of the Serb minority was abolished, while the application of other suspended provisions was provided. The law differentiates between large minorities (proportional representation guaranteed on all levels of the state) and small minorities (the new enumeration including for the first time the Muslim-Bosniaks in Croatia, whose status was the subject of considerable political struggle).

According to the "Law on Self-governing National Communities in Slovenia", the right by the autochthonous minorities (Italians and Hungarians) to self-government has been guaranteed. These self-governing institutions of national minorities decide about internal problems in their group. On the national level, Italian and Hungarian "self-governing minority communities" have been established that participate in the full range of decision-making on issues concerning the entire community.[16] However, these far-reaching provisions are only guaranteed for the two autochthonous above-mentioned minority groups and not for other minorities living in the country, such as Roma or Serbs, Croats or Bosniaks.

Drafts of a general legislative act on national minorities proposed by different national minorities exist and were submitted to the Parliament in Romania, but even after the democratic coalition government came to power such a law was promised but not adopted.

Secondly, in the absence of a general minority law, minority-related provisions may be regulated through articles in the acts on the fields relevant to minorities, from the electoral law through language legislation to the law on education (Romania, Bulgaria, Macedonia) or through specific acts. There are laws on education[17] and laws on local

---

15   Constitutional Law on the Amendment of the Constitutional Law on Human Rights and Freedoms as well as on the Rights of Ethnic and National Communities or Minorities in the Republic of Croatia, of 11 May 2000, Narodne Novine 200, no 51, pos. 1127. See also H. Küpper: Minority Rights: Current Developments in Central and South-eastern European States, Paper prepared for the VI ICCEES World Congress, Tampere Finland, 29/30 August 2000, p. 8.

16   Council of Europe, Replies on the questionnaire (Slovenia).

17   Law on Primary and Law on Secondary Education in Macedonia (Official Gazette of the Republic of Macedonia Nr. 44/95); Law on Education in Romania (Law no. 84 of 1995 which is being amended and supplemented now by the Parliament); Law on Education and National Education Act in Bulgaria. Also worth mentioning is the Law of the confirmation of the European Charter on Regional or Minority Languages in Croatia (The National Gazette, Inter. Agreements 18/97), according to which there is no obligation for Croatia to organise higher education level studies in regional or minority languages, as it is exempt from Art. 8. par. 1.1 of this Convention.

self-government,[18] as well as acts on the media[19] that contain provisions regarding minority language use in the different fields in all the analysed countries. The use of minority languages in public and within the administration is generally regulated by special laws on language use (like the very recent law adopted in Croatia) or by laws on local self-government or local authorities (Romania, Macedonia). In the case of FYROM the Law on Local Self Government envisages in those units of self-government where a majority (over 50 per cent) or a significant (over 20 per cent) part of the population are minorities that the language and alphabet of the minority concerned are also in official use (in addition to the Macedonian language and Cyrillic alphabet) within the municipal council. Where the minority population constitutes a majority, the minority language is in official use also in public service institutions.[20]

Good practices

There are special arrangements for *minority representation* and *effective participation in the decision-making* in Romania, where a particular model of applying a specific threshold for minority parties in national parliamentary elections is in force. Here parties registered as organisations of citizens belonging to a national minority gain a seat if they win at least 5 per cent of the average number of votes cast for one deputy. This allows also for small minorities to be represented in the parliament. Other countries in the region have *reserved seats* in the national parliament for minority representatives. This is the case in Slovenia, where the Hungarian and Italian national minorities elect their own deputies to the National Assembly, or in the case of Croatia.

In most of the countries in the region, there are *parliamentary committees for minority issues*,[21] mostly in the framework of the general human rights questions. In some countries the *institution of ombudsman* was established with a mandate covering misconduct on the part of the authorities in human rights and/or minority rights questions.

18 Law on General Administrative Procedure and Law on Municipality Statutes in Croatia, Law on the Local Public Administration in Romania (Law No. 6971991, ammended by Law No. 24/1996); Law on Local Self-government in Macedonia (Official Gazette No. 52/95).

19 Radio and Television Act in Bulgaria, Law on Croatian Radio-Television in Croatia, Law on Radio and Television Broadcasting in Romania (Law No. 48/1992).

20 Art. 25 of the Law on Local Self-government.

21 Committee for Human Rights and the Rights of Ethnic and National Communities or Minorities in Croatia; Commission for Ethnic Communities of the Slovenian Parliament, chaired by minority representatives; Council for Inter-Ethnic Relations as a permanent working body of the Parliament of Macedonia.

Those bodies or ombudsmen appointed by parliament have the task of monitoring the activities of public bodies and protecting human rights in general by investigating complaints. This is the mandate of the Croatian, Macedonian and also the Romanian ombudsman. The ombudsman of the Republic of Croatia has played a significant role in the protection of minority rights in the framework of his authority (although without too much real power).[22]

Government offices on/for national minorities. In Romania, a Minister for National Minorities in the Prime Minister's Office has been appointed, the minister himself being a Hungarian delegated by the Democratic Alliance of Hungarians in Romania. In 1998 an Inter-Ministerial Committee for National Minorities was established (although neither the minister nor the Committee was, for example, informed about the elaboration of a state report on the enforcement of the Framework Convention – prepared exclusively by the foreign ministry). A National Council on Ethnic and Demographic Issues has existed in Bulgaria since December 1997 in charge of both ethnic minorities and Bulgarians abroad. Similar institutions exist in almost all the analysed countries in the region, such as the Office for National Minorities of the Government and of the Council for National Minorities in Croatia (established in 1998), as well as the Council on inter-ethnic relations in the case of Macedonia. The Council for Inter-ethnic Relations in Macedonia was established in 1993. The members of this Council are appointed by the Parliament (two Macedonians, two Albanians, two Turks, two Vlachs, two Roma, one Serb and one Moslem) and it is chaired by the President of the Parliament, being both a parliamentary body and one of the state administration.

The sub-commissions on minorities of the joint intergovernmental commissions monitoring implementation of the bilateral treaties were entrusted with the task of informing the relevant partners of the implementation of the treaty, of addressing concrete situations involving minorities, and of preparing recommendations for the respective governments on the further realisation and/or modification of the provisions of the treaty. An often-debated question regarding the work of these sub-committees refers to the involvement of the minorities in the implementation mechanism as well as in the work of the committees. Sub-committees on minority issues were established between Hungary and Romania, Romania and Ukraine, Croatia and Hungary, and Slovenia and Hungary. These sub-committees quite actively address timely practical issues in the relations of the minority-majority-kin-state dynamic. According to the minutes and joint declarations of the sub-committees on minorities, they are adopting concrete recommendations in the field of education, cross-border co-operation, the

---

22 Data from September 1999, Report on the Implementation of the Framework Convention, Croatian Helsinki Committee.

opening of new border crossing posts and culture (e.g., recommendations of the Slovenian-Hungarian sub-committee). As a positive sign, these recommendations are very comprehensive and detailed and drafted in such a way as to enable their realisation in the short term.

The role of minority organisations/parties in coalition governments. In most cases where democratic forces are in the government as a result in elections in the mid-90s, it is interesting to see that the most important and powerful minority organisations have become part of the government coalitions. These improvements were mostly due to the fact that the democratic parties would not have been able to form a government without the votes of the minority organisations. They were regarded as representing the balance in the coalition government, having clear programmes and representing voters with stable voting preferences. This is the case in Romania, where the Democratic Alliance of Hungarians has been a member of the coalition government since 1996. In FYROM, one of the coalition parties is the party of the Albanian ethnic minority, first the Party for Democratic Prosperity (PDP) and later the Democratic Party of Albanians (DPA).

Especially important is *minority representation in local self-government.* In several cases (Romania, Macedonia, Slovenia) the application of laws on local self-government or electoral laws enabled the alliances representing minority communities to hold power. This actually means that at least in certain municipalities the principle of subsidiarity can be implemented.

The opportunity to become part of a coalition government is a very important factor in the overall promotion of the minority identity in a given country. Minorities have received an opportunity for the first time in decades to become part of the ruling elite of a certain state without total assimilation or integration, by representing the programme of their minority association and promoting the aims of their particular community. This is an important factor in stopping the constant decrease of the minority population due to immigration or assimilation. It is also a chance for minority intellectuals to apply for jobs in the central or municipal governments. Through these developments, the role of tertiary education in the mother tongue has become even more important for the minority communities.

Questioned or even denied tertiary, especially university education caused tensions in Bulgaria, Macedonia and in Romania. However, in Romania the establishment of the Petoefi-Schiller Multicultural University and the announcement of the Hungarian government that it would finance a Hungarian private university helped to calm down the tensions in this regard. In Macedonia, a new law on higher education is in preparation that would most probably solve some of the conflicts regarding an Albanian language teaching university. The initiative of the OSCE High Commissioner on National Minorities regarding the establishment of a trilingual (English, Macedonian, Albanian) private Higher Education Centre for Public Administration and Business[23] will also have an important impact in this regard not only in Macedonia but in the whole region. The Macedonian parliament legalised in July 2000 the underground Albanian-language Tetovo University as an accredited private institution. The Tetovo University question is one of the most divisive in Macedonian politics. The OSCE-sponsored measure envisions the university as an institution for training teachers and civil servants, who will have to demonstrate proficiency in Macedonian as well as in Albanian.[24]

One basic precondition for the realisation of the rights regarding identity protection and promotion for national minorities is the possibility of *being informed in one's mother tongue*. In this regard, significant results have been achieved in the last years in all countries in Southeastern Europe in language programmes on both state and private television or radio stations (in particular the local private stations are extremely useful in this regard). Good examples can be found in Bulgaria, Croatia, Macedonia (Albanian and Turkish), Romania (especially Hungarian and German) and in Slovenia.

The NGOs dealing with human rights, minority issues and conflict prevention in the region are an important factor in the effective management of inter-ethnic relations. NGOs often replace the duties and take on the tasks of the authorities and contribute to the development of a civil society, the spread of democratic principles and rule of law. Members of minority communities become aware of their rights and possibilities mostly through NGO work and less through governmental sources. This is the case quite recently with the implementation and monitoring of the Framework Convention.

Shortcomings

Coalition governments can also be considered one of the most sensitive issues in minority-majority relations. The contradictory aims of coalition parties and inconsistent government programmes often lead to unclear, vague and difficult to implement legislative acts. At times, they have not resulted in legislative acts at all, but rather remained *coalition agreements on paper without any outcome in practice*. Or, as in the case of Romania, the government had to pursue the more generous provisions of minority protection through emergency decrees, such as the Amendment of the Education Act (1997) or the Amendment of the Local Administration Act (1997), as the parliament was less prepared and willing to adopt these measures. These negative results and experiences

---

23   Press Release of the OSCE High Commissioner on National Minorities on inter-ethnic issues in the FYR of Macedonia, 10 November 1998.
24   /RFE/RLNewsline of 27 July 2000.

cause serious frustrations in society in general and in minority communities in particular. The question of leaving the government coalition comes up from time to time with much vehemence.

There is a clear *lack of will to ratify the Language Charter* in most of the states in Southeastern Europe, despite the international undertakings made in this regard, most probably due to their standards on language use in education (especially tertiary education) and before public authorities.

The *reliability of official census data* is requested regularly when minority protection is analysed in these countries. Especially relevant is the number of Roma in almost all of the countries in the region, but also the so-called "problematic" minorities for certain states, such as Bulgarian speaking Muslims (Pomaks) or Macedonians in the case of the Bulgarian census. An additional problem is the recognition of national minorities by the state (in the case of Bulgaria, especially regarding Pomaks and Macedonians[25] or the Csango-Hungarian minority in Romania[26]). In the case of Slovenia and Croatia, the status of non-Slovene or non-Croat former permanent residents who are denied citizenship is very problematic. These groups are not effectively protected by the government and are often the victims of serious human rights violations.

The *return of property* confiscated during nationalisation in the period of communism, the return of property confiscated during the wars after 1991 and the return of refugees in certain countries in Southeast Europe causes tensions in inter-ethnic relations. Although national programmes exist for the return of refugees and their property, they are being carried out neither in Croatia nor in Bosnia-Herzegovina. Entities that recently became minorities in these countries on either side are not able to return. Authorities are neither carrying out their duties nor acting according to the regulations. Hostile steps are taken also by society in this regard. Especially the Roma are affected.[27]

Although all international undertakings listed and analysed above refer equally to the Roma ethnic communities, their rights are far from being effectively protected to the same extent in Slovenia or Romania as in Macedonia or Bulgaria. Even worse is the case of Bosnia-Herzegovina, despite serious government projects or initiatives in this regard, such as the decision of the Council of Ministers in Bulgaria (April 1999) to adopt a Framework Program for Equal Participation of Roma in Bulgarian Society, which envisages among others the establishment of a special governmental body to deal with ethnic discrimination. These ethnic groups suffer from serious discrimination by state

25 Shadow report prepared by the Bulgarian Helsinki Committee, September 1999.
26 Shadow report prepared by the Romanian Helsinki Committee, September 1999.
27 Shadow reports, Helsinki Committee For Human Rights in Bosnia-Herzegovina, in: Republika Srpska, Croatian Helsinki Committee. Data from September 1999.

authorities, but also by society and even by other minority communities. It ranges from discrimination in education starting with elementary education (few of them attend elementary schools, they are forced to attend schools for mentally disabled children, or their parents cannot provide for elementary preconditions for school attendance as in Bosnia-Herzegovina, or the maltreatment of Roma children at elementary schools), to employment (in all the countries in Southeastern Europe unemployment is highest among Roma people, in particular in Bosnia-Herzegovina because of the huge economic problems) and administration, as well as before courts, the police (maltreatment, harassment) and the media.

V Conclusion: Risks and recommendations for the EU

Looking at the impressive number of laws, decrees or government programmes dealing with the protection of national minorities in Southeastern Europe, one could easily assess that a positive process is taking place and that minorities in most of the countries in the region are adequately protected. However, as a conclusion of this study, it is more appropriate to insist that despite the adoption of constitutional principles and domestic legislation and the establishment of a legal framework for adequate minority protection, they have not fulfilled their obligations in this regard in practice. Therefore, we cannot speak yet (with the exception of a very few examples) about an institutionalised and applied minority protection system in the region or about effectively implemented standards. There has traditionally been a large discrepancy in several countries between what is written in the law and the actual situation. Indeed, legal provisions can be curtailed by government decrees or circumvented by local decrees.

In some of the countries, further measures will be needed in order to be able to make the generous standards applicable in practice. Here minority issues cannot be seen only as an issue of the legal framework or just of political will. In addition, inter-ethnic tensions caused by economic problems (such as a lack of financial resources and unemployment), delayed modernisation and regional underdevelopment need to be addressed. The actual condition of inter-ethnic relations in society is a more complicated process, which often relates to perceptions of own history and the history of the neighbours (in the communist decades or the inter-war period) and perceptions of national identity.

Furthermore, it also has to be emphasised that "the multiethnic state" has a different meaning in this part of Europe than the classical concept of multi-ethnicity and multiculturalism. Traditional particularities, the burden of the past and bad experiences have to be taken into account while planning the common future of Europe.

Fortunately, the risks assessed in the countries analysed above are soft risks that might have the potential to turn into more serious tensions without raising awareness and adequate preventive measures. Still, the problems listed below are far from being hard security risks or stability risks at this stage. This fact might give hope for further developments in the field of inter-ethnic co-existence, despite the geopolitical heritage full of ethnic tensions and despite serious wars and ethnic cleansing that have taken place in the Balkans during the last decade.

Assessed soft security risks and recommendations

1. There is a discrepancy between legal framework and practice. Provisions of certain legislative acts (laws or government decrees) are either not implemented or the space for discretion in the hands of state authorities is too large, in this way hindering adequate and effective implementation of already guaranteed rights. Moreover, if a national consensus is absent about laws or decrees on minority rights, the *rejection on side of society or administration* can hinder even the most appropriate and generous legislation, or governments are more likely to adopt soft law regulations instead of applicable hard law (announcing government programmes without any legislation to implement them). The constitutional definition of the titular nation and state, as well as of the description of the status of co-existing national and ethnic minorities, determines the position of these communities within the overall legal-institutional framework and within political and economic life. It also has a strong impact on the attitude of the administration towards the application and implementation of the legislative acts in this regard. If the constitution stipulates the idea of one nation – one state, it is difficult to find any justification for differentiation in favour of minority groups and to adopt special laws in this regard.

2. Lack of minimal finances could render even the most generously guaranteed rights meaningless and hinder implementation of even the basic international standards. This creates frustration and therefore tension in the whole society between minorities and majority, but also between the opposition and government. Transparency and a clear system of minority policy in the context of allocation and distribution of funds, as well as openness towards the economic problems of minority communities, could help to overcome the general problems. Local taxes used within the respective locality and also for minority purposes can largely improve co-existence on the local or regional level. Mobilisation of the private sector, especially of small and medium-size enterprises, could take over the duties of central financing from case to case.

3. Dissemination of negative stereotypes related to national minorities through the

media, as well as political statements using hateful language that could easily be regarded as incitement, are promoting hatred and intolerance. Although these are strictly forbidden by domestic laws and by all relevant international binding documents, the phenomenon still exists and is quite common in Southeastern Europe. It causes tension between the different ethnic groups despite all legal restrictions due to lack of appropriate practical measures taken by administrative bodies. In addition, there are registered cases of misuse of the freedom of speech. Political forces often (especially during elections) use the participation of a minority organisation in the local and general elections as a pretext to incite hostility against these minorities (for example, in the case of the Albanian mayors in Gostivar and Tetovo in Macedonia or during the recent local elections in cities like Cluj or Targu Mure in Romania, partly inhabited by Hungarians).

4. To a large extent, demographic processes influence inter-ethnic relations and can therefore solve or generate tensions across Europe (see the situation in Northern Ireland), but these are especially relevant in the region of Southeastern Europe. One aspect of ethnic tensions in the region is the high birth-rate of the Albanian population outside Albania (practically everywhere, the Albanian minorities have higher birth rates than the rest of the population). This feelings of an increasing demographic imbalance (in Macedonia and some parts of Montenegro).[28] The same feelings are present regarding the Roma population in almost all of the countries in the region.

5. Unemployment is one of the major tension-causing factors both for minorities and the majority in the region, especially in FYROM, Bulgaria, or Bosnia-Herzegovina. Due to the very high rate of unemployment, social tensions can easily turn into ethnic tensions without adequate programmes and measures to help mitigate the effects. In addition, considerable workplace discrimination exists against several minorities. As one of the main tools for overcoming unemployment and workplace discriminations is strongly linked to the existence of well-prepared minority intellectuals, secondary and tertiary education has become a key issue during recent years. High level education for minorities in the minority language could help them receive important positions and become part of the elite, potentially halting the emmigration process of the young generation.

6. The Roma issue is and will be one of the core issues of overall minority protection in the region of Southeastern Europe. The focus during recent years was mainly on national minorities and less on ethnic minorities in these countries, although the

---

28   H. Küpper: Minority Rights: Current Developments in Central and Southeastern European States, Paper prepared for the VI ICCEES World Congress, Tampere Finland, 29/30 August 2000.

issue of the Roma would have to be addressed by any multiethnic society promoting diversity. Economic discrimination leads to a vicious circle where unemployment and therefore poverty contributes to a high crime rate which in turn contributes to discrimination against minorities, which is one major cause of their poverty (all countries in Southeastern Europe). Unsolved or neglected problems in this field have the potential to escalate into serious conflicts between Roma communities and the rest of the society.

7. Cross-border co-operation is either missing or is at a very low level among the states in the region, despite mutual kinship, home states, and traditions for several minorities. Special agreements on the basis of bilateral agreements can to a large extent improve inter-ethnic coexistence along the borders. An important burden on the central or local government can be lifted by cross-border co-operation regarding mother tongue education, especially secondary and tertiary education, cultural needs (such as library sharing and joint maintenance of cultural institutions like minority theatres and research centres). Cultural co-operation is the less problematic issue in the very tense neighbouring relations of these countries, therefore initiatives in the field of culture could lead to stronger co-operation in other important fields. Lively cross-border co-operation may positively influence small or medium sized joint, minority-majority-kin-state enterprises.

8. *Lack of bilateral agreements* between several neighbouring states (Bulgaria – FYROM, Greece – Bosnia-Herzegovina – neighbouring countries) may also be regarded as a potential risk for stability in the region. Even if some agreements exist, these do not address inter-ethnic issues or foresee the protection of national minorities (Romania and Bulgaria). Bilateral treaties might contribute to a common basis to address tense issues between neighbouring states. The joint inter-governmental bodies have to deal with practical questions (such as the development of communication networks and the establishment of border crossing points). It would be easier to overcome historical grievances through small, practice-oriented steps. It is essential for the minorities living in these countries that their home states and kin states do not allow the past to get in the way of a better future. (Note the promising tendencies in Romanian-Hungarian relations.)

9. Even in those cases where bilateral relations have improved during recent years on the basis of such treaties, the contradicting tendencies foreseen in the bilateral agreements and EU requirements (Schengen Agreement) may generate tension in the relations between neighbouring states, minorities and their kin states. Co-operation in the fields of minority protection, cross-border co-operation, emerging border regions on the one hand (bilateral treaties), strict visa requirements on the other hand (the borders of these Southeast European countries are becoming outside borders of the

Union), need to be addressed in time and in a way satisfactory for both the governments and minorities most affected. Especially important are good relations where the enlargement process and its border crossing requirements raise fear and frustrations among the population in those countries that are not in the first group of accession states, or that are not likely to become part of the enlargement process in the near future. The European Commission could help with expertise and clear concepts to overcome the difficult position of governments in the accession negotiations.

Suggestions for Further Reading

Hatschikjan, Magarditsch, Tröbst, Stefan (eds.): Südosteuropa – Ein Handbuch, München 1999.

Neuss Jurczek, Hilz (ed.): Transformationsprozesse im südlichen Mitteleuropa, Occasional Papers Nr. 20, Europäisches Zentrum für Föderalismus-Forschung, Tübingen.

The Present-Day Educational System for National Minorities in Romania, Ministry for National Education in Romania, General Educational Directorate for National Minorities, 1999.

Report of the Special Delegation of Council of Europe Advisers, Stability Pact for Southeastern Europe, Working Table I on: Democratisation and Human Rights, Strasbourg, 6 March 2000.

Regular Report from the Commission on Progress towards Accession by each of the candidate countries, October 13 1999, European Commission.

Bosnia-Herzegovina

International Helsinki Federation for Human Rights, Annual Report 1999:
  [http://www.ihf-hr.org/reports/ar99/ar99bos.htm]

Bulgaria

Bulgarian Helsinki Committee, Report Submitted Pursuant to Article 25, Paragraph 1 of the Framework Convention for the Protection of National Minorities, September 1999: *[http://www.riga.lv/minelres/reports/bulgaria/bulgaria_NGO.htm]*
International Helsinki Federation for Human Rights, Annual Report 1999: *[http://www.ihf-hr.org/reports/ar99/ar99bul.htm]*

Croatia

Report Submitted By Croatia Pursuant to Article 25, Paragraph 1 of the Framework Convention for the Protection of National Minorities, 16 March 1999, Council of Europe, ACFC/SR (99) 5.
Croatian Helsinki Committee, Report on the Implementation of the Framework Convention for the Protection of National Minorities in Republic of Croatia, September 1999:
http://www.riga.lv/minelres/reports/croatia/croatia_NGO.htm
International Helsinki Federation for Human Rights, Annual Report 1999: *[http://www.ihf-hr.org/reports/ar99/ar99cro.htm]*

Former Yugoslav Republic of Macedonia

Contribution of the Republic of Macedonia to the Final Document of the Conference on Inter-Ethnic Relations and Minorities in Southeastern Europe Within Stability Pact Working Table I, Ministry of Foreign Affairs, Republic of Macedonia, Skopje, March 2000.
Helsinki Committee for Human Rights in the Republic of Macedonia, Report on Minority Rights in the Republic of Macedonia, September 1999:
[http://www.riga.lv/minelres/reports/macedonia/macedonia_NGO.htm]
International Helsinki Federation for Human Rights, Annual Report 1999: *[http://www.ihf-hr.org/reports/ar99/ar99mac.htm]*

175

Romania

Report Submitted by Romania Pursuant to Article 25, Paragraph 1 of the Framework Convention for the Protection of National Minorities, 24 June 1999, Council of Europe, ACFC/SR (99) 11.

Shadow Report, Gabriel Andreescu, October 1999:
[http://www.riga.lv/minelres/reports/romania/romania_NGO.htm]

International Helsinki Federation for Human Rights, Annual Report 1999:
[http://www.ihf-hr.org/reports/ar99/ar99rom.htm]

Slovenia

International Helsinki Federation for Human Rights, Annual Report 1999:
[http://www.ihf-hr.org/reports/ar99/ar9slv.htm]

Border Regimes in Southeastern Europe

Daniela Heimerl, Ivanka Petkova

I Introduction

Southeastern Europe has always been a polymorphous space characterised by a hetero-clite geography favouring small-state building, by its intermediate position between Europe and Asia, the Occident and the Orient, and by the expansionist aspirations of neighbouring states and extra-regional powers. The conflicts in the Balkan Peninsula are watched over anxiously and the idea of the precariousness of borders plays an important role in the cultural and political memory of the different peoples and communities. Borders sometimes resemble temporary fictions as products of historical "rapports" questioned again and again.

Since the Second World War, the former Yugoslavia has been the quintessence of the kaleidoscope of the peoples and cultures which Southeastern Europe comprises, creating a heterogeneous world within federal borders. In a general way, the countries of Southeastern Europe have been a microcosm of the geopolitical fractures of the post-war period until 1989/1990. Except for the former Yugoslavia, the region was not very integrated due to a number of non-economic factors including the existence of the CMEA[1] (of which Bulgaria and Romania were members), the specific situation of Federal Republic of Yugoslavia (FRY) and the autarkic policies of Albania. Today, the Southeast European countries are still less economically integrated than ten years ago. Moreover, economic interests again might not be the primary factor in determining economic relations and trade patterns, for contradictory elements of the historical past

---

1 Council of Mutual Economic Assistance (Bulgaria, Czechoslovakia, GDR, Hungary, Poland, Romania, USSR, Cuba, Mongolia, Vietnam).

are reflected in present economic realities and relations within the region. Wars, embargoes, sanction regimes and politically motivated trade wars have largely determined trade flows.

Multilateral regional co-operation was only launched in the 1970s and 1980s, remaining an abstract idea between countries where the list of inter-state problems is inexhaustible, thus bearing on the setting up of border regimes and the permeability of state borders in general. Relations between neighbouring countries are being formed on a bilateral basis, with the passage from bilateral co-operation to regional co-operation being a protracted process.

The European Union has a two-sided task in managing borders with this region: On the one hand, it has to maintain open access for goods and people to facilitate the economic integration that is beneficial for both the EU and the Southeastern region. On the other hand, it wants to control cross-border movements in order to regulate trade and, more controversially, to try to reduce criminal activity. Can it maintain the right balance between these two conflicting aims? Policy measures addressing these two tasks seem to be drifting apart. The hyperactivity of EU policy-makers in creating an internal security agenda since Amsterdam has at present caused the border-control side of the equation to run ahead of the trade- and travel-liberalising side.

The inherent tension between the external and internal EU policies towards Southeastern Europe (what some experts already call the "acquis border",[2] which is comprised in the EU internal security agenda and has its implications on visa policies and trade regimes) implies a paradox indeed: As the EU dismantles border controls between its own member states in order to allow people and goods to travel freely, it is working overtime to make checks on its external borders between EU member states and third countries as watertight as possible. Previously, each member state controlled goods and people when they came in or out of the country, so they were less worried about what their neighbours were doing. With the single market, they feel that if there is one weak link or preferential treatment in just one area, it can affect anything. As controls at the internal borders disappear, customs services in member states are carrying out more duties on the Union's external borders on behalf of other EU countries. The many regulations in place are designed to stop illegal immigration or miscellaneous trafficking, to clamp down on counterfeit goods and to check that imports meet EU public health, environmental and veterinary standards. According to one estimate, customs officers have to ensure that up to 400 separate import controls are respected.[3]

2   Heather Grabbe: The Sharp Edges of Europe: Security Implications of Extending EU Border Policies Eastwards, March 2000, p. 9 (Institute for Security Studies Western European Union, Occasional papers, 13).
3   European Dialogue, January–February, 2000/1, p. 3.

Concerning border regimes in general, there is a daunting amount of legislation which must be processed and implemented by the candidate countries of the region (Slovenia, Bulgaria and Romania) who have to do 90 per cent themselves, with the EU helping with 10 per cent.[4] Although national customs and administrations are separate and independent services, they all operate within the same legal framework and are linked by an extensive computer network. This can be used to provide regular updates from Brussels on tariff provisions, while a separate computerised system – which will also link four candidate countries, Hungary, Slovakia, Czech Republic and Poland – is being developed to stamp out transit fraud. The drive to improve customs procedures in the candidate countries to meet EU standards and prevent any chinks appearing in the external borders is a prerequisite for membership.

According to the EU, this process is taking place against a background of insufficient infrastructure, a lack of harmonised practices, a high level of crime, a paucity of well-trained, motivated personnel and increasing traffic flows. The main instrument for helping to improve border crossings and access roads and equipment, as well as to facilitate institution building, training staff, fighting corruption, etc., is the Phare programme. For instance, in 1999, Romania received around US-$ 9 million to help secure its border. To raise standards to a uniform level, the EU has drawn up a gap analysis for each candidate country (i.e., for Slovenia, Bulgaria and Romania) to identify where extra work is required, as well as a needs analysis to establish which shortfalls would need to be remedied by EU assistance. It has also created blueprints for each of the 13 customs sectors: legislation, border and inland control, investigation and enforcement, organisation and management, ethics, human resource management, training, revenue collection and accounting, trade facilitation, transit and movement of goods, customs laboratories, infrastructure and equipment, and computerisation. The new future members will have to act in the customs area as if they had always been in the EU.

This study focuses on the strong connection that exists between the need for communication and exchange within Southeastern Europe and for access from the outside, with interesting synergies, yet also contradictions. The second section deals with visa policies, namely the EU perspective towards the Southeast European countries, as well as the approaches the countries of the region have adopted among themselves. The third section assesses trade flows, patterns and regimes between the EU and the Southeast European countries and among the latter. The fourth section deals with trade routes and drug trafficking in the region.

---

4   European Dialogue, January–February, 2000/1, p. 3.

II Visa policies

Borders have become multi-functional. They are seen as something to be overcome (through cross-border co-operation for example) but also as a discriminatory division between peoples (visa policies). The EU's external security concerns have caused it to encourage regional integration at all levels, but at the same time its emerging internal security policies (from migration to transnational crime to asylum policies and police co-operation) are having contrary effects by reinforcing barriers between countries.

Extending the Schengen agreement eastward implies a bargain: freer movement westward at the price of not allowing free movement from the East. This is not a simple trade-off between different types of border control, however, because becoming the external border of the EU has much wider legal and financial implications. The countries on the outer rim of the Schengen zone not only have to control traffic through these borders more thoroughly, but they also have to develop a sophisticated infrastructure for keeping data on who and what is crossing their borders, as well as a legal apparatus to deal with asylum claims and refugees. These countries thus take on major responsibilities, both economic and legal. They become in one respect a new form of buffer-zone for the EU, namely with regard to immigration.

EU visa policies towards Southeastern Europe

Citizens from EU member states can currently travel freely to all Southeast European countries, with the exception of the Federal Republic of Yugoslavia, for a period not exceeding 90 days. With regard to the latter, the Republic of Montenegro has adopted a liberal visa policy allowing EU citizens to enter without a visa.

Non-applicant countries: With regard to the so-called non-applicant Southeast European countries, namely Croatia, Bosnia-Herzegovina, Macedonia, FRY and Albania, the EU has so far adopted a fragmented visa policy. Croatian citizens do not need a visa to enter EU countries (a very liberal border-crossing regime is established with Italy, where citizens can travel back and forth with only their identity cards) with the exception of Denmark (and also Norway[5]), which imposed visa restrictions in May and June 1999 to limit applicants for political asylum – mainly Serbs with Croatian nationality – arriving from Eastern Slavonia, a region which was conquered by Serbian separatists

---

5   In 1998, approximately 2,000 Croatian Serbs sought asylum in Norway.

during the Croatian-Serbian war in 1991 and reintegrated into Croatia in January 1998 after having been administered by the United Nations since 1996. Great Britain introduced visas for Croatian citizens in September 1999 for the same reason. During the first six months of 1999, more than 1,500 applicants from Eastern Slavonia, arriving by regular flights from Croatia, were registered by the British authorities. It should be emphasised that Bosnian Croats, namely from Herzegovina, many of whom have a Croatian passport, benefit from the liberal EU policy in contrast to their Bosnian compatriots. In this respect, EU policy is creating a dividing line with important psychological and emotional repercussions.

Macedonian, Yugoslavian, and Bosnia-Herzegovina nationals (including diplomats) cannot enter EU countries (with the exception of Austria and Greece) without a visa. Italy, Germany and France do not ask for a visa for Macedonians having diplomatic and service passports. It should be mentioned that since the beginning of 2000, Macedonia no longer asks for visas for Greek citizens who want to travel to the country.

Applicant countries: On 1 July 1999, all ten EU countries of the Schengen group signed bilateral visa-free agreements with the eight applicants on the EU's visa "white list" whose nationals need no visa to enter the EU. Not all applicants have benefited from taking on EU border policies, as Bulgaria and Romania remain on the EU's visa "black list".[6] By only putting a part of the accession candidates on the "white list", the EU is drawing a distinct geographical and political dividing line between Central Europe and Southeastern Europe (or the Eastern Balkans as these two countries are still called sometimes). The EU's invitation in to Romania and Bulgaria to start accession negotiations, extended in December 1999, raised hopes that the visa "black list" might be revised, and the European Commission recommended to the Council of Ministers in January 2000 that visa restrictions on these two countries be removed. However, it is not clear whether the Council will agree to this step, despite the symbolic importance of demonstrating inclusiveness in opening accession negotiations with all the Helsinki countries in February 2000.

One of the ways to measure potential migration risks of applicant countries' citizens to EU member states after the introduction of a non-visa regime is the number of requests for asylum submitted by citizens of a particular country. In the case of Bulgaria, for example, the peak of asylum requests by Bulgarian citizens was reached in the early

---

6 An important factor that influences migration is that Romanians and Bulgarians are not mobile nations. In general they would prefer to live and work in their country. For instance, a survey made by BBSS Gallup International indicates that 62.2 per cent of the surveyed group wants to work in Bulgaria and 72.2 per cent wants to live in Bulgaria.

90s and has since diminished substantially.[7] This shows that Bulgaria cannot be considered as a potential risk country. Ten years of data support the argument that if the visa-free regime were introduced for Bulgarians, the number of asylum requests would not change significantly. Another important statistical source of risk assessment is the number of citizens filed under criminal statistics. If we take the example of Bulgarian citizens and Germany as the primary country of destination, slightly more fake documents were identified in 1999 (126) compared to 1998 (115). These data do not point to a high risk potential. They are, however, a strong signal to the political authorities to take preventive measures.

Thus, at present, Bulgarian and Romanian citizens and especially businessmen increase their transaction costs when applying for visas to travel to EU countries. First, it is a time-consuming procedure. Second, it requires additional documentation, which has to be translated and confirmed by state bodies. Third, invitations from the counterpart in the particular EU state sometimes require payment.

The EU's current discriminatory visa policy towards Bulgaria and Romania is causing problems for policy-makers, who want to avoid having to impose a similar visa regime on neighbouring countries. For example, in the Czech Republic, there was a clash when Foreign Minister Jan Kavan publicly criticised an interior ministry proposal to introduce visas for Bulgarians and Romanians in June 1999. But this policy is also having other unintended consequences. In Bulgaria and Romania, there is a widespread perception that the only reason why their nationals are subject to the visa restrictions is that the EU fears a flood of Roma from the East, exciting accusations of double standards when the EU demands better treatment of the Roma in Southeast and Central European countries.

On 2 December 1999 in Brussels, the Council of Justice and Home Affairs examined the annual report on the situation at the exterior borders of the EU member states that enacted the Schengen Convention. It stated that immigration, especially from countries like Romania and Yugoslav successor states, has reached a peak at the border between Italy and Slovenia. The border between Austria and Hungary is very much affected by migratory pressure, contrary to the border between Austria and Slovenia where hardly any pressure is observed. At the Greek-Bulgarian and Greek-Macedonian borders, migratory pressure has diminished considerably.[8]

One thing is clear: New EU members will not be allowed to opt out of all or parts of

---

7 According to UNHCR statistics about all 25 European countries monitored, the total amount of requests for asylum submitted by Bulgarian citizens in 1999 was 1,710 requests, or 0.4 per cent of the total amount of requests (39th place in ranking). Bulgaria is behind Poland (0.7 per cent) and Slovakia (1.2 per cent).

8 Europolitique, 22 December 1999.

the Schengen acquis,[9] which requires a range of measures to build the necessary institutions, as well as the policies to implement it. Schengen has developed into a system both for abolishing internal border controls and for regulating controls at external borders. It has developed a common visa regime, common regulations for procedures at land and coastal borders and airports, and extensive police co-operation that includes the Schengen Information System (SIS) database. The tasks that the European Commission sets in its policy documents consist of specific measures with a clear timetable – for example, setting up new reception centres for asylum seekers – and also general guidelines on how to improve border management. The responsibilities are set out in a common manual, which lays down procedures, and a common set of consular instructions, listing those countries whose nationals require a visa to enter the Union. The responsibilities set out in the Schengen Convention were further defined by EU leaders at their December 1998 Vienna summit, when the EU leaders adopted an action plan to establish "an area of freedom, security and justice" as foreseen in the Amsterdam Treaty. As part of the pre-accession preparation, the extent to which each of the candidates is putting into place the hundreds of pages of Schengen rules is being carefully examined during the screening process. It is possible, however, that even if a candidate country has ratified all the necessary measures and has become an EU member, its inhabitants might not enjoy free movement. To achieve this ultimate aim, each new member will have to demonstrate that it is capable of policing effectively those of its own borders which have become the EU's new external border. According to the EU, "The basic rule is that the principle of free movement is not in force when ratification is finished, but only when the country concerned is deemed ready to apply all the Schengen provisions. So there could be a discrepancy between joining the EU and lifting border controls at the internal borders." This is something candidate countries like Bulgaria and Romania will have to keep in mind.

One area of co-operation which the future new members will have to join from Day One is the Schengen Information System – a highly sophisticated and costly computer data exchange network based in Strasbourg. It allows the police and the judiciary in member states to share vital information on visa applications, illegal immigrants and wanted and missing persons. It depends on confidentiality, discretion and absolute mutual trust between different states for its efficiency.

Another responsibility, with which the new managers of external EU borders will have to come to terms, is implementing the EU visa policy. In theory, borders with Schengen countries become softer as applicant countries are drawn towards the common border zone, but these concessions on their western borders are only made if they

---

9   Britain and Ireland negotiated their flexibility during the drafting of the Amsterdam Treaty.

apply harder controls on their eastern borders. This is an unpalatable reality for countries like Hungary which have close ties with neighbours and high cross-border traffic and will have to ensure that Romanians comply with existing EU rules and have visas. Similarly, Romania and Bulgaria – the only two candidate countries which are still on the EU's visa list – will have to comply with EU rules if they become members after Hungary.

The EU's expectations of the standards candidate countries will need to meet were spelled out in more detail in political guidelines adopted by EU leaders at their informal summit in mid-October 1999 in Tampere (Finland) on the controls that should be put into place at an enlarged Union's external borders. Leaders emphasised that controlling external borders in a balanced and uniform manner does not mean preventing the entry of legitimate asylum seekers. In addition, while special border crossing points can be established for small border traffic, all traffic crossing an external border must still be controlled. The candidates were told they had to settle any existing border disputes and establish working co-operation with their neighbours. They were informed that a police authority with trustworthy resources – and not armed forces – should ensure land and sea controls as well as checks at harbours and airports. At the same time, EU leaders pointed out that co-operation between present and future member states and their neighbours should not be treated as a military matter or as a sub-regional security arrangement.

In this context, a major step has been taken to comply with the requirements of the Schengen Agreement with regards to the safety of identity documents in Bulgaria. According to the law on new identity documents which came into force in April 1999, a replacement of Bulgarian identity documents is foreseen by March 2001. One of the goals is to prevent forgery. Progress has also been achieved in border management as one of the short-term priorities of accession partnership. Bulgaria continues to demilitarise its border control. The number of conscripts employed is decreasing. Conscripts are no longer assigned to green and blue borders. These border control posts are now staffed exclusively by police officers. Means of detecting forged documents have been installed gradually at the border check points.

For the three Southeastern European applicants Slovenia, Romania and Bulgaria, legal obscurity still clouds the issue of which conditions must be fulfilled before accession and which can be left until later. There are different views on whether Schengen has to be simultaneous with accession to the EU. The timing of the application of EU visa policies is vital to whether they become new dividing lines between countries. Moreover, timing will determine whether the applicants start to gain the benefits of Schengen before accession, as opposed to simply receiving the disadvantages (in terms of disrupting integration with their eastern neighbours).

In addition, the Schengen acquis is not the only means which affects border policies in the region. Because of the extensive intergovernmental and extra-EU agreements governing this area, applicant countries have to take on the emerging EU refugee and asylum regime as well. The countries have been unilaterally incorporated into this regime through the extension of the EU redistributive system for handling asylum claims, as well as exporting border control and practices to strengthen their eastern borders. The redistributive system rests both on a series of readmission agreements that ensure the return of migrants to their country of nationality or their original country of entry and on the "safe country doctrine". For example, Greece has signed an active agreement on readmission agreement with Croatia. Germany and Bulgaria signed an agreement which came into effect in January 1995 and has played a significant role in crime detection. It should be noted that apart from Germany, Greece is targeted by Bulgarian citizens for migration. The majority of illegal migrants from Bulgaria consists of seasonal agricultural workers, construction workers and housemaids. There is a high potential for bilateral co-operation with Greece on curbing illegal immigration. The know-how from the bilateral co-operation with Germany could be used in order to find efficient measures.

Visa policies between Southeast European countries

Relatively new countries like the successor states of the former Yugoslavia had to develop their own customs authorities from scratch, a process which at times required settling demarcation disputes with their neighbours. Slovenia and Croatia needed new border crossings following their independence; their border will become one of the EU external borders after Slovenian accession. For these new countries, the organisation required in effectively policing and managing the EU's external borders may involve a heavier burden than for longer-established countries like Hungary.

One phenomenon driving the erection of Schengen-inspired border controls has been anticipatory adjustments of applicants. This form of policy adoption – whereby the applicants take on what they perceive as EU norms in advance of formal EU pressure to do so – has been increasingly prevalent over the past three years. In fact, applicants such as Slovenia or Hungary are merely "consumers" of EU policies and cannot contribute to them. They are in a kind of "twilight zone" with regard to EU obligations. They are adopting EU member state relations without being member states, and implementing policies without being able to influence their formulation.

The former Iron Curtain became the external border of the Schengen zone when Austria and Italy began applying the Schengen Agreement to their borders between

October 1997 and April 1998. Fearful of the impact of the new border controls on cross-border relations with these two countries, the Slovenian border authorities took pre-emptive action by persuading their government to adopt a Schengen-type identity and customs checks at the Croatian border. The aim was to convince the Italian and Austrian authorities that Schengen had been implemented along Slovenia's non-EU borders, thus allowing a more flexible and open approach by the EU countries to their Slovene borders even after Schengen became fully operational on 1 April 1998. This was only partly successful. There are still long queues at the borders with Austria and Italy. Compliance with Schengen norms in the case of Slovenia has been accompanied by increasing unease among Southeast European countries about the implications of these norms for bilateral relations and the fact that applicants cannot participate in formulating these norms. While Bernard Kouchner, head of UNMIK, has lately praised the Macedonians for offering "an open door where everybody can enter and leave", the Macedonian press has vehement criticised the fact that Macedonian citizens need a visa for all Schengen countries, especially with regard to Slovenia, whose new visa system also prevents Macedonians from travelling freely.[10]

On 10 February 2000, the Slovenian government discussed the situation following the introduction of entry visas, especially concerning Romania. Visas for Romanians were introduced as part of harmonisation of Slovenia's visa policy with that of the EU in the framework of Slovenia's accession efforts. Certain decisions were taken at the government session, namely that Romanian truck drivers may obtain visas with longer validity and multiple entries at the appropriate Slovenian diplomatic or consular missions. The principle of reciprocity is expected to be applied. Until a Slovenian embassy is opened in Romania, citizens of Romania will be able to obtain transit and single-entry visas at Slovenian border crossings. Slavko Debelak, State Secretary at the Ministry of Internal Affairs, explained that visas represent a safeguard, as waves of migration are quite strong. Certain visa policy privileges that Slovenia grants to Russia and Turkey (benefits for Bulgaria are temporarily suspended) are still allowed under the Schengen policy. Citizens of those countries that also have a residential permit for one of the EU or EFTA countries are thus free of such visa obligations for stays of up to ten days. The same principle includes those citizens that possess a type C Schengen visa, which allows them to move freely around all Schengen countries.[11]

With the appointment of a co-ordinating group that will make preparations for the establishment of security, customs and inspections at the future EU border between Slovenia and Croatia, the Slovenian government on 27 July 2000 began the project of

10 Nova Makedonija, in: Le Courrier international, 6–12 January 2000.
11 Slovenia Weekly, 7–13 February 2000 p. 6.

186

establishing a Schengen border between the two countries. It was delayed with respect to both time and scope. Minister of Interior Peter Jambrek said that the EU-quality supervisory system on the border has to be established by the time Slovenia is ready for membership in the EU on 1 January 2003. The project will encompass a whole range of ministries, local communities, economic bodies, airports, the port of Koper and others. It will demand a great deal of funding, some of which will come from the EU – 1,200 additional police officers will have to be employed and equipped. The project also means the building of new facilities at border crossings. The minister stressed that the project meant some sort of tool to address illegal migration. In a rather blunt statement, he underlined that the Bosnian-Croatian border is currently almost completely permeable.[12] Sarajevo airport, he added, is the biggest problem for illegal migration, "from which tourists from all Muslim countries of the world enter without a visa".[13] Jambrek said also that nothing much will change for Slovenian nationals who cross the Schengen border.

For Hungary, the main concern about Schengen is the impact of EU policies on access of the ethnic Hungarians living in surrounding countries, and especially in the Southeast European countries. These "external minorities" total 3 to 3.5 million people. At present, ethnic Hungarians who are citizens of Romania, Slovakia, Ukraine or one of the former Yugoslav countries (especially Yugoslav citizens living in the northern province of Vojvodina bordering on Hungary) can travel and work in Hungary without visas. Ensuring the welfare of these communities is a main tenant of Hungarian foreign policy and is a central issue in its bilateral relations with its neighbours. Hungary has so far resisted pressure from EU member states to introduce a travel visa regime for neighbouring countries. However, there is a growing awareness that Austria will not abolish controls on its border with Hungary unless it has a guarantee that third-country citizens cannot travel freely through Hungary. A number of proposals has been put forward to deal with the problem of admitting ethnic Hungarians without a visa. One is a "national visa" permitting a stay of 90 days for citizens of neighbouring countries, but in Hungary alone. Another possibility: long-term visas to be given to ethnic Hungarians or people with dual citizenship. The government is concerned that this would cause legal and political complications and that such favourable treatment could result in resentment against ethnic Hungarians, for instance in Romania. Even if Hungary does not have to introduce visas for its neighbours prior to accession, the EU's tightening of border controls is having an impact on cross-border trade and investment. Since 1 Sep-

12 This statement is rather in contradiction to the strict identity controls which are currently applied at border crossings between the two countries.
13 Slovenia Weekly, 1 August 2000, p. 7.

tember 1999, all people crossing borders in either direction (whether Hungarian or foreign) have to be registered, the data is stored for 90 days. This caused an unwanted additional complication in Hungarian-Romanian relations shortly before elections in Romania, as it is the home of the largest external minority with more than two million ethnic Hungarians. If the EU lifts visa restrictions for Romanian citizens, one of the biggest problems of current Hungarian foreign policy would be resolved. All depends on whether the EU wants to favour politics or security. In the EU perspective, the currently permeable Romanian-Moldavian border is considered a source of serious danger. However, no Romanian politician is ready to introduce visas for Moldavian citizens. External border controls with co-applicants like Slovenia are to be erected only if the EU says that they are necessary, which is unlikely as the EU has a bilateral visa-free travel regime with this country. The two countries, Slovenia and Hungary, signed a treaty in February 1999 on the return of illegal immigrants to the original country of entry.[14]

As the EU pressures the applicants to impose visa regimes on neighbouring countries, the bargain of harder external borders in return for free movement of people is increasingly difficult to sell domestically, even if political leaders remain committed to EU integration. Changing status and permeability of non-EU borders could reawaken many unresolved issues over borders between applicants (Romania and Hungary), between applicants and member states (Austria and Slovenia) and between applicants and non-applicants (Slovenia and Croatia). For instance, whereas Slovenia and Croatia generally found themselves in agreement when they were part of former Yugoslavia, relations between them have been cool since the break-up of the federation. Of particular concern is the question of sovereignty over border issues, particularly the Bay of Piran, which represents Slovenia's outlet to the high seas. Although the dogmatic line pursued by the late Croatian president Franjo Tudjman has represented one of the main barriers to negotiations in the past, objections from the Slovene side held up ratification of a treaty in December 1999. The National Assembly refused to endorse an agreement on border traffic and co-operation that had already been passed by the Croatian parliament. This measure was one of the less contentious disputes between the two countries and had been expected to provide a springboard for talks on more difficult subjects.

Bulgaria and Romania have also introduced measures to tighten border controls and to impose visa regimes on third countries. Their motivations for adjusting to EU norms are not confined to anticipation of EU entry requirements, but also rooted in their desire to leave the EU's "black list" of countries whose nationals require a visa to enter the

---

14   MTI, Bulletin hebdomadaire, p. 11.

EU. The Romanian government took anticipatory measures to reassure the EU ahead of the revision of the visa "black list", in the hope of being taken off the list by showing "a significant reduction of transit migration from third countries through Romanian territory". By late 1999, Romania had joined 57 agreements with regard to preventing and fighting organised crime, and is negotiating another 35, in addition to 31 re-admission agreements. Furthermore, a bill was passed providing for the withdrawal of passports from criminals convicted abroad. New security features have been added to identity papers to prevent forgery, and restrictive visa requirements are being applied to 85 countries that have "significant illegal migration potential". A new law on refugees modelled on European practice is being adopted. Under the new EU-aligned border law, Romania was to stop issuing entry visas at its border crossing points as of 1 January 2000. However, the lack of resources and infrastructure remains a major problem. The Romanian Interior Ministry told the Justice and Home Affairs Council in autumn 1998 that co-operation with neighbouring countries was essential for effective control of borders owing to the inadequacy of infrastructure for Romanian police forces to carry out the task.

It should be noted that the development of bilateral economic relations between Greece and Albania is currently heavily supported by a significant number of Albanian expatriates (estimated at 500,000) in the Greek labour market. In 1996, the Simitis government abandoned the practice of massively expelling Albanians who immigrated illegally. The remittances of this community contribute considerably to the Albanian economy.[15]

The visa policies which the different countries are currently applying in Southeastern Europe are a reflection of EU visa policy and the various contradictory lines of political development that have characterised the region in the last decade. However, as a survival strategy, some countries have kept their borders remarkably open for the time being.

Slovenia has the most restrictive visa policy towards neighbouring countries, which is quite contrary to the role it wants to assume as a link between the West and the "Balkans", having recently been quite active in developing and strengthening ties with the countries of the region. Transit and tourist visas are required for citizens of Albania and FRY (with the latter diplomatic relations have not yet been established!). Until recently, no visas were required for Romanian and Bulgarian citizens, but in compliance with the EU "black list" visas have been introduced, even though Bulgaria is not considered a risk country by Slovenian authorities. Macedonians also need a visa: visa policy is especially strict towards citizens from Bosnia-Herzegovina. Transit and tourist

---

15   R. King, G. Lazarides and C. Tsardanides (eds.): Eldorado or Fortress? Migration in Southern Europe, London 2000, pp. 170–185.

visas are required unless one has a resident card with a working permit in one of the EU or Schengen countries. If someone living in one of the EU member states has refugee status, he or she need a visa.

Croatia's policy is more liberal than Slovenia's. Transit and tourist visas are required for Albanians, Moldavians and for citizens of FRY (there was an agreement of mutual recognition between the two countries in August 1996, although the status of the Prevlaka Peninsula, which is being supervised by the UN military observer mission to Prevlaka, remains contentious). No visas are required for citizens of Bulgaria, Romania, Hungary, Slovenia, Macedonia and Bosnia-Herzegovina. Since June 2000, citizens from Bosnia-Herzegovina can travel to Croatia with their identity card and are no longer required to obtain the very costly passport from their authorities. Croatia has facilitated access for Bosnian nationals to boost its tourism industry, which is still lagging far behind its pre-war level. Furthermore, the Croatian and Hungarian prime ministers signed an agreement in May 2000, according to which Croatian and Hungarian citizens will be able to cross the borders with their identity cards only. Croatia already has such a liberal border-crossing regime with Slovenia and Italy.

Bosnia-Herzegovina does not ask for visas from Croatian, Macedonian, Hungarian and Yugoslav citizens. However, Bosnian citizens need a visa to travel to Bulgaria, Romania and Albania. Bosnia-Herzegovina introduced visa requirements in November 1999 for Bulgaria and the following countries: Cuba, Armenia, Azerbaijan, Kazakhstan, Kirgistan, Uzbekistan, Tajikistan and Turkmenistan!

Macedonia does not require visas from Bulgarian, Romanian, Hungarian, Croatian, Bosnian and Yugoslavian citizens. Since 1 February 2000, Slovenia and the Czech Republic require a visa for Macedonian citizens. Albanians need a visa, too.

Yugoslav citizens can travel visa-free to Bosnia-Herzegovina, to Macedonia and to Hungary.

All in all, the candidate country *Hungary* applies the most liberal visa policy in Southeastern Europe for the time being, mandating visas for Albanian citizens only. If visa policies have evolved rapidly during the last five years in the region, it seems that there are some major changes to come with the accession status of Hungary, which is already preparing a stricter visa policy. It will especially concern Macedonia and Bosnia-Herzegovina, where visa restrictions will be introduced within the next two years. Croatia will be excluded from this measure as, for the time being, it is on the "white list" of the EU. Most interestingly, FRY will be excluded as well, as the Hungarian government is founding its policy on the convention of 1966 which institutionalised visa-free circulation between Hungary and FRY. Though diplomats say that the possibility of imposing visas is not entirely excluded even if there are no political changes in FRY, the matter is not considered as urgent as the cases of Macedonia and Bosnia-

Herzegovina. Romania is considered an "exceptional case" and has been mentioned expressly by the Hungarian negotiators in a distinct declaration during the accession negotiations of Chapter 23 in Brussels. For the time being, Hungary does not foresee a lifting of the visa restrictions for Romania by the EU, a move further emphasised by the European Parliament in Strasbourg. While diplomats can envisage visa restrictions for Bulgarian citizens, though relations with this country are proclaimed as excellent (the case has not been expressly mentioned during the negotiations of Chapter 23), it seems that with regard to Romania there exists an unsolvable dilemma. Hungary's visa decisions will have an important impact on regional relations and other country's visa policies (namely Croatia's) and will very clearly indicate where the future Europe might end, creating a zone of *excluded* countries comprised of Albania, Macedonia and Bosnia-Herzegovina. The case of FRY is being left open.

Table 1: Visa policies in Southeastern Europe

	Slovenia	Croatia	BiH	Macedonia	FRY	Hungary	Romania	Bulgaria	Albania
Slovenia		–	+	+	+	–	+	+	+
Croatia	–		–	–	+	–	–	–	+
BiH	+	–		–	–	–	+	+	+
Macedonia	+	–	–		–	–	–	–	+
FRY	+	+	–	–		–	+	+	+
Hungary	–	–	–	–	–		–	–	+
Romania	+	–	+	–	+	–		–	+
Bulgaria	+	–	+	–	+	–	–		+
Albania	+	+	+	+	+	+	+	+	

+ = visa is necessary

– = no visa is necessary

(information valid as of August 2000)

Recommendations

EU border and visa policies raise a number of questions and generate serious risks in Southeastern Europe. These include the risk of creating a buffer-zone at the outer rim of the Schengen zone. As such, defining where the "outer border" of Schengen should be situated seems to be at the core of the problem. The EU has to state rapidly and clearly where its future external borders will finally lie in this respect.

EU border and visa policies foster a range of dilemmas in the foreign relations of the countries of the region, particularly concerning constructive engagement with their non-applicant neighbours with regard to visa and minorities. Thus, the differentiation or compartmentalisation caused by EU policies has a negative impact on regional foreign relations. In particular, the imposition of EU-driven policies and visa-regimes is inhibiting the ability of local and regional actors to co-operate on a range of sensitive issues, including minority relations, migration, local economic infrastructure and institution-building. In fact, current EU policies for dealing with external borders (including migration and asylum) are having restrictive effects on the movement of goods and people that are at odds with the emphasis on regional integration and co-operation as a means of ensuring long-term stability and security. A more sophisticated and realistic approach to border management is thus needed.

The EU should compensate those countries which muster the political will to liberalise their visa policies with their neighbours, and as such, contribute actively to regional co-operation.

III Trade flows, patterns and regimes

Trade integration is one of the most important components of the Stability Pact for Southeastern Europe, as it focuses its efforts on the liberalisation and facilitation of trade through the reduction and elimination of tariff and non-tariff barriers. A number of Quick Start projects announced during the March 2000 Stability Regional Funding Conference is intended to facilitate trade in Southeastern Europe. At the third meeting in Skopje, Macedonia, in June 2000, the Working Group on Trade Issues adopted the Guidelines for a Study of Free Trade Agreements among countries of the region. It also agreed to conduct a study of non-tariff barriers in the region.[16] The World Bank Regional Strategy paper of March 2000[17] underlines the need for regional trade liberalisation. It emphasises this while freely admitting that access to EU markets is much more important. Specifically, the paper calls for the creation of a Free Trade Area in Southeastern Europe, for free access to EU markets and for gradually opening Southeast European markets to competition from the EU.

There is, however, no analysis of the costs and benefits of this trade policy. There is no indication whether it would not have a different impact on the different countries of

---

16 The group, which has met twice under Macedonian chairmanship, has not been able as of August 2000 to collect all the existing Free Trade Agreements among the countries of the region. This is however a major precondition to make recommendations to harmonise them in order to promote regional trade. SCP, Current Activities, Regional Table, Thessaloniki, 8 June 2000.

17 The Road to Stability and Prosperity in Southeastern Europe. A Regional Strategy, 13 March 2000.

192

the region. The twin goals of intra-regional trade liberalisation and integration depend on a complex mix of economic and policy issues, not least of which concerns the absence of Serbia, which is at the centre of the region's trade and transport links. It is impossible to have a comprehensive and coherent reconstruction programme for Southeastern Europe excluding Serbia. Furthermore, the bulk of the money collected at the Regional Funding Conference in March 2000 has been earmarked for infrastructure projects, not addressing the issues of de-industrialisation, unemployment and the fact that, taking the industrial and agricultural sectors into account, Southeastern Europe is in several respects a developing region. Taking into account their initial vulnerability, the consequences of the Kosovo war have economically weakened the countries of the region even further.

Trade between the EU and Southeastern Europe

Past efforts of the EU to stabilise the region have had some serious deficiencies whose consequences are being felt today. They did not pay enough attention to the "Eastern Balkans", thus neglecting the stabilising potential of Bulgaria and Romania for the region as a whole. Furthermore, they focused mainly on bilateral relations. The so-called regional approaches have in fact been based on strict bilateralism, undermining the essence of such initiatives. If access to EU markets is already duty-free for many Southeastern European products, EU conditionality and ad hoc policies have had a direct impact on economic performance and progress and, of course, an indirect impact on trade flows.

Over the past ten years, the EU has become the most important trading partner for most of the Southeastern European countries. Albania, Bulgaria and Romania have re-oriented their trade towards the EU. In 1989 the former Yugoslav Federation traded mostly with the European Community, and for the newly created states the EU is also their most important trading partner. However, a closer look shows that the trade position of the different member states in the region is very unequal. Germany, Italy, Austria and Greece have a strong position with certain countries (Austria with Slovenia and Croatia in the north, Greece with Albania, Bulgaria and Macedonia in the south),[18] underlining the idea of a sub-regionalisation of trade patterns in the region.

Lately, the EU has designed a new form of contractual relations, the Stabilisation

---

18 D. Heimerl, Y. Rizopoulos, N. Vukadinovic: Contradictions et limites des politiques de reconstruction dans les Balkans, Revue d'Études Comparatives Est-Ouest, 1999, No. 4, p. 215.

and Association Agreement (SAA), for the countries in the so-called "Western Balkans". The content is similar to the usual Europe Agreements which have been signed with Slovenia, Bulgaria and Romania, but the SAA does not contain a promise of future membership. It has many of the features of a Europe Agreement such as staged measures to improve legislation and the quality of civil service, and the liberalisation of trade and co-operation over such areas as customs, administration and science, but does side-step the issue of EU accession.

Thus, there are different prospects for different countries with respect to European integration, from the start of negotiations with Macedonia for a SAA and the imminent start with Croatia after the change of government at the beginning of this year to the difficulties detected thus far by the EU regarding the feasibility of opening negotiations for such an agreement with Albania (which already has a trade and co-operation agreement with the EU, though it is less extensive than the one in force with Macedonia). Croatia and FRY still have no permanent trade agreement with the EU (though some trade concessions were approved in 1996 and 1997). Furthermore, the EU has invited Bulgaria and Romania, the two countries in the region that have signed Europe Agreements, to start negotiations for membership in December 1999, whereas Slovenia has been involved in accession negotiations proper since November 1998.

Table 2: Trade arrangements with the EU

	Year	Agreement
Albania	1991	TECA
Bulgaria	1993	EA
Romania	1993	EA
Slovenia	1993/1996	TECA/EA
Bosnia-Herzegovina	1996	ATP
Croatia	1996	ATP
Macedonia	1996	TECA
FRY	1997	ATP (withdrawn in 1998)

TECA: Trade and Economic Co-operation Agreement, EA: Europe Agreement, ATP: Autonomous Trade Preferences taken over from the 1980 Trade and Co-operation Agreement

Slovenia: Despite the political divide between the old establishment and those opposing the former communists, a broad cross-party consensus exists on Slovenia's foreign policy priorities, including rapid EU accession. The country has already benefited from considerable trade liberalisation under the Europe Agreement which came into force in

February 1999.[19] The re-orienting of trade with the EU after independence is quite spectacular. Since 1993, Slovenia has benefited from a Co-operation Agreement with the EU, which has abolished most duties on Slovenian products. A plan for a free-trade zone with the EU began to be implemented in January 1997 as part of the Europe Agreement. Full trade liberalisation with the EU is planned for 2001, and in 2002 Slovenia is planning to bring its tariffs with regard to non-EU countries fully into line with the EU common external tariff, which will especially hamper regional trade relations with neighbouring Croatia. Although much progress has been made in liberalising trade with the EU in industrial goods, trade in agricultural goods still faces a plethora of restrictions. As far as the product range of exported merchandise is concerned, many manufacturing activities are involved, intent particularly on finding niche markets, principally in the EU and other Western markets.

Croatia's official foreign policy is to strengthen its ties with Western institutions so as to speed up its long-term goals of accession to the EU and NATO. But this position has been persistently undermined by tensions with the United States and the EU over its relationship with Bosnia-Herzegovina. The Croatian government has done little to encourage the Bosnian Croats to support the political and economic reintegration of this country. Instead, Croatia's late president Franjo Tudjman openly expressed doubts about its prospects for long-term survival and, at times, he appeared to seek an understanding with FRY on partitioning Bosnia-Herzegovina. There has been a lack of financial transparency in Croatia's support for the Bosnian Croats.

As a result of its poor international relations, Croatia has been denied many assistance programmes such as the EU Phare programme. This has also ruled out an EU Europe Agreement, with the result that Croatian companies are at a relative disadvantage in exporting to the EU. The declining competitiveness of Croatian exports is

---

19   Relations with Italy, historically tense, have tended to fluctuate depending on the government in power in Rome. In 1992, Italy officially acknowledged Slovenia as a successor to all relevant agreements made between Rome and the former Yugoslavia. These included the treaties of Osimo of 1975, which regulated the new borders, and subsequent arrangements for compensation to Italians dispossessed by the Slovene authorities after the Second World War. Italy's precondition was that those Italians who had lived in the region acquired by Slovenia after the War should be given the right to purchase property in Slovenia, a right constitutionally denied to all foreigners at the time. Slovenia has changed its constitution since. Although some issues have remained unresolved, including the question of legal protection for the ethnic minority in Italy, relations have improved with Italy in the aftermath of the NATO war against FRY, when Slovenia was rewarded for its unequivocal backing of the West's policy. Relations with Austria were initially cordial as the Austrian government fully supported Slovenia's bid for independence in 1991. However, relations have become more ambivalent as the right-wing Freedom Party entered a coalition government in early 2000 with the conservative People's Party. Slovenia fears that the new Austrian government might step up pressure on Slovenia to officially recognize its German-speaking minority of Austrian descent and pay compensation to ethnic Germans, now living in Austria, whose property was confiscated by the Yugoslav communists after the war. Endowed with a veto in EU institutions, Austria could try to make these and similar issues a precondition for Slovenia's accession to the EU.

evident by the fall in the percentage of exports to the EU, although it remains the country's most important market. In 1994, the EU accounted for 59.4 per cent of exports compared with 47.6 per cent in 1998. In 1998, 59.4 per cent of imports came from the EU, a slightly higher proportion than in 1994 when the EU presented 59.2 per cent of imports. In D-mark terms, exports to the EU grew by 30 per cent in 1999 due to the EU GDP growth.

The new Croatian government is enjoying a honeymoon with the EU and the USA. Negotiations on a SAA which would formalise Croatia's relationship should begin soon, as the European Commission adopted a proposition to that effect in July 2000. Western countries are keen that Croatia provide a conspicuous example of the benefits of rejecting nationalist extremism for voters in Bosnia-Herzegovina and FRY, and the West appears to be giving the new government more latitude than might otherwise be the case.

The constitution of *Bosnia-Herzegovina*, which was promulgated as part of the Dayton peace agreement in 1995, makes the central state responsible for foreign affairs, customs and foreign trade, monetary policy and other areas. Furthermore, the constitution allows the two entities to enter separate parallel relations with Serbia and Croatia.

A new trade regime offering exporters from Bosnia-Herzegovina more favourable access to the EU came into effect on 1 January 2000. For the first time since the break-up of the Agreement on Co-operation and Trade between the EU and former Yugoslavia in November 1991, the country is being treated as a separate entity rather than as part of the global quota of trade allocated by the EU to former Yugoslavia. The latest agreement will last until 31 December 2001. It has significantly increased the range of products exempt from tariffs and simplified the administrative procedure. Before the war, Bosnia-Herzegovina had a trade surplus and the EU was one of its most important trading partners. Much of its export capacity was wiped out during the war and exports in 1998 were only one-fifth of the pre-war level. The latest measure, which is part of the EU's new strategy as embodied in the SAA for the Balkans, could provide an important impetus to exporters.

Macedonia signed a Trade and Co-operation Agreement with the EU in November 1997. In 1998, there was a sharp expansion in EU markets for Macedonian exporters. Prime Minister Ljubco Georgievski requested the elaboration of an EU Europe Agreement and to be treated like Romania and Bulgaria, namely as a candidate for EU membership. In return, in May 1999 the EU proposed an SAA (in July 1999 the EU formally agreed to open negotiations). Since the SAAs are designed for former Yugoslav republics and Albania, this will reinforce Macedonia's existing status. Macedonia and the EU started negotiations for an SAA in April 2000. There is a difference in how long it would take to reach the associate status (the EU proposes two phases of five years each, Macedonia wants two phases of four years each). Upgrading the office of the EU resident envoy to a permanent delegation has been a compensation for the country's disappointments. Macedonian's officials have also been disappointed by what they view as a lack of tangible support. They had lobbied the European Commission to locate the Reconstruction Agency for Kosovo in Skopje, but lost out to Thessaloniki.

Macedonia's existing Trade and Co-operation Agreement with the EU already gives it substantial access to EU markets. Trade in certain products however, – including important export sectors such as textiles, iron and steel – was subject to EU protectionist measures until recently. In the first two months of 2000, exports to the EU member states, Macedonia's largest trading partners, rose by 18 per cent. An anti-dumping dispute over iron and steel exports has been resolved and the export of lamb to the traditional Italian market has been resumed after a three-year pause. The countries of the European Free Trade Association (EFTA) could become more significant trading partners once a free-trade agreement is finalised in 2000. Germany is still Macedonia's largest trading partner, followed by FRY.

FRY enjoys a prime crossroad location at the heart of the Balkans, being the quickest road link between western Europe and the Middle East. However, it has been unable to capitalise on its geography over the past decade.[20] It has been subject to a variety of economic sanctions since 1992. Sanctions have been the centrepiece of Western policy towards Serbia for the best part of a decade. The trade sanctions which were imposed in 1992 for Serbia's role in the war in Bosnia were lifted after the Dayton Agreement (November 1995), but an "outer wall" of financial sanctions and denial of access to multilateral funding remained in place from 1996 to 1999. After the lifting of the sanctions in 1996, international transport began to be restored, but the reintegration of Yugoslav carriers into the international transport system was still impeded. Foreign maritime, inland waterway and road carriers continued to enjoy a high share in the transport of goods exported from and imported into FRY. There was no significant increase in the transit traffic on Yugoslav roads and highways either. New sanctions were imposed in 1998 (the EU revoked access to trade preferences, having restored them

---

20 Transport priorities: repair the damage caused by NATO bombing; complete the trans-Serbia motorway linking the Yugoslav-Hungarian border with the Yugoslav-Bulgarian and the Yugoslav-Macedonian Borders (about 300 km); build the Belgrade-Bar motorway linking Serbia with the only Yugoslav port, Bar in Montenegro (570 km); extend the Belgrade-Yugoslav-Croatian border motorway (40 km); and link Belgrade with the Romanian border (100 km). The realisation of these projects depends to a large measure on international loans and foreign investors for all above projects. Legislation is in place for the government to offer 30-year concessions to foreign investors for all the above projects, pending lifting of the international investment ban. A proposed high-speed trans-Serbia railway connecting Subotica, near the Hungarian border, with Dimitrovgrad on the Bulgarian border (504 km) and with Macedonia, would link central and western Europe with Turkey and Greece. EIU, Country Profile Yugoslavia 1999–2000, p. 22.

in April 1997, suspended them in December 1997, restored them and suspended them again in 1998) and again in 1999 as the Kosovo conflict heated up. In addition to new US-initiated sanctions, including a ban on oil sales and a freeze of government assets abroad, the EU has also banned government-backed credits and investments in Serbia and denied landing rights to Yugoslav airlines. The EU has also imposed a visa ban on more than 300 senior Serbian politicians, army and police officers, as well as on businessmen considered to have close ties to the Yugoslav president Slobodan Milosevic. This ban was extended to almost 800 individuals in February 2000. The sanction regime also entails exclusion from the Stability Pact framework that is developed to help the whole Southeast European region.

Finland, which assumed the EU presidency in July 1999, wanted the international community to act quickly to lift at least part of the sanctions, including bans on oil imports and airplane flights. Sanctions should gradually be lifted because they were hindering efforts aimed at stabilising the Balkans and encouraging democracy in the region, according to Perrti Torstila, political director of the Finnish Ministry of Foreign Affairs.[21] Ahitissari stated that aid to Serbia should not be tied to the issue of Milosevic's removal, as this would bring new suffering to innocent Yugoslavs and hamper the development of democracy in Serbia. At the end of July 1999, the EU and the US disagreed over whether to provide Serbia with energy aid. EU foreign ministers backed a Greek-Dutch proposal to provide "energy for democracy" – fuel and essential supplies to run electricity plants and machinery in Serb towns "actively working for greater democracy". However, US opposition reportedly frustrated the plan. In August 1999, the EU lifted the oil and airline flight embargoes against Montenegro and Kosovo. On 13 September 1999, the EU foreign ministers expressed their willingness to support democratic forces in Serbia, particularly in cities governed by parties that oppose the Milosevic regime. However, the proposal to provide energy aid only to opposition-controlled municipalities in Serbia was not thought through: it implied that the residents of opposition-controlled Nis would have heating in the winter, whereas those of nearby SPS-controlled Leskovac would not. It has not been explained how the EU delivered the aid to towns of its choice, bypassing Yugoslav customs and the central government.

The tough stance upheld by the US and the UK came under pressure from the Serbian opposition as well as from some dissonant voices in the EU. Critics of the policy argued that sanctions actually played into the regime's hands by alienating ordinary Serbs, by undermining the Serbian opposition, by encouraging the black market, by stifling competition in the economy and by concentrating power in the hands of the ruling elite. In November 1999, Hans Koschnik, the German emissary to Bosnia-Herze-

---

21   EIU, Country Report, 3rd quarter, Yugoslavia, p. 28.

govina, said that sanctions should be lifted and replaced with "intensive co-operation" with the Serbian opposition. By demanding an immediate lifting of all sanctions in autumn 1999 as soon as it had reached a formal agreement with Milosevic to hold early elections, the opposition presented the West with a virtual ultimatum. But the friction between the EU and the opposition was exposed in December 1999, when the main opposition leaders boycotted an invitation to meet EU ministers in Luxembourg. The ban on airline flights was finally lifted in February 2000, as this merely isolated the general population from the outside world and fed government propaganda that the West was punishing ordinary Serbs. In April 2000, the EU tightened trade sanctions by blacklisting firms, seeking to ban business with Serbian firms connected with the government.[22] This, however, will also hit ordinary citizens and will eventually lead to a blacklisting inside Serbia of those companies which are "white-listed" in the West.

In May 2000, the UN Economic Commission for Europe said that international sanctions were counterproductive. It argued that the regenerative Stability Pact for Southeastern Europe needed the recovery of the Yugoslav economy and FRY's involvement in regional programmes. According to the report, sanctions serve only to stimulate the region's black market economy and keep FRY's population poor and socially vulnerable while the elite accumulates wealth. The verdict followed an initiative at the beginning of February 2000 by businessmen from a wide range of countries, urging the US to lift sanctions, which they said supported crime and corruption in the whole region.

Despite the fear of EU opprobrium, many of FRY's neighbours (still awaiting promised post-Kosovo funding from the West) are willing sanctions-busters and trade intermediaries (as was the case during the UN trade embargo against FRY between 1992 and 1995). But loopholes mitigate rather than remove the considerable costs. Another unintended consequence of sanctions has been to encourage the further disintegration of FRY, contrary to the professed wishes of the EU. The Western policy of isolating Serbia while lifting sanctions on Montenegro and promising it aid is fuelling Montenegro's drive for independence. In Iraq, sanctions have the proclaimed objective of trying to modify government behaviour (to make it desist from developing weapons of mass destruction). In Serbia's case, no specific actions are demanded from the government

---

22   The new measures prohibit EU firms from conducting any business with Yugoslav firms linked to the government. In order for them to trade with the EU, the burden of proof falls on Serbian companies to show that they have no connections with the Milosevic regime. By contrast, companies from Montenegro are to be presumed to be unconnected with the regime unless it is proven otherwise. It is difficult to believe that any company in FRY would risk the wrath of the government by advertising its independence or opposition by applying to be included on the EU's White List. There is confusion about how to implement the new ban. For instance, the Yugoslav companies have to prove that they do not financially aid the government, but does paying taxes and customs duties constitute financial aid?

other than to step down. Those in the West who believe that Serbia is indeed a dictator-ship are in effect expecting the population to engage in insurrection against a formidable political, security and military apparatus.

Since they are politically ineffective and harm ordinary citizens, why are the sanctions maintained by the EU? The sanctions are a sign most of all of frustration with a failure to achieve goals – in FRY's case, the removal of the regime.

In sum, trade between the EU and the region can be characterised by the EU's emergence as the most important trading partner for a majority of countries in this region. However, this statement has to be geographically diversified with regard to the important volume of trade of a certain number of member states with the region. Simultaneously, there is an on-going fragmentation process because of a differentiated treatment by the EU of individual Southeast European countries and because of various sanction regimes.

Trade between the countries of Southeastern Europe

The question of compatible economies in the perspective of ten years of change is of course underlying the development of mutual and regional trade in the region. A specific feature of these countries is that around 50 per cent of their exports remain commodity-based. This feature makes exports much dependent on the physical crossing of borders.

There is no reliable source of foreign trade statistics for all Southeast European countries. International publications reporting the foreign trade of these countries are often not complete (omitting Bosnia-Herzegovina and FRY or giving only partial data, not including for example Bosnian trade between the Republika Srpska and FRY). As such, they distort the trade figures of the region, present a wrong état de lieu and lead to incorrect conclusions. Figures in this study are mostly drawn from Milica Uvalic's article, which gives the most complete data of trade in this region.[23]

In 1998, for Albania, Bulgaria and Romania, trade with Southeast European countries was of marginal importance. However, for most of the successor states of former Yugoslavia, trade with the other Southeast European countries represents a rather significant portion of overall trade. Intra-regional trade showed signs of recovery in 1989.[24] This tendency was interrupted by the disintegration of the former Yugoslavia leading to the creation of five separate states, which set up various restrictions on trade

---

23 M. Uvalic: Regional Co-operation in South-Eastern Europe, in: Southeast Europe and Black Sea Studies, Vol. 1, 2000.

24 D. Heimerl, Y. Rizopoulos, N. Vukadinovic: Contradictions et limites des politiques de reconstruction dans les Balkans, Revue d'Études Comparatives Est-Ouest, 1999, No. 4, p. 215.

with their former trading partners, though the level of integration among the regions of the former Yugoslavia is at present evaluated by experts to have been similar to that of countries inside a common market. This evolution has been quite contrary to the general trend of trade liberalisation elsewhere that is supported by the EU.

Despite drastic reduction in the overall level of trade among the newly created states, most states maintained some trade with their former trading partners. Regarding Bosnia-Herzegovina, Macedonia and FRY, the potential for regional co-operation is rather significant. Mutual trade plays an important role for the successor states of former Yugoslavia (with the exception of Slovenia, though it has somewhat increased its share of exports to the Southeastern European region in recent years). This is especially true for export. If one considers Southeastern Europe as one regional trading partner, Bosnia-Herzegovina traded more with the other Southeast European countries in 1998 than with the EU, both in terms of exports (67 per cent) and imports (53 per cent). FRY in 1998 also exported more to other SEE countries (35 per cent) than to the EU (33 per cent), though its imports from the EU (39 per cent) were more than double the share of imports from Southeastern Europe (16 per cent).

From the perspective of Southeastern Europe as one regional trading partner, several specific features must be taken into consideration:

Trade barriers: There has been a movement towards fragmentation of the trading space in recent years. Economic interests are not the primary factor determining trade flows in Southeastern Europe. Various new restrictions on trade with former trading partners have been imposed. Despite appeals to develop regional co-operation by international organisations and the EU during the last year, there seems to have been an ongoing process of fragmentation in the region instead. It is often said by EU officials that the Southeast European countries should trade more freely with each other and with applicant countries. This was Chris Patten's advice to Croatia's complaint in March 2000. Croatia faced new tariff barriers from the EU accession candidates that had felt under pressure to align their rates with union levels before accession.[25] This clearly underlines the contradictory approach in EU trading policy towards the region.

Risk of trade according to ethnic lines (Kosovo, internal borders of Bosnia-Herzegovina): This is a consequence of the formation and organisation of new and prevalently mono-ethnic entities aspiring to the consolidation of their internal and external "ethnic security" (reflected in political terms in the election of ethnic parties) through demands for the status of independence or substantial autonomy.

Interior sanctions: one typical example is Serbia and Montenegro (see below).

The fragmentation of trading space can be exemplified by the following measures:

---

25   Financial Times, 30 March 2000.

The *sanction regime* partially lifted, maintained and reinforced against the Federal Republic of Yugoslavia by the EU and the United States (see above).

NATO bombed eight Danube bridges last spring. Shipping through the blocked stretches of the river has been halted. The International Danube Commission emphasised that any final plan of clearing the waterway would have to include building at least one temporary bridge over the Danube in Novi Sad (FRY). Danube transport reached its peak in 1987 (the annual volume of goods transported was 100m tonnes). The collapse of the Soviet Union and the embargo against FRY during the war in Bosnia brought transport to a standstill. A slow recovery started in 1994, which brought up transport volume to 35m–40m tonnes in 1998. The closure of the Danube has had a major impact not only on FRY, but also on Macedonia, Bulgaria and Romania, much of whose trade passed by road or river through Serbia.

Establishment of alternative transport routes around Serbia: After nine years of bickering, Romania and Bulgaria have agreed on a site for a Danube River bridge that will allow trans-Balkan traffic to bypass Serbia. The agreement signed in Bucharest on 27 March 2000 is one of the first concrete results of the Stability Pact for Southeastern Europe. The bridge is a vital link in an EU project known as Pan European Corridor IV. The project aims to create a major north-south transport route linking Greece and Western Europe through Bulgaria, Romania and Hungary. The new bridge will cross the Danube about 20 km east of Serbia in Vidin (Bulgaria) and the Romanian river port of Calafat. Currently, the main road and rail routes between Western Europe and the Balkans pass through FRY. Even before the NATO air strikes, the EU had been eager to create alternative transport routes bypassing Serbia.

Kosovo: Certain measures, which cannot all be outlined here, represent major violations of Yugoslav sovereignty in Kosovo. UN Security Council Resolution 1244 reaffirms Yugoslav (not Serbian!) sovereignty over Kosovo and calls for substantial autonomy for the province.[26] Kosovo has de facto been detached from Serbia for the time being and is run as a protectorate of an even purer form than the arrangement in Bosnia-Herzegovina.

By August 1999, Kosovo payment systems were still in the hands of Serbian banks. The National Bank of Yugoslavia insisted that the Dinar is the legal tender for the whole country and any other currency would be illegal. In autumn 1999, UNMIK abandoned the Yugoslav Dinar as the official currency in circulation in favour of the D-mark and started to set up a customs service at the border with Macedonia and Al-

---

26 FRY submitted a 25-page memorandum to the UN Security Council protesting namely that in numerous ways, including introducing a new currency, setting up a customs service, and organizing a census, the UN is usurping authority from the Yugoslav State.

bania, two key steps in severing ties between the province and FRY. No Serbs are employed in the customs service and all taxes are collected in D-marks and will not be sent to Belgrade. At the end of 1999, the United States had been pressing, with support from Kouchner, for approval of a regulation giving the UN office in Kosovo the right to issue temporary travel documents – in effect passports – to Kosovo residents. On 17 November 1999, the UN administration took steps towards setting up a banking system for the province by establishing the Banking and Payments Authority for Kosovo (BPK), which will have many of the traditional duties of a central bank, but will not issue its own currency.

Montenegro: Montenegro has been threatening to proclaim its independence since 1997 when Milo Djukanovic was elected president. On 29 December 1998, the Montenegrin cabinet adopted an economic policy for 1999, which committed the Republic to adopting independent monetary, pricing and foreign trade policies:

- Trade representative offices and missions are opened in 1999 and 2000 (Brussels, London, Paris, Ljubljana, Bonn, Milan, Sarajevo). By the end of 2000, offices are planned for Zagreb, Skopje, Berlin and Moscow.
- In January 1999, Montenegro announces that it is planning to take over the conduct of foreign trade from the federal government.
- In early February 1999, following Montenegro's unilateral decision to reopen the border with Croatia without consulting Belgrade, the first shipment of goods crosses the border.
- In mid-February 1999, Montenegrin businessmen are advised not to transport their goods to Serbia, which is accused of waging a trade and customs war by setting up tax collection points along the border and detaining Montenegrin trucks for inspection in a bid to control the flow of goods between Serbia and Montenegro.
- By mid-1999, Djukanovic's police forces have almost entire control over the republic's borders with Albania, Croatia and the Adriatic Coast.
- In August 1999, a meeting of Montenegrin clans in the north of the republic promises to defend Yugoslavia by all means and secede from Montenegro should that republic withdraw from the Yugoslav Federation. The Montenegrin Interior Ministry reacts by saying that the government would firmly oppose any attempt by the clans to secede from Montenegro and attach the territory they inhabit to Serbia.
- In autumn 1999, political tensions between Belgrade and Podgorica develop into tit-for-tat economic warfare. The row is increasingly affecting economic ties between the two republics. On 24 September 1999, Montenegro announces that it will introduce its own customs system in response to Serbian threats to block shipments of food and other goods to Montenegro. Serbia justifies the measures by federal loss of control of Montenegro's external borders. Belgrade also says that it will only allow

payment transactions to firms that regularly pay taxes to the federal state. Montenegro's government is encouraging the republic's companies not to pay such taxes in protest against FRY's refusal to hand over Montenegro's share of the federation's customs revenue. About 70 per cent of Montenegrin payment operations are conducted with Serbia. Montenegro has in turn said that Montenegrin firms may start collecting payments from Serbia in hard currency.

– These interior sanctions and counter sanctions are taking place at the border between Montenegro and Serbia in a region, Sandzak, which straddles southwestern Serbia and northern Montenegro, comprising about 350,000 people, around one-half of whom are Muslim Slavs (some of their leaders are demanding greater autonomy or independence from Serbia).

– On 3 November 1999, the D-mark becomes legal tender in Montenegro, in a first step towards establishing an independent monetary system. Serbia retaliates by virtually closing its markets to Montenegrin companies. The National Bank of Yugoslavia imposes restrictions on fund transfers between firms in Montenegro and Serbia.

– On 25 February 2000, Montenegro and Albania open their borders, without consultation with Belgrade at the check point Bozaj/Hani I Hotit. This decision follows a series of diplomatic efforts between the two countries to prepare common projects in the framework of the Stability Pact. Montenegrins can get a visa for Albania directly at the border, and Albanians only need their passport stamped by the police on Montenegrin territory.

– On 6 March 2000, the Serbian police seal off the border with Montenegro, causing long queues of trucks and cars at all border crossings.

– On 23 July 2000, the Yugoslav Army blocks the checkpoint Bozaj/Hani I Hotit, preventing Albanians from entering Montenegro.

Against this background of fragmentation of the trading space, it is appropriate to take a closer look at the trade relations between the Southeastern European countries.

Slovenia aims to be a trading hub at the crossroads of Central Europe. For this reason the government is implementing an ambitious road-building programme. The east-west link connects Central Europe with Slovenia's main port of Koper, which is already Austria's main maritime outlet and serves other Central European countries for both their export and import trade.

Slovenia is a very open economy with foreign trade accounting for 115 per cent of GDP (1998). Among the states of former Yugoslavia, only Croatia remains a significant trading partner. Recent statistics point to a stabilisation in exports to Croatia, which is Slovenia's largest export market outside the EU. Slovenia signed a free-trade agreement with Croatia in October 1997, which came into force in January 1998. The rate of expansion of exports to Bosnia-Herzegovina, which has been one of Slovenia's fastest growing export markets since the end of the 1992–1995 war, slowed down in 1999.[27]

Exports dropped substantially in 1991 because of the loss of Yugoslav markets, which was not made up by gains elsewhere. On the import side, the loss of markets in former Yugoslavia has been particularly felt in respect of production materials. Germany alone has consistently accounted for 30 per cent of exports since 1993, which has left Slovenia heavily exposed to economic developments in just one country. Efforts to diversify export markets seem to have borne some fruit recently (France, Italy and the UK). Efforts to recapture markets within the former Soviet Union have been less successful. However, trade with the countries of the CEFTA (Slovenia has been a member since 1996) picked up in 1999 but remains below potential. CEFTA has pledged to reduce customs duties among member countries. A 1997 CEFTA summit in Slovenia produced agreement on the liberalisation of trade in agricultural goods and the opening of membership talks with Bulgaria.

An agreement between Italy, Hungary and Slovenia on co-operation in economy, transport and communications and military was signed in 1997. Contacts between Slovenian and Serbian businessmen have been maintained, but a large-scale resumption of trading between the two countries will require the resolution of political and financial problems.

The *Croatian* authorities are sensitive to any perception that Croatia is being consigned to the Balkan sphere. Nevertheless, the importance of relations within the region is recognised. Croatia has pushed for a special relationship with the Federation of Bosnia-Herzegovina (Federation), but Bosnian Muslim leaders, who are still wary of Croatian intentions in Bosnia-Herzegovina, have reacted with suspicion. Limited Croat-Muslim co-operation against the Bosnian Serbs during the last years of the war did not translate into the integration of Croat- and Muslim-controlled areas in the half of

---

27 Several Slovene companies have announced plans to invest abroad, particularly in other parts of former Yugoslavia. The second largest bank, SKB Banka, has said that it intends to open a bank in Montenegro, as well as to take stakes in existing institutions in Bosnia-Herzegovina and Macedonia. In February 2000, Slovenia's largest food retailer, Mercator, announced that it was planning to set up shopping centers in Bosnia-Herzegovina and in Croatia. A Slovene meat producer, Perutnina from Ptuj, is planning to set up a joint venture in Velika Kladusa in the region of Bihac, by taking control of a local poultry processing plant. In March 2000, Fructal, which makes fruit juices and other drinks, invested in Macedonia by taking an 86 per cent stake in the drinks producer Konzeks. It hopes to use this as a spring-board for exports to Bulgaria, Romania, FRY, Greece and Albania. Some Slovene companies have invested abroad to recapture markets that they lost after the break-up of former Yugoslavia; some of the deals represent new relationships. Slovene consumer goods producers have realised that they will face greater competition from abroad, particularly the EU, when all trade barriers are removed. Investing abroad offers them a way into markets that are likely to experience more rapid growth. It also allows them, in some cases, to take control of potential competitors at very low prices.

Bosnia-Herzegovina assigned to them after the Dayton peace accord. The two sides have remained bitterly divided, with the Croat-controlled area more closely integrated into Croatia. In early 1999, hard-line Croats launched a campaign for the creation of a third entity within the country.

The geographical diversity of the country was compounded by the varying experience of the war in different parts of the country, as a result of which very different patterns of economic development have emerged in recent years. For instance, Dalmatia has been effected by its close proximity to the core Croat-controlled areas of Bosnia, centred on western Herzegovina. Widespread avoidance of taxes and customs duties there has negatively affected businesses in Dalmatia.

Foreign trade fell sharply when war broke out at the beginning of the 90s. An upturn in 1992 mainly represented the reclassification of transactions with other former Yugoslav republics that had hitherto been domestic trade. Although Croatia's military campaigns in 1995 and the Dayton Peace Agreement in December 1995 allowed the country to restore trade routes severed from 1991 to 1995, exports of goods declined in 1996 and 1997. In 1998, exports rose by 9 per cent per year, still slightly below the level of 1992.

It is no coincidence that the stagnation of Croatian exports has been accompanied by resurgence in the rest of the region. Croatian companies lost their markets to other transition countries because of limited restructuring. The higher level of wages and taxes combined with the EU's refusal to sign a Europe agreement has put all of its exporters to a disadvantage against competitors from the rest of the region. The proportion of exports destined for other former Yugoslav states has altered little. It was 25.6 per cent in 1998, compared with 24.7 per cent in 1993. However, there has been a steady decline in exports to Slovenia (in 1993 18.2 per cent of the total to 9.5 per cent of the total in 1998). Bosnia-Herzegovina has displaced Slovenia as the third largest market for Croatian goods, exports there totalling US-$ 653 million in 1998. Much of Croatia's trade with this country is with the bordering Croat-controlled areas in Herzegovina. The border has been poorly controlled, and accurate figures for trade have been lacking. Former Yugoslav republics have declined in significance, accounting for 10.4 per cent of imports in 1998 (16.6 per cent in 1993). However, imports from Slovenia have fallen considerably less than Croatian exports to Slovenia. The most striking change has been the increase in imports from Hungary (up 171 per cent in 1993–1998) and the Czech Republic (up 332 per cent in 1993–1998).

In 1999, exports began to recover despite disappointing sales in Western markets and a collapse in exports to Bosnia-Herzegovina, which had been the third largest market in 1998 (minus 16.3 per cent in 1999). The main reason has been the decision of the Federation to revoke an agreement allowing free-duty trade with Croatia in May

1999. This was a big blow to many Croatian companies, particularly consumer goods producers. Many of their products are of too low a quality to be sold anywhere else, but they have built up captive markets among Bosnian Croats and saw a strong rise in sales after the end of the 1992–1995 war. The abolition of the preferential trading relationship between the Federation and Croatia is probably the main factor behind the 39 per cent fall in imports from Bosnia-Herzegovina – since Croatia erected tariff barriers of its own when the Federation revoked the two sides' free-trade agreement. Croatia has signed a bilateral free-trade agreement with Hungary. The EU lobbied the Hungarian government not to go ahead with this.

The new government's economic programme includes the aim that free-trade agreements will be signed within two years with the EU, the EFTA and all present signatories of the Central European Free Trade Agreement. It also appears to make some progress in securing a free trade agreement with Bosnia-Herzegovina. The Croatian side expects a new accord which would cover all of Bosnia-Herzegovina and not only the Federation, like the agreement that had operated between 1996 and 1999, when it was revoked by the Federation under international pressure.

The instability of the region, which was heightened by the escalation of the conflict in Kosovo in March–June 1999, poses the main threat to *Bosnia-Herzegovina*. It has an immediate impact on party politics in the Republika Srpska and the economic impact has been significant through the loss of trade and interruption of business and commercial flows within the wider region. In the longer term the success of the Kosovo Albanians in achieving a very high degree of autonomy or independence could rekindle separatist claims on part of Bosnian Croats and Serbs.

At the end of the war Bosnia-Herzegovina comprised three distinct economic zones, each with a different currency. In 1998, massive efforts were made to unify payment operations in the Federation and between the entities. The existence of multiple layers of government, compounded by the ethnic divide, the dominance of nationalist parties, combined with substantial regional differences in development, raises the risk of economic grievances translating into ethnic animosities.

At its Madrid meeting, held in December 1998, the Peace Implementation Council had called for the creation of a joint border service. If successful, this will be a huge step towards strengthening the sovereignty of the country. The joint institutions of the country have made some progress on the issue of border control. In June 1999, the presidency reached an agreement on a joint border service, and new units were deployed by 1 October 1999. A similar agreement between the Muslims and the Croats for a joint border service on the Federation's borders has never been implemented. Both entities intend to continue customs reform. Currently, they are setting up customs enforcement divisions within their customs services with backing from the EU. Other plans include the enactment of additional legislation to deal with customs offences and penalties, while setting up a joint Bosnia-Herzegovinian border police to deter border crime.

The data from the two entities' statistics institutes can be considered a rough estimate only. Even when combined with other sources, they do not provide a full picture of the foreign trade flows, which tend to be underreported. The IMF's Direction of Trade Statistics does not include trade with FRY, which is the main trading partner for the Republika Srpska and is also becoming a more important export destination for the Federation. The accuracy of the Federal Institute's trade data is undermined by its poor coverage of Croat-controlled areas, where many factories restarted production between 1996 and 1998. For instance, the aluminium plant in Mostar – which exports most of its output – recently reported that it was operating at full capacity. As this factory is controlled by hard-liners in the Croatian Democratic Union of Bosnia-Herzegovina, it almost certainly does not provide data to the Muslim-controlled Federal Institute. Likewise, the Federal Institute's data probably exclude the large amount of unrecorded trade. In recent years, consumer goods – especially processed food and cigarettes – have been smuggled from Croatia into western Herzegovina. Much of this has been re-exported back to its country of origin by Croatians buying from duty-free shops in the coastal town of Neum, thereby avoiding Croatian excise duty and value-added tax.

Furthermore, reconstruction supported by a strong inflow of foreign assistance sucked in imports that could not be recorded accurately, owing to the country's division into three ethnically controlled territories and its permeable borders with Croatia and FRY.[28]

Towards a full implementation of Bosnia-Herzegovina's Customs Law: The budgetary strains facing the two entities have been partly offset by strong growth in customs revenue since May 1999, when they ended their preferential trade agreements with Croatia and FRY. Goods entering are now charged the same customs duty regardless of the country of origin or point of entry. The entities had previously levied different levels of customs tariffs, and while the Federation allowed customs-free imports from Croatia, the Republika Srpska gave the same privilege to goods from FRY. The implementation of the new customs law sets tariffs at four different rates, from zero to 15 per cent, in line with international trade practices. In order for the country to receive the second portion of its IMF stand-by, the entities had to pass their budgets for 1999 and abandon

---

28 Post-war reconstruction began seriously only in 1998 in the Republika Srpska, following the inauguration of a more moderate government. At the fifth donors' conference in Brussels in May 1999, emergency budgetary support was approved for the Republika Srpska to help to cover a budget gap provoked by the escalation of the conflict in Kosovo.

preferential trading relationships with Croatia and FRY. The preferential trade agreements, compounded by the impact of widespread fraud and customs avoidance, deprived entity budgets of significant revenue: the cost of customs and tax fraud in 1998 was estimated at (convertible marka) KM 1 billion. The effective existence of three separate customs administrations had evidently obstructed the enforcement of state customs law.

New import duties, which were laid down under state legislation passed in 1998, came into effect in the two entities on March 1999 after they reached an agreement on additional import duties. The stumbling block in the negotiations was the question of which commodities would be subject to these additional import duties, which are intended to protect local industry. Before the agreement, each entity applied its own excise duties – thereby breaching the country's constitution which makes customs policy the responsibility of state institutions, even though the entities are responsible for implementing customs policy. The agreement on additional import duties replaced the entities' illegal customs practices and allowed for unified duties to be applied across the country.

In December 1999, after the failure of the Council of Ministers to extend the decree it had passed on additional import duties for 1999, the high representative Wolfgang Petritsch, whose intervention was sought by the prime ministers of both entities, issued a decree extending additional import duties after 31 December 1999, when they were due to expire. The two prime ministers were concerned that if the additional import duties were abolished they would lose substantial amounts of government revenue and domestic producers would suffer a loss of competitiveness.

The post-war recovery of domestic production in Bosnia-Herzegovina has been fragile. The country continues to record large imports, the taxation of which provides an important substitute for the meagre local tax revenue.

Relations with Croatia: In December 1998, the Federation signed an agreement on special relations with Croatia as well as a second agreement on the use of the port of Ploce and the passage through Neum. These two issues have been under discussion since 1994, when the Bosnian Croats and Muslims signed the Washington Agreement, paving the way for the creation of the Federation. They have been delayed because of ambivalence on the part of the Bosniak Party for Democratic Action, which has feared that, since the agreement provides for confederal links with Croatia, the signing of a similar accord between the Republika Srpska and Serbia could lead to the dissolution of the country in the long run. Although the Bosnian Muslims eventually agreed to both agreements, the most sensitive aspects being dealt with in annexes have not yet been approved by the Federation's House of Representatives or the parliament of Bosnia-Herzegovina.

Another potential source of confrontation is the country's coastline.[29] In northern Bosnia, the reconstructed bridge across the Sava river, which links Orasje and Zupanja, was officially opened in December 1998 in order to significantly improve the flow of traffic between the two countries, which had been disrupted due to the destruction of the bridge during the war.

Relations between the Republika Srpska and FRY: The Republika Srpska was under the sway of the authorities of FRY in the aftermath of the war. But their grip waned in January 1998, when a moderate government came to power. It has amended its rules for financial transactions and trade with FRY after the latter's decision on 1 February 1999 to treat trade with the Republika Srpska as foreign trade. Until then, transactions between the two had been treated as domestic on the basis of a protocol that was, however, never confirmed by the parliament of Bosnia-Herzegovina. As of 1 February 1999, exports from the Republika Srpska to FRY have to follow the standard customs procedure and be registered with the National Bank of Yugoslavia. Imports of goods from the Republika Srpska remain duty-free and payments can be settled in hard currency or Yugoslav Dinars (YuD).

FRY changed the trading regime in response to the decision by the entity's authorities in November 1998 to lower the YuD-KM exchange rate at which it would process transactions. It halted all payment transactions in response to this, resuming them only after the authorities revoked their decision. The finance minister of the Republika Srpska declared that an exchange rate of YuD 8.5:KM 1 would apply from 1 February 1999. The unfavorable exchange rate had been detrimental to the Republika Srpska, given that over 70 per cent of its trade is with Yugoslavia. The package announced in February was in fact the first step in abolishing the preferential treatment Yugoslavia had enjoyed in trade so far.

The lingering dispute between the Republika Srpska and FRY triggered by the decision in 1999 to lower the YuD-DM rate that the entity uses, came to a head in November 1999. The Republika Srpska said it was banning the use of the dinar for domestic payments pending an agreement with Belgrade on how cross-border financial transactions would be conducted. The ban was introduced in response to the Yugoslav government's freeze of February 1999 on financial transactions with the Republika Srpska, following the decision on the dinar exchange rate. The Yugoslav government consequently revoked the freeze, but cross-border payment transactions have remained controversial.

Although no foreign trade data for the Republika Srpska have been published recent-

---

29 Next to the coastal town of Neum, the Hotel Stella, which was built by the force of Zenica, was lately privatised by Croatians and is not to be recuperated by its legal proprietor.

ly, anecdotal evidence indicates that it was running a large trade deficit in the final quarter of 1999, albeit smaller than during the war in Kosovo. The disruption of production and trading links with FRY that occurred during the Kosovo war has been compounded by the Republika Srpska's government's decision – under pressure from the central bank – to suspend payments in Yugoslav dinars. Companies' have lost many of their traditional Yugoslav markets, because of the depressed level of living standards in FRY, while their prospects of reorienting their sales are constrained by a weak level of purchasing power in the Federation and by higher quality standards demanded in Slovenia and Croatia.

Trade evolution: In 1998, Federation trade was concentrated on a number of countries, with Croatia and Slovenia the most important export markets. In the first 11 months of 1999, Italy has become the Federation's largest single export market. Negotiations on a trade agreement between Croatia and Bosnia-Herzegovina started in March 1999, on the basis of a proposal drawn up by Croatia to replace the bilateral trade agreement that was suspended by the Federation's prime minister in December 1998.

Exports to Croatia, its second largest market, stood just 44,000 dollars below the level of exports to Italy. However, there was a 25 per cent year-on-year fall in exports to Croatia, largely because of the abolition of trade privileges in May 1999. The data also point to a high level of trade with FRY, which was the Federation's sixth-largest export market (US-$ 28 million) in January–November 1999 (for the second year consecutively). Italy and Germany were the second and fourth most important suppliers of imports. However, the Federation's trade has become increasingly orientated towards Eastern European markets, which together accounted for just under half of all imports. Apart from Croatia, major suppliers are Slovenia, Hungary and the Czech Republic.

Politicians in the Federation have grown concerned about the extent of the bilateral trade deficits they have been running with Croatia and Slovenia. They have occasionally complained that Federation exporters face non-tariff barriers. The obstacles to potentially buoyant trade between these two countries are particularly important in the case of Slovenia.

There was a significant change in the territorial composition of the Federation's foreign trade in January and February 2000. The single largest increase was registered in exports to FRY, and total exports there exceeded exports to Croatia, the Federation's second largest market in 1999, and Slovenia, another important destination. In January and February 2000 exports to FRY rose by more than 600 per cent, while exports to Croatia fell by 56 per cent. The increase made FRY the Federation's fourth-largest export market in these months. The slump in exports to Croatia was largely due to the termination of its trade agreement with the Federation in May 1999.

The escalation of the Kosovo conflict had a substantial effect on Bosnia-Herzegovina. Trade throughout the country was disrupted. The Republika Srpska bore the brunt of the war as, in contrast to the Federation, FRY had been its largest export market. Industry has been further handicapped by damage to infrastructure. In bombing a railway in Serbia, NATO severed one of the main transport links between Bosnia-Herzegovina and Serbia. Some factories will find it hard to resume production, such as Cajavec Holding in Banja Luka. It produces components, the bulk of which had been sold to Zastava, a car factory in Serbia, which was destroyed by air strikes. It will take time for the Republika Srpska to find new export markets. Most manufacturers produce low quality products that cannot be sold abroad. Agricultural producers have been hoping for some time to export to Croatia. They will be held back however by the likely outcome of negotiations with Croatia on a trade agreement. In December 1998, the Croatian government submitted a draft agreement in which it recommended a free regime for industrial goods but a restrictive one for agricultural goods.

Trade between entities: In 2000, trade between the two entities has continued to rise sharply, albeit from a very low base. Rising trade between the two entities is one of the main reasons for the 48 per cent year-on-year rise in wholesale trade in the third quarter of 1999. Strong growth in inter-entity trade reflects an overall improvement in the business climate between the two entities and in particular the Republika Srpska's greater orientation to the Federation market, owing to the decline in transactions with FRY, which has lately operated a ban on food exports to this entity.

Transport: The 1,030 km rail network was the most important means of transporting goods before the war. The main routes ran north-south (between the port of Ploce in Croatia and Doboj in Republika Srpska) and east-west (between Bihac in the Federation and Zvornik in Republika Srpska). The network, substantially damaged during the war, has been divided by three ethnic groups and is controlled by three different companies, although the Dayton agreement stipulates that a state-level public corporation should be set up to control the entire network. There are plans to expand the road network and to improve connections with neighbouring countries. One proposal is to build a motorway from Osijek in Croatia along Bosnia-Herzegovina's north-south axis through Sarajevo and Mostar to the port of Ploce. Although Bosnia-Herzegovina has a 20-km coastline, its main access to the sea is the Croatian port of Ploce. Before the war, the supply of raw materials for heavy industry in central Bosnia passed through Ploce, which was also a conduit for exports of finished goods. The Bosnian Croats denied the other two communities access to the port until September 1998, when Bosnia-Herzegovina and Croatia reached an agreement on its use. The other important port for Bosnia-Herzegovina is on the river Sava at Brcko in Republika Srpska. Enterprises in the Federation have been denied access to it because of tensions between the two entities. In March 1999, Brcko was officially proclaimed a neutral district. The town has been demilitarised, a joint police force has been set up and a programme for the speedier return of refugees put in place. Efforts have been made to revive the town's economy to make the whole concept of Brcko's existence as a neutral district sustainable. This will help enterprises in the Tuzla region, which used the port heavily in the past.

As a landlocked country, *Macedonia* depends on its neighbours for trade routes. It has adequate road and rail links to FRY and Greece but poor connections to Albania to the west and Bulgaria to the east. Freight and passenger services have been interrupted for long periods, first during the disruption that accompanied the outbreak of war in Bosnia-Herzegovina and then during the Greek-imposed trade blockade, when the service was restricted to the Skopje-Belgrade portion of the route. After the launch of NATO airstrikes in March 1999, the service ran from Vranje in southern Serbia and terminated in Thessaloniki.

The country has faced three major challenges to its stability and existence in the 1990s. It steered past the first of these – the break-up of FRY and imposition of international trade sanctions on Serbia and Montenegro – by reaching a peaceful state of affairs with the Serbs. Its relaxed attitude to enforcing the sanctions made it a conduit for trade with FRY, thereby mitigating the economic downturn in the early part of the decade. A second challenge arose when Greece imposed a trade blockade on Macedonia, although this was lifted after 18 months. Unlike these two challenges, the escalation of the conflict in the Serbian province of Kosovo has undermined the inter-ethnic relations in the country, and the security of Macedonia's northern and western borders could come under serious threat in the case of increased violence in southern Serbia between the ethnic Albanian majority and the Serbian security services.

Macedonia's export receipts stagnated from 1990 to 1994 because of the effects of the break-up of Yugoslavia, the imposition of the trade sanctions on this country and the trade embargo introduced by Greece in early 1994. Receipts have risen only slowly since then, even though both, trade sanctions on FRY and the Greek embargo, have been lifted. Exports to FRY picked up sharply after the war, when it became Macedonia's most important export market in 1996/1997. Macedonia's export performance in the other former Yugoslav republics has been disappointing, however, collapsing in the case of Slovenia from US-$ 82 million in 1996 to US-$ 41 million in 1997. Exports to Croatia rose from US-$ 34 million in 1996 to US-$ 54 million in 1998, but still represent only a fraction of the pre-independence level of trade.

The strong growth in exports to FRY was fostered by the liberalisation of trade between the two countries after tariffs on goods traded between the two countries were eliminated in October 1997. A uniform 1 per cent registration fee replaced variable customs fees ranging up to 7.5 per cent. In 1998, FRY ran into balance-of-payments problems and introduced a series of protectionist measures, hampering Macedonian exporters.

In fact, relations with FRY deteriorated in 1998/1999 because of Macedonia's agreement to the stationing of the NATO Extraction Force. FRY, Macedonia's then second-largest export market, made its displeasure felt by frustrating plans for a more liberal trading relationship between the two countries. In January 1999, FRY asked for the proposed free-trade zone between the two countries to be delayed for an intermittent period. This mini-trade war was at first not expected to escalate given that FRY was using Macedonia as an alternative base for its national carrier Jat in order to evade the EU flight ban which was then in force. Belgrade also received other trading advantages from routing traffic through its southern neighbour. Macedonia, meanwhile, was unlikely to strike back.

The NATO bombing campaign severed natural trade routes with FRY and northern Europe. It deprived Macedonia of the Yugoslav market that accounted for 18 per cent of its receipts in 1998 (second-largest market). It also severed the natural trade links by blocking the main transport route with all EU countries apart from Greece (in the second quarter of 1999, exports to Greece rose by 15.5 per cent year-on-year), which together accounted for a further 37 per cent of the country's exports in 1998 (railway links that were suspended soon after the launch of the NATO air campaign were restored only on 14 September 1999). A large proportion of exports are bulky goods with low levels of value added, and the additional cost of transport made them uncompetitive.

The sharpest decline in trade has been in exports to FRY. Much of the trade between the two countries had to be suspended, not only because of the NATO bombing, but also because the main road and railway lines between them pass through Kosovo. In addition, the Yugoslav government instituted a series of restrictions on trade. Trade began to recover in June 1999 after the air strikes stopped and the Yugoslav government abolished wartime measures. Even so, much of the trade had to be diverted away from Kosovo to the eastern half of Serbia. Total export receipts recovered strongly in July, resulting from a further resumption of exports to FRY – including Kosovo. Exports will also be lifted by a barter agreement reached in principle in August 1999 between Macedonia and FRY. The latter will supply wheat in return for sheet metal, oil products and cigars.

Exports have recovered strongly in the third quarter of 2000, spurred by a sharp expansion in exports to Kosovo. As no formal border controls were put in place after Yugoslav troops withdrew, there were at first few barriers to trade. The Macedonians' success may also have reflected contracts secured by ethnic Albanian traders in western Macedonia, overcoming the Kosovo Albanians' cultural resistance to Slav Macedonians – whom they view as pro-Serb. Macedonian companies' position in the market will hinge on whether they are subject to customs duties that have been levied by UNMIK.

The Macedonian government claims that they should be exempt since Macedonia's free-trade agreement with FRY, of which Kosovo remains a part, remains in force. It provides for duty-free trade, with exports subject only to a 1 per cent administration charge. In September 1999, Macedonia claimed that UNMIK had agreed to this position. In October, however, some Macedonian exporters complained that duties were being applied to their goods in an arbitrary way. An agreement has been reached with UNMIK to start exports via Kosovo in April 2000. However, in May it appeared that a "transport corridor" to guarantee safe passage through what is still an insecure (if shorter) route had not been established. Once established, the route could also be used for trade with Bosnia and Croatia. There could be a further decline in Macedonian exports to the rest of FRY – a large portion of which are foods, drinks and tobacco – after the Serbian authorities announced plans in February 2000 to erect barriers to trade in agricultural goods. But there is also the potential for export to Montenegro.

Despite a number of niggling disputes between Croatia and Macedonia, the level of trade with Croatia in 1998 has increased over 1997. Exports increased by around 50 per cent, while imports from Croatia in the same period declined by nearly 8 per cent. In March 1999, Macedonia signed a free-trade agreement with Croatia, which came into force on 1 January 2000. These developments were offset by a deterioration of Macedonia's trade position with Slovenia, with Macedonia registering a deficit of just under US-$ 96 million. Imports from Slovenia in 1998 were US-$ 14,9 million, while exports to Slovenia came to just US-$ 41 million. There have been numerous attempts to remedy the situation and also charges that Slovenia is not respecting the free-trade agreement signed between the two countries. It is hoped that the construction of a pharmaceutical plant in Skopje by the Slovene company Lek will reduce the import bill for drugs from Slovenia and provide Macedonia with a source of export revenue from the sale of pharmaceuticals to other countries in the region in the future.

Macedonia's relations with Greece have improved greatly under Georgievski, particularly since Costas Simitis became the Greek prime minister. This is shown by both the rising volume of Greek investment in Macedonia and the increasing ease with a country whose existence Greece until recently considered a threat to its sovereignty.

In February 1999, Georgievski agreed to sign a free trade accord with Bulgaria that came into force on 1 January 2000. Although trade between the two countries has been markedly down over the past two years on account of the collapse of the Bulgarian economy, there is potential for an increase if regional stability can be assured. Plans to improve transport links will encourage this. The agreement with Bulgaria covers around 90 per cent of trade in goods and paves the way for a three-stage liberalisation in trade. Agricultural goods are not covered by the agreement. Both Macedonia and Bulgaria hope this will pave the way for a substantial recovery in trade, which increased during the 1994/1995 Greek embargo, but subsided thereafter and collapsed after Bulgaria's 1996/1997 financial crisis.

In September 1999, Macedonia signed a free-trade agreement with Turkey. In August 1999, the construction of the Skopje export-processing zone, the first free-trade zone in Macedonia, was inaugurated.

All in all, there are promising signs that co-operation is improving between Macedonia and its neighbours, except FRY. There have been vicissitudes in Macedonian relations with this country. In February 2000, FRY banned imports of Macedonian agricultural products, only to lift the ban in April. A serious threat to the relationship came at the end of February, when the EU added the Yugoslav ambassador in Skopje, Zoran Janackovic, to the list of those unable to enter the EU. Macedonia has not asked him to leave and is caught between supporting EU policy and starting a diplomatic incident with FRY. In mid-March, Macedonia announced that it would open a consulate general in Podgorica in Montenegro. In May, Yugoslav police were turning Macedonians with UNMIK stamps in their passports back at the border. This is a serious development as it could stop trucks carrying goods via FRY, an important transit route for Macedonia. However, on the export side, the most significant rise in early 2000 was to the republics of former Yugoslavia, which accounted for 27 per cent of all exports. Exports to the republics of former Yugoslavia rose by 87 per cent. Serbia proper is also an important trading partner. Historical ties have left the two economies complementary, with a high level of mutual investment of trade.

IV Trade routes and drug trafficking in Southeastern Europe

The backbone of the transport infrastructure (railway and highway) of the region, not only of the former Yugoslavia but as a connection between continents, has been the Zagreb/Belgrade route which has been closed now for almost ten years, independently of the sanction regime imposed on the FRY (sometimes opened for diplomatic purposes but generally closed). This route connects Central Europe but also Western Europe to Southeastern Europe down to Turkey and the Middle East.

Being closed down, traffic had to be rerouted, either to the north or to the south. In both cases, the province of Kosovo has become an important passage of trade.

There is also rerouting by the sea but it is much more expensive. All of the humanitarian aid is shipped from Bari (Italy) to Bar (Montenegro).

There is also the question of internal and external air traffic and the question of airports in the region. Under the international embargo of 1992–1995 air connections with FRY were banned, but services resumed to most major European cities in 1996. In mid-1998, the US and EU denied landing rights to the JAT. Air connections were again halted because of NATO airstrikes in 1999. After NATO bombed hangars at the Surcin Airport near Belgrade, JAT transferred its fleet of airliners to Romania (it has 37 aircraft). In normal times, JAT has regular, daily flights to Podgorica and Iivat in Montenegro and Pristina in Kosovo.

In this context, one should note that with the rerouting of traffic a coherent customs policy is not possible. According to Belgrade, more than 250,000 non-Albanians have been driven out of Kosovo. An equal number of foreign nationals has entered illegally because of inadequate border protection by KFOR and the UN administration. Illegal traffic (stolen cars) is prospering in Montenegro, Albania, Bosnia-Herzegovina and Kosovo (where car registration has not yet been imposed). The illegal cigarette trade is also flourishing and has had quite disastrous effects on the local tobacco industry. Cigarette smuggling has been especially prevalent at the border between Montenegro and western Herzegovina. As Romanian President Emil Constantinescu pointed out in May 2000, "a war among local Mafias" was currently raging in the countries of former Yugoslavia: "One has to look at the situation differently. There is no longer an inter-ethnic war but a war among local mafias which are organised along ethnic lines."[30]

Furthermore, the increase in drug production and trafficking[31] in the Balkans can be seen as a response to the economic crisis, especially in Albania. It was also an offshoot of the wars in the former Yugoslavia. Local production of drugs such as cannabis and opium poppies, virtually non-existent before the conflicts broke out, is now a fact of life in Bosnia (Mostar), Albania (the southern part of the country) and Macedonia (Vardar Valley, the northern part of Skopje). Greece has become an ideal place for laundering money. This mushrooming drug production, both spurred and cloaked by the geopolitical clashes in the region, has already had very serious consequences in all the Balkan countries, where consumption is sky-rocketing. The war in former Yugoslavia has thus produced its share of spin-off effects: all the belligerents have experienced the benefits of an informal economy, financed arms purchases with drug money, set up new organised crime structures, and established contacts with their counterparts in the rest of Europe.

The "Balkans route" now encompasses all the countries in the region. Alternative routes passing through Bulgaria, Macedonia, Greece and Albania have been grafted onto the traditional trunk route through Serbia, which was disrupted by the conflict. As in the neighbouring regions of the Caucasus and the Middle East, drug traders have taken advantage of economic embargoes to infiltrate their merchandise into the more

---

30   AFP, 21 Mai 2000.
31   All information on drugs has been drawn from the reports of the Observatoire géopolitique des drogues (rapports 1995/1996 et 1997/1998).

"respectable" smuggling of basis necessities, oil, arms and illegal immigrants. In Albania, drug trade has made informal banking operations permanent and at the same time facilitated the linkup between the Albanian clans and Italian criminal organisations. Bosnian and Croatian warlords, who were deeply implicated in drug trafficking, at first simply to supply local demand in times of war, have seen their role expand until they are now involved on an international scale. In Serbia, the secret service networks have refashioned themselves as drug operators. The fact that those taking part in the trade were actively involved in the war, that some of them control entire regions (especially in Bosnia) and have a special relationship with the authorities that makes it practically impossible for law enforcement agencies to root them out. At the same time, the international community, especially Europe, is demonstrating a continuing lack of political will to put an end to the illicit activities in Kosovo, Macedonia and Albania that allowed them to flourish.[32]

Bosnia-Herzegovina

The end of the war in Bosnia has speeded up drug trafficking. The war itself, the way it was fought and the armed groups who waged it were the levers that transformed the drug scene in this part of Europe. Bosnia-Herzegovina, a traditional transit area on the Balkan smuggling route, has become a production and processing centre for some drugs, while consumption is growing at an unprecedented rate.

FRY

The new Federal Republic of Yugoslavia had to learn to live under a blockade practically as soon as it was created. In the early years of the conflict in Bosnia-Herzegovina, the traditional drug trafficking routes in the Balkans diverted north to Bulgaria, Romania and Hungary and south into Greece, Macedonia and Albania. The war and the resulting blockade, which put the old traffickers out of business, quickly generated new networks that are far more diversified and perform far better. As soon as the blockade stopped, traditional criminals became active again, while a boom in hard drug

32 Observatoire géopolitique des drogues (www.ogd.org, rapport 1995/1996). For example, in the case of Mostar where a group of Croatian organised criminals, led by veritable warlords with connections in Zagreb, Croatia's capital, and North America, is especially active. The connection between organised crime, the Mostar police and the Bosnian wing of the HDZ seems very clear, but there was want of sufficient support from European and American governments to expose the connections.

consumption occurred and marijuana use became commonplace. The bulk of the drug trade is handled by three state organisations: the SID (the foreign information and documentation service); the SDB (the interior ministry secret police); and the KOS (the defence ministry counter-espionage service). The Belgrade police protects highly placed traffickers, whether they deal in drugs, cigarettes, alcohol or currencies. Drug business and politics are closely intertwined, to the extent that some military officers, politicians, war profiteers, embargo-busters and businessmen have been killed for trying to cut their links to the Serb secret services. These links between politics and drug trafficking are also evident on the other side, among Albanians in Kosovo. Several of Arkan's "political" victims in 1994–1995 were in fact rival dealers who got in the way of commercial activities. But in the Albanian community the role of the secret services is played by clans that specialise in transporting drugs to Europe and selling them there. In Montenegro the situation is somewhat different. As in Albania, it is mainly Italian organised crime that has a strong hold on the drug traffic. Arms, cocaine and synthetic drugs are still reaching the former Yugoslavia from Italy, through Montenegro.

The end of hostilities in Bosnia, the lifting of the embargo against Serbia and the re-opening of the Belgrade-Zagreb highway handed over fresh opportunities to the new generation of traffickers. They have the advantage of being battle-hardened, headed by politicians and backed up by well-run legal business operations. They are continuing to collaborate with each other even when they belong to enemy camps, as they did throughout the war. In short, they can rely on all resources normally available to a country's secret service.

Independent of these "new networks", the now classical Istanbul–Sofia–Belgrade route in the hands of the Turkish "Babas" has started to function again. But it appears that this older route is shadowed by a new one, which was created during the three-year embargo and dealt in merchandise as varied as basic goods, oil and heroin. The new route links Bulgaria to Montenegro via Macedonia, the Serbian province of Kosovo and/or Albania. Both these routes can lead into Slovenia that, with its "lax" drug laws, has become a must for land routes targeting Italy and Austria, as well as a significant consumer market for illicit drugs. It seems that the new FRY has become a significant shipment point, with traffickers using a strategy of transferring drugs from TIR trucks to private car or tourist buses. Smaller heroin shipments are distributed among a larger number of vehicles that first have to cross Slovenia and Hungary before reaching their final destination, the countries of the Schengen area.

Albania

Albania had scarcely emerged from the financial isolation imposed by the Communist regime when its economic opportunities were blocked by the various embargoes against its neighbours. Smuggling aimed at getting round those embargoes soon became the country's most lucrative activity. According to a special report,[33] Albania's organised crime has been expanding in Kosovo and is thriving in the face of an inadequate UN police force, taking full advantage of Kosovo's open border with Albania. The Albanian mafia is considered Europe's fastest-growing one. The Albanian-speaking region (comprised of Albania, southern Macedonia and the Serbian province of Kosovo) increasingly seems to be playing the part of a dispatching centre for the whole of Europe, in particular for the German-speaking countries.

Macedonia

Before the collapse of Yugoslavia and the independence of Macedonia, poppy growing and opium production were subject to very precise rules. Stimulated by the Balkan Route and the profits it generates, cannabis and poppy crops have mushroomed in Southeastern Macedonia during the last two years. For some, drug plant cropping is necessary for survival, for others it is a lucrative international business. The country's chemical industry, deprived of its outlets in the former Yugoslavia and in some East European countries, tends to turn to producing precursors which are mainly destined for Turkish traffickers. Heroin production, processing and marketing are mainly in the hands of ethnic Albanians from Macedonia. While it cannot be denied that the Albanian population is the most involved in heroin trafficking – but also the most affected by heroin use – it is also true that any drug-related crime is treated more severely when the culprit is an Albanian.

Romania

Since the embargo against countries of the former Yugoslavia has been lifted, traffickers no longer restrict their activities to running drugs across the border with Hungary. Large stocks have been built up and are now being distributed in all directions, especially using the traditional Balkan route running through Bulgaria and Serbia but also the

33   The Sunday Telegraph, 5 September 1999.

most recent Ukrainian and Moldavian transit routes. Both channel drugs to the Schengen area via Poland and the Czech Republic.

V Conclusions and recommendations

It is of vital importance to improve the EU's access to Southeastern Europe and especially the Balkan peninsula. Routes from the north (through Italy and Austria) require, in addition to the renovation of the railway lines, the construction of a highway in the west from Trieste to Rijeka (through Dalmatia to Zagreb) and in the east from Maribor to Zagreb. But above all, a highway is needed from Ljubljana to Zagreb and on to Bosnia-Herzegovina and Serbia. The route from the Aegean (Thessaloniki) is the only one that provides a decent railway link towards Macedonia and Serbia; the road network in that direction is also good; however, the road links between Greece and Albania are unsatisfactory.

Reaching the Balkans from the Adriatic is easy but almost all ground links that lead inland from ports, especially in the southern Adriatic, are either poor or currently blocked: the rail link from the port of Ploce to Sarajevo/Tuzla/Samac has not been completely activated; the line from the port of Bar to Belgrade is sometimes cut off, sometimes difficult to use for political reasons; from the port of Durres, the railroad is currently hard to use, and is in any case not linked to Macedonia, while the line to Montenegro is still cut off. Road links are still insufficient (barely acceptable from Ploce and Bar, inadequate from Durres). While improvement of the road and railroad links from Ploce towards Bosnia-Herzegovina and from Bar towards Kosovo and Serbia would respond to the growing traffic needs, reactivation of the Albanian railroad line and modernisation of the road network seem to be essential for the very development of the Albanian economy. Bringing Albania out of its isolation would mean being able to reach the Balkan inland area from Durres by improving roads from Durres to the Albanian border and, from there, to Gostivar in Macedonia, linking the Albanian border with the Macedonian network (Kafasan-Kicevo) and modernising the line towards Skopje. These initiatives would open up connections across the Adriatic, through Albania, Macedonia, Serbia and Bulgaria.

In economic terms, it is not a "normal" economic situation that these countries are facing. Available statistics underestimate the actual volume of trade between them. There is a high percentage of invisible trade that should be legalised, with the exception of criminal activities. Wars and trade embargoes have produced a substantial amount of smuggling, especially across the "soft" borders (between Serbia and Republika Srpska, Albania and Kosovo, Croatia and Herzegovina). The statistics do not reflect this illegal trade, which sometimes takes place in barter form. The amount of intra-regional trade is supposed to be much higher than reported, even with corrected data.

Some specialists recommend that the revival of economic relations offers realistic possibilities for new links in the mid-term future and that re-establishing political and inter-ethnic relations is more complex and uncertain. They argue that the influence of economic relations can sometimes be so important over time that it markedly improves inter-state relations. However, in the Southeastern European context, it seems that everything should be done first to remove the political obstacles (imposed from inside and outside, like visa restrictions) which hamper these relations. Otherwise, trade and economic ties cannot be revived. We must look at these countries as partners and not as markets!

A bilateral approach conditional on multilateral economic relations and initial integration into the European framework should be implemented.[34] A multilateral economic opening towards interested countries should be organised on a very low level of political conditionality, but be well-defined with regard to the "mercantile" framework it intends to favour. The terms of the bilateral agreement between the EU and the country could include the granting of financial assistance and, if necessary, financing for reconstruction; the definition of a programme for new communications infrastructures in those markets; unilateral liberalisation of the EU import regime (a total one for industrial products coming from these countries – on the basis of the EU regulations on the origin of products – and a partial one for agricultural products) – through instruments and aids similar to those foreseen for the associated transition countries of the EU. The bilateral agreement should at the same time commit each country to starting a process of trade liberalisation (a total one for industrial products, a partial one for agricultural products) with the other countries in the region with whom agreements have been signed; a free trade zone should be set up in five years at the most; links in the energy, telecommunications, road and railroad sectors with the countries involved in the agreements should be revitalised and developed, providing specific guarantees on the freedom of movement and transit and non-discrimination in terms of tariffs and taxes. Thus, insertion into the framework of European integration is immediate for those countries willing to open up economic relations among themselves according to scheduled dates. At the same time, it creates greater opportunities for the export of these countries, making it possible for certain sectors of their industry to grow through international co-operation.

The residual industrial capacities of these countries should not generate too much

34 For this proposal cf. Tito Favaretto: Paving the way for possible Balkan regional co-operation, in: The International Spectator, January–March 2000, p. 77.

concern within member states. The same could hold true for agricultural products with the adoption of a system of samples, quotas and tariffs following the model used during the association of the countries of Cenral and Eastern Europe, but the partial liberalisation would be of major importance to the region considering the importance of the agricultural sector in their GDP and, conversely, the low share of exports with respect to imports on total trade. At the same time, the scheduled liberalisation of trade would organise, foster and partially synchronise a trend towards opening that has already begun to appear between countries (agreements among Macedonia, Croatia, Bulgaria and Turkey; requests by Albania for trade liberalisation with Macedonia and Bulgaria, etc.). The commitment to freedom of transit from and through third countries and the guarantee of non-discriminatory tariffs and taxes is complex but could initiate a process in which production, trade and transport would gradually be organised into a coherent regional context of tariffs and movement of goods. Liberalisation processes both by the EU and by the countries of the region would create conditions for greater interest by foreign economic operators.

There seem to be two schools: the one underlining the importance of trade with EU (Gligorov, Wittkowsky[35]) and the other emphasising the role of mutual trade and regional co-operation (Uvalic). The latter argues that one of the first steps for increasing economic links among the countries of Southeastern Europe is to promote mutual trade. The majority of the countries of Southeastern Europe have already, on different grounds, more or less differentiated access to markets of other regions and retain a number of trade barriers between themselves. Currently there are no institutional arrangements through which they could exploit the potential of their own region, in the interest of their own development. There are potentials, as has been shown above, for expanding trade among some Southeast European countries, especially among the successor states of former Yugoslavia. Considering that over the last few years, Southeast European exports to the EU have been stagnating or declining – the only exception being Romania – sluggish performance on Western markets could be compensated by increasing exports to Southeast European markets. Some positive steps have been taken in this direction as bilateral free-trade agreements have been signed by a number of Southeast European countries.[36]

35 A. Wittkowsky: Südosteuropa und die Europäische Union – Stabilität durch Integration, in: Südosteuropa, Heft 3–4, 2000, p. 169.
36 For these proposals cf.: M. Uvalic: Regional Co-operation in Southeastern Europe, in: Southeast Europe and Black Sea Studies, Vol. 1, 2000.

Cross-Border Co-operation in Southeastern Europe

Fabian Schmidt, Milica Uvalic

I Introduction

Regional co-operation in Southeastern Europe, embracing various forms of bilateral and multilateral cross-border co-operation among individual countries, has been one of the main pillars of the Stability Pact for Southeastern Europe adopted in Cologne on 10 June 1999 after the end of the military conflict in Kosovo. In line with this initiative, the European Union has launched the Stabilisation and Association Process specifically for Southeastern Europe as a follow-up of the earlier developed Regional Approach for the five countries of the Western Balkans. Both processes emphasise the importance of regional and cross-border co-operation as one of the fundamental elements and instruments for achieving more permanent peace, stability and development in Southeastern Europe. As was the case with countries in Central and Eastern Europe in the early 1990s, which were encouraged to collaborate and intensify intra-regional co-operation by signing the Central European Free Trade Agreement (CEFTA), the European Commission is encouraging Southeast European countries to go through a similar process of first intensifying co-operation among themselves while preparing for future EU membership and integration with EU structures.

There are, however, some main differences between the two processes in Central and Eastern Europe and Southeastern Europe. Today's encouragement of cross-border co-operation in Southeastern Europe is taking place as a direct consequence, at least in part, of the 1999 military conflict, since most of these initiatives in favour of Southeastern Europe would not have been launched had the war in Kosovo not taken place. The second main difference is that many previous attempts to intensify regional co-operation

225

in Southeastern Europe have failed or have had limited success[1], whereas CEFTA, despite not leading to a significant increase in intra-regional trade, has nevertheless had a certain role to play in the pre-accession period of members.[2] These are precisely the reasons why regional/cross-border co-operation is even more important today in Southeastern Europe than it was in Central and Eastern Europe in the early 1990s. Regional and cross-border co-operation at all levels and in various fields should contribute to achieving the most important objectives of the international community in Southeastern Europe, which previously were not achieved or which were achieved only very partially, in this way also facilitating the future integration of this region into a wider EU.

The present paper evaluates the current initiatives in Southeastern Europe, primarily in cross-border co-operation (rather than regional co-operation).[3] Although these two terms are frequently used indistinguishably, we define cross-border co-operation as all forms of co-operation at the sub-state level (rather than the state level, as in the case of regional co-operation) between various types of professional agents and institutions (NGOs, professional groups, organisations or associations, therefore excluding personal individual contacts), whether bilateral or multilateral (i.e., involving agents from only two or from more countries respectively). As to geographical coverage, Southeastern Europe will include seven transition countries: Albania, Bosnia-Herzegovina, Bulgaria, Croatia, Former Yugoslav Republic of Macedonia (FYROM), Romania and the Federal Republic of Yugoslavia (FRY). The paper is structured as follows. Section II gives an overview and initial assessment of past experiences with cross-border co-operation in Southeastern Europe. Section III discusses the strategies and priorities regarding cross-border co-operation of the major international organisations. Section IV presents a synthesis of on-going cross-border co-operation initiatives within the framework of the Stability Pact, presently undertaken in different fields (a detailed list is provided in the appendix). Section V discusses some critical issues regarding EU policies and cross-border co-operation in Southeastern Europe. The last section (section VI) makes several recommendations for improvement of EU policy, taking into account the structural problems of cross-border co-operation in Southeastern Europe.

1   M. Uvalic: Regional Co-operation in South-East Europe, in: Southeast Europe and Black Sea Studies, Vol. 1, pp. 64–84.
2   A. Inotai: The Czech Republic, Hungary, Poland, the Slovak Republic and Slovenia, in: H. Tang (ed.): Winners and Losers of EU Integration – Policy Issues for Central and Eastern Europe, Washington, D.C., The World Bank, pp. 17–51.
3   Regional co-operation is discussed in detail by P. Simic in this volume.

II Past experiences in cross-border co-operation in Southeastern Europe

There has been a wide range of initiatives stimulating regional and cross-border co-operation in Southeastern Europe. While many of these initiatives have been launched after the 1999 military conflict in Kosovo within the framework of the Stability Pact for Southeastern Europe, not all initiatives are of such recent origin. In addition to the EU 1995 Royaumont Process and its 1996 Regional Approach developed for the five countries of the so-called Western Balkans (Albania, Bosnia-Herzegovina, Croatia, FYROM and FRY), there have been others which ought to be mentioned, such as the 1989 Central European Initiative (CEI), the 1992 Black Sea Co-operation Initiative (BSEC), the 1996 South-East European Co-operation Initiative (SECI), and the 1996 Conference on Stability and Good Neighbourliness in Southeast Europe (CSEE).[4] Although these initiatives were all launched at the highest level, usually involving governments of Southeast European (and other) countries and thereby representing forms of regional co-operation, their objectives and specific tasks were aimed to stimulate various forms of cross-border co-operation among agents and institutions of participating states.

Table 1: Participation of Southeast European countries in multilateral initiatives of regional co-operation[5]

Country	CEI (1989)	CEFTA (1992)	BSEC (1992)	CSEE (1996)	RP (1995)	EU-RA (1996)	SECI (1996)	SP (1999)	Total
Albania	+	–	+	+	+	+	+	+	7
B&H	+	–	–	Obs.	+	+	+	+	5+1 Obs.
Bulgaria	+	+	+	+	+	–	+	+	7
Croatia	+	–	–	Obs.	+	+	Obs.	+	4+2 Obs.
FYROM	+	–	–	+	+	+	+	+	6
Romania	+	+	+	+	+	–	+	+	7
FRY	–	–	–	+	+	+	–	–	3

CEI: Central European Initiative; CEFTA: Central European Free Trade Agreement; BSEC: Black Sea Economic Co-operation; CSEE: Conference on Stability and Good Neighbourliness in SEE; RP: Royaumont Process; EU-RA: European Union Regional Approach; SECI: South East Europe Co-operation Initiative; SP: Stability Pact for SEE.
+: Participant; –: Non-participant; Obs.: Observer.

Within the framework of the above and other less formalised initiatives of regional co-operation in Southeastern Europe, there have been a variety of cross-border co-operation projects during the past decade undertaken in different areas.

---

4   M. Uvalic: op. cit., or D. Lopandic: Multilateral Co-operation in Southeastern Europe, in: J. Mimic (ed.): Southeastern Europe 2000 – A View from Serbia (Belgrade: Stubovi Kulture), 1999, pp. 67–84.

5   Source: M. Uvalic: op. cit., mainly based on D. Lopandic: op. cit., p. 79 with some minor modifications.

Among the oldest forms of cross-border co-operation are those aimed at developing civil society, such as those in place since 1991 between peace groups in the different parts of former Yugoslavia. These groups sprung up in reaction to the war and rising nationalism and managed to maintain contacts by developing the Zamir E-mail network (long before the development of proper Internet access throughout the region). The peace groups – most notably the Anti Ratna Kampanja in Zagreb and the Centar za Antiratnu Akciju in Belgrade – managed to maintain contacts among non-nationalists in Southeastern Europe. They became an important contact point for other NGOs looking for partners throughout the region.

Cross-border co-operation among the non-nationalist media in the different parts of the former Yugoslavia has been established in part through mechanisms set up by the peace movements. One self-sustaining initiative that grew out of these activities was the Alternativna Informativna Mreza (AIM) created in October 1992 as a network of journalists which included all countries of the former Yugoslavia and Albania. The network contributed a common pool of articles to be used by different news media both in the Balkans and elsewhere.

Many media institutions, especially local news agencies, have maintained co-operation agreements with their other regional partners. This applies both to public/state-owned as to private news agencies that worked to develop links of exchange with other private agencies throughout the region. The quality of news exchanged was sometimes not competitive with respect to the large international news agencies, which delayed the development of a news market.

Foreign initiatives with a cross-border dimension involved both the Budapest based Regional Media Program of the Open Society Institute, which operates through its local offices, and the activities of the Institute for War and Peace Reporting, which had set up offices throughout the region and thus developed a modest network of news gathering and distribution. Other media related NGOs, often financed by various donors – such as different EU governments or agencies – have frequently developed professional contacts between journalists throughout the region, even though these barely resulted in a vivid institutionalised exchange of news and information.

Other outside initiatives to promote the communication and exchange among local NGOs and representatives from Southeastern Europe include the efforts of the Aspen Institute Berlin during 1997–99 to bring together major intellectuals from the Balkans to discuss the unresolved problems in Southeastern Europe and evaluate the Carnegie Foundation's Report "Unfinished Peace"[6]. Since then, the Aspen Institute has launched an alumni programme targeting young intellectuals from Southeastern Europe, in order

6   International Commission on the Balkans (1996).

to promote the exchange of ideas and discussion about regional co-operation issues. The large variety of activities and conferences organised in numerous fields by the Soros Foundation has also frequently brought together NGO representatives from throughout the region, working in a variety of fields.

A broad variety of current projects in the civil society sector builds on continuous efforts in that field undertaken in the past. The remaining difficulties, such as doubling of efforts or lack of co-operation, will only be overcome through better contacts between NGOs on the ground.

Due to the character of the ethnic conflicts in Southeastern Europe, there have been few cross-border initiatives to address minority conflicts and ethnic relations. Most countries in the region were reluctant to support cross-border activities in the field of minority rights, since that was potentially regarded as interference in internal affairs. The main exception was the co-operation of smaller human rights NGOs, and most notably those within the International Helsinki Federation for Human Rights, whose activists have not shied away from crossing borders and addressing human and minority rights problems across the region. The OSCE also, especially through its High Commissioner on National Minorities, Max van der Stoel, has been active in improving minority rights in the region. Nevertheless, most of these initiatives were clearly focused on one country and had no explicit cross-border dimension.

Parallel to the efforts to strengthen civil society were the attempts to improve governance. The efforts in this field go back to the involvement of the Council of Europe in helping countries draft laws that help them establish democratic institutions after the end of Communism. Numerous projects have taken place in the past, also through the OSCE's Office for Democratic Institutions and Human Rights, but most of these projects clearly focused on one particular country and its legislative reform and did little to stimulate cross-border co-operation. The Council of Europe has also taken the lead in the area of public administration. The OECD, in particular through its SIGMA Program for Support for Improvement in Governance and Management in Central and Eastern Europe, has given substantial support to individual countries in the field during the process of drafting legislation.

Parliamentary co-operation throughout Southeastern Europe has focused mainly on the Council of Europe and the parliamentary assemblies of other international bodies and, as far as political parties were concerned, the different umbrella organisations of European parties. The main process boosting inter-parliamentary co-operation in Southeastern Europe on an institutionalised level was the Royaumont Process (which also today leads the task force on inter-parliamentary co-operation of the Stability Pact at Working Table I).

In the field of security, the main cross-border co-operation initiatives included the work of the "Partnership for Peace Program" of NATO. The programme has focused on the holding of numerous joint exercises over the past decade and on training and exchange programmes for officers from the armies of all participating countries. The involvement of units from the different Southeast European countries within SFOR and KFOR peacekeeping troops, as well as in other international organisations engaged in creating a secure environment, can be considered as very practical examples of multinational cross-border co-operation. Other institutions promoting similar aims include the UN agencies and the OSCE, which played an important role in supporting regional stability. There have also been other multilateral initiatives, such as "Mission Alba" in Albania in 1997 or the WEU's MAPE mission, that can also be considered as forms of cross-border co-operation in the broader sense since they involved military and police contingents from different Western and Southeast European states co-operating on a common task.

In the field of education,[7] there have been several initiatives contributing to cross-border co-operation during the 1990s. One important project deals with the joint writing of history textbooks. Another one is the PETNICA centre in Valjevo (Serbia), which regularly organises summer camps for gifted students from neighbouring countries in the fields of science and technology for innovative ways of learning. The Soros Foundation's networks also include regional education programmes in all Southeast European countries. In particular, the Central European University in Budapest and the Open Society Institute Regional Centre in Budapest have considerably contributed to cross-border co-operation in the field of education over the last decade. They are actually the only organisations that have been present in Southeastern Europe throughout the 1990s, albeit with a specific agenda. Through its immediate local activities, the Soros education development programmes have considerably contributed to cross-border co-operation, in particular by linking universities and other institutions to the internet. Also, the exchange of students has become an important and successful part of cross-border co-operation. The activities of the Open Society Fund, enabling exchange of experiences and ideas among people living in different Southeast European countries, have considerably contributed to cross-border co-operation in various fields.

The EU multi-country Phare and TEMPUS programmes in higher education have also promoted cross-border co-operation in Southeastern Europe, but were not inclusive of all countries (Croatia and the FRY were excluded). The University of Athens has been administering a network of Southeast European universities that offers a Master's degree in Southeast European studies. In 1992, the University of Bologna set up a multidisciplin-

---

7   The authors would like to thank S. Uvalic-Trumbic from the UNESCO office in Paris for having provided useful information on co-operation among SEE countries in the field of education.

ary network "Europe and the Balkans" dealing with problems in politics, international relations, economics and history. It has also been regularly organising a Summer School in Cervia (Italy), bringing over students from all countries in Southeastern Europe. The Aspen Institute organised several ad hoc gatherings within the Unfinished Peace Report of the International Commission on the Balkans, which also included education.[8] The Salzburg Seminar of American Studies, within its universities project, also brought together representatives of Southeast European universities with colleagues from US universities.

There have also been some other limited (and usually rather unobserved) cross-border co-operation initiatives among some Southeast European countries. Such initiatives include those of the European Movement for Serbia, which has been conducting research projects and seminars about the possibilities of creating regional frameworks. One such network is the "Zrenjanin Initiative", a programme launched in 1997 for supporting the development of private small-scale enterprises and entrepreneurship in Southeastern Europe. Numerous other activities have also been undertaken by various NGOs throughout the 1990s on a scholarly level.

Due to the project-related character of many NGO programmes on the ground, however, these initiatives usually did not have a more permanent effect, in the sense of creating self-sustaining co-operation structures throughout Southeastern Europe, but were merely important starting points towards getting people together and discussing practical co-operation issues. Nevertheless, NGOs have played an extremely important role, also political, throughout these years in developing civil society, thus offering support to groups of citizens, organising seminars, exchanges and other types of activities.

The basic past cross-border co-operation initiatives in the field of economic co-operation included the work of the chambers of commerce and umbrella organisations of the various industries. Business contacts have been maintained, even during the wars of the 1990s, although they have clearly significantly diminished with respect to the past due to the conflicts, imposition of trade and other barriers and local crises, while smuggling and organised crime profited from the absence of rule of law and institutions capable of enforcing the law.

Due to weak markets and other specific economic (and political) problems, however, economic co-operation within the region and between Southeast European and Western countries has focused mainly on trade and foreign direct investment. Most active have been the Italian, Austrian, Turkish, Greek and German institutions, who also are among the leading investors in the region. In total, however, the overall flow of foreign direct investment to the region southeast of Hungary has been extremely low. Over the whole

---

8 The Tuzla conference in Bosnia-Herzegovina in 1998, and the Budapest conference in 1999.

1989–1998 period, net inflows of foreign direct investment into four Southeast European countries (Albania, Croatia, Macedonia and FRY, thus excluding Bosnia for which comparable data are not available) have amounted to only US-$ 3.672 million, which represents only 4.5 per cent of total foreign direct investment that has gone into 27 transition economies[9].

There have been more positive examples of cross-border co-operation, such as the free trade agreement between FYROM and FRY signed in 1997 or similar agreements concluded in recent years among some other countries in Southeastern Europe. Slovenia has a free trade agreement with Bosnia-Herzegovina, Croatia and FYROM, and similarly FYROM has a free trade agreement with all neighbouring countries (including Bulgaria).

The most significant example of really indigenous cross-border co-operation in Southeastern Europe, besides business contacts – including forms of organised crime – is the strong integration of Herzeg-Bosna with Croatia during the Tudjman era, which indeed implied very close integration in terms of military policy, finance, the pensions system and other areas. Similarly, there was close integration between the Republika Srpska and FRY during the years of the war in Bosnia (1992–1995). In both cases, many forms of co-operation – such as in the field of trade – have remained important still today. Both of these models, however, rather than helping democracy and the rule of law in the region, can be better described as systems detrimental to the integration of Southeastern Europe. The existence of these parallel systems was a very strong obstacle to the integration of Bosnia-Herzegovina. Despite an apparent change in politics over the last few years, their profound negative consequences are still today very much felt.

The EU Regional Approach as well as the efforts of SECI before 1999 have contributed to developing cross-border co-operation in the economic sphere only to a very limited extent. Some projects in the field of infrastructure were initiated already under the umbrella of SECI, which set up a project group to improve the development of transport infrastructure along the main international routes. The participating states concluded a Memorandum of Understanding on the Facilitation of International Road Transport of Goods in the SECI region. Considering the large differences regarding the state and quality of infrastructure in the respective Southeast European countries, in the future it is paramount to improve transport, railways and telecommunication links, particularly in the underdeveloped areas (Albania, Kosovo, Montenegro, certain parts of Bosnia, Dalmatia, southern Serbia, Romania and Bulgaria).

One example of positive experience in cross-border co-operation from outside Southeastern Europe is that of the German-Polish border town of Guben/Gubin which is

9   EBRD (1999).

part of a "Euroregion". In these towns, both sides have closely integrated their respective municipal fire departments, which means that both sides jointly co-ordinate the purchase of new equipment in order to make it mutually compatible. They also hold joint exercises. The towns have established a special border crossing to which the two city mayors have keys. This enables the fire departments to cross the border without any bureaucracy whatsoever in case of emergencies. This example shows that for such immediate forms of cross-border co-operation, central governments need to pass a certain amount of authority to the local level in order to make cross-border co-operation work. Unfortunately, there are no such examples in the Balkans and the central governments are usually hesitant to give up sovereignty in similar areas. On the other hand, local governments often do not dare request greater liberties and authority but tend to look towards their respective capitals for support, rather than seek ways to develop their own capacities.

What do these very different experiences with cross-border co-operation in Southeastern Europe during the past decade suggest? While the experiences with cross-border co-operation were positive in those cases where the initiatives got off the ground, the overall social and political impact has been rather limited and is becoming noticeable only perhaps today, and rather gradually. In many cases cross-border co-operation in Southeast European countries suffered from a lack of sincerity of the sides involved or a lack of interest and political vision. Those initiatives dependent on foreign donors have often not proven sustainable once the funding ended.

The international organisations operating in the field often failed to co-operate and inform each other about their own activities, leading to a doubling of efforts and to competition between international NGOs, who themselves compete for internationally funded projects. Another problem is posed by the incompatibility of the interests of different players such as NGOs inside and outside the region, governments, regional players and economic interest groups.

The most important institutional factors which today seem detrimental to cross-border co-operation in Southeastern Europe include: the lack of legal security, which is having a direct negative impact on investment, trade and other fields of cross-border co-operation; insufficient integration of legal standards; failure to implement the rule of law; visa requirements and excessively long waiting periods; non-transparent, large, and unreformed bureaucracies; and unclear constitutional frameworks in some states or regional entities (e. g., Montenegro or Kosovo).

Among the cultural and political factors impeding closer links among Southeast European countries we should mention the lack of interest among the main actors in Southeastern Europe to implement cross-border co-operation; the frequent focus on short-term issues and the lack of vision and clear prospective; the profound and long-lasting effects of nationalist feelings and ideology; the low degree of specialist training among local actors in some countries; and the patronage systems and diffused corruption. Although there are enormous differences among the attitudes of the individual Southeast European countries, there is still a dominant tendency to give preference to contacts between the national and Western governments, rather than to co-operation within the region at a decentralised level.

The key problems in education remain those in the field of school and university exchanges and in the field of nationalist history teaching. An often antiquated pedagogic approach to teaching that does not convey contradictions and pluralistic views remains an important factor detrimental to cross-border co-operation. The general co-operation between education institutions has been weak. However, the existing international exchange programmes for students from other countries have also only had limited attraction. This has been particularly true since the wars in the former Yugoslavia, with the possible exception of Albania, which always maintained a large number of university slots for Kosovar students.

There are also economic factors which have hampered cross-border co-operation in Southeastern Europe and still represent an important obstacle for including: the unstable economic framework; unfavourable investment conditions due to the high political risk in the whole region; loss of regional markets through disintegration and wars; high customs duties and other trade barriers; high levels of taxation; corruption at all levels; unreliable conduct of business; high interest rates; and inefficient banking systems. There are generally very limited financial resources to implement cross-border programmes. In some Southeast European countries, this is also due to rather centralised systems of governance (e.g., in Croatia or FYROM) which limits the budgetary autonomy of local authorities and prevents them from collecting local taxes. Under such circumstances, there is often no willingness to use the limited resources for cross-border initiatives, as there are usually priorities which are considered to be more important. However, not all of these factors apply equally to all of the states in Southeastern Europe.

Regarding the political actors, the key problem areas for progress with cross-border co-operation are found in Serbia, Bosnia-Herzegovina, Kosovo and Montenegro. The role of each of these actors is very different, however, but the key detrimental factor remains Serbia. As long as the country continues to be governed by the political parties presently in power, which do not seem willing to actively contribute to improving relations with their neighbours, little progress can be achieved in cross-border co-operation in Southeastern Europe.

In Bosnia-Herzegovina, Kosovo and Montenegro, the unresolved constitutional status and fragile institutional systems play an important role in impeding closer cross-

234

border co-operation. These three entities, however, are represented at the Stability Pact – Bosnia-Herzegovina as a sovereign state, Kosovo through the UN, while Montenegro for the moment only has observer status but has the right to participate in the working tables. These actors have all expressed their desire to promote and support cross-border co-operation, so in theory, the main precondition for its implementation – political readiness – seems to be present (the notable exception, as already mentioned, being Serbia). Overall, there are a number of structural problems, other than wars and institutional barriers, which have hampered cross-border co-operation in Southeastern Europe during the past decade. However, there are also a limited number of factors beneficial for cross-border co-operation. While the institutional framework and the judiciary in many countries still pose severe problems, the political class in most Southeast European countries has understood that the future and welfare of their countries depends on fast moves to improve the institutions, promote regional and European integration, and get actively involved in the Stability Pact process, although in some countries this is taking somewhat longer than in others. All Southeast European countries (except Serbia) are presently active in promoting cross-border co-operation through the Stability Pact initiatives, and all sovereign countries (except FRY) are also members in the NATO Partnership for Peace Program and have been holding numerous joint exercises throughout the Balkans region. The positive economic and cultural factors include: the inherited or newly established trade links among some Southeast European countries; the clear willingness to overcome regional isolation in border regions; promotion of regional economy and cultural life; and the expressed interest to improve infrastructure connections throughout the Balkans. The main groups promoting cross-border co-operation include the business community, the intellectual elite and potentially the younger generation.

III Strategies of major international organisations

Several international organisations have been engaged in promoting cross-border co-operation in Southeastern Europe. Before 1999, the best-known initiatives were the EU Regional Approach, which also involved infrastructure and aid programmes such as Phare, OBNOVA, TAFKO and ECHO. In addition, a major initiative to promote cross-border co-operation in this region was and remains SECI. Since December 1999, the new CARA programme of the EU has taken effect (recently renamed CARDS), through which some US-$ 5 billion is to be provided over the 2001–2006 period for the five countries of the Western Balkans. The Agency for the Reconstruction of Southeastern Europe has also set up office in Thessaloniki and is going to take over the tasks from some of the other EU institutions.

While most of these programmes are primarily focusing on internal reconstruction and humanitarian aid, the infrastructure projects are of fundamental importance for cross-border co-operation, as there are many projects which do have a cross-border character, involving two or more countries from Southeastern Europe. This also applies to the assistance offered for institution-building through other projects, such as the WEU's MAPE in Albania, or the various programmes of the Council of Europe or the OSCE in advising legislators or officials in the government and public administration. A key element in these EU and other European initiatives is the direct link between infrastructure development programmes and cross-border projects, a principle that has often been implemented and is becoming common practice.

SECI, initiated by the USA in 1996, was similar in its concept, but it never really was able to gather the massive support that the Stability Pact received, in part because the circumstances a few years ago were quite different from today's. SECI's objective was to enhance regional co-operation, and thus stability among the countries of Southeastern Europe "by encouraging co-operative and trans-boundary solutions to shared economic and environmental problems."[10] Under the auspices of the participating countries, SECI seeks to address relevant development aspects of the region by improving information exchange, planning multi-state programmes and attracting private capital to complement bilateral and multilateral sources of funding.

SECI sees itself not as "an integration group" but as "a flexible framework for launching and executing concrete projects and programmes of interest to the participating states."[11] Its participants identify, through the work of the Agenda Committee, projects of interest to two or more countries which are consistent and not duplicating work underway in other economic initiatives. SECI then tries to create the environment conducive to the implementation of these projects and seeks to secure the means to implement them.

Other important institutions have also been involved in cross-border co-operation initiatives, such as the UN Economic Commission for Europe (UN-ECE), which is offering technical support.[12] Through its network of contacts throughout the region and its conventions, norms, standards and guidelines, the UN-ECE has the means to facilitate and simplify transfrontier operations and to provide mechanisms for solving problems. SECI has kept its activities to a manageable number of well-defined proj-

---

10 SECI; Methods of Work, http://www.unece.org/seci/sec_meth.htm.
11 SECI; Methods of Work, http://www.unece.org/seci/sec_meth.htm.
12 M. Uvalic: Regional Co-operation – Lessons Learned, Paper prepared for the UN-ECE Annual Conference, Geneva, 4 May 2000; revised version forthcoming in a special issue on EU enlargement of the International Political Science Review.

ects which have shown positive results, largely because a precondition for pursuing these projects was the explicit interest of the parties involved.

Both institutions are now closely co-operating within the Stability Pact, and SECI may be integrated into the Stability Pact. One essential difference between SECI and the Stability Pact is that while SECI worked to bring local actors together at points of common interest, with the intention to create permanent joint institutions and mechanisms of co-operation among these countries, the Stability Pact can be considered as more of an institutionalised declaration of intent by the EU and G7 regarding South-eastern Europe.

In this sense SECI had a demand-driven approach in which a common prior understanding of the participants was the starting point for SECI initiatives. The Stability Pact follows a more supply-driven approach, in the sense that international donors have pledged large funds. The Stability Pact is charged with finding appropriate partners for implementation of given projects. At the same time, the round-table character of the Stability Pact gives the recipient countries and some larger NGOs the ability to give feedback to donors and Stability Pact partners. In this sense the Stability Pact is more patronising than SECI, largely due to its central mediating role and strong influence between donors and recipients.

The Stability Pact is under massive public and political pressure to present successful outcomes of its operations. For this purpose it had to identify problems from the perspective of the donors, who usually have clear guidelines for spending their money and then try to find appropriate partners for the implementation. These partners are often either the national governments or international organisations, which then perform the role of a mediator between the donors and the local NGOs or initiatives by other organisations. SECI, in contrast, could afford to bring the local actors to the table first and then formulate a strategy and to look for possible donors after finding a common ground.

There is a fine line between both approaches, however, determined more by time, public pressure to provide concrete results and by the presence of funds than by the general mission or strategy of either SECI or the Stability Pact, which are similar. With the planned stronger integration of SECI into the Stability Pact, the demand-driven approach of SECI and the supply-driven approach of the Stability Pact are going to provide a more complete and supplementary framework.

The Stability Pact's staff of roughly two-dozen people attempts to co-ordinate the efforts of donors with players on the ground, NGOs and international organisations, thus functioning as a clearing house between those involved in a broader process of development and integration. The reasons for this shift can be found in the Kosovo crisis and the subsequent understanding by the G7 and the EU that a strategic approach is needed toward stabilisation of the entire region. This was also a lesson learned from the failure to prevent the conflict in Kosovo. Therefore the shift from a demand-driven to a supply-driven approach also derived from the understanding that delays in implementation are counterproductive for overall regional stability.

The main instrument of the Stability Pact is the Regional Table, which is the principal co-ordinating body, including the governments participating in the Table as well as international financial and other institutions. Under the level of the Regional Table, three Working Tables exist on the issues of Democratisation and Human Rights (Working Table I), Economic Reconstruction, Development and Co-operation (Working Table II) and Security Issues (Working Table III). Those aspects that touch upon the competencies of more than one working table are presented to the Regional Table which deals with cross-table issues.

The list of projects of the Stability Pact looks impressive compared to those of SECI, but one should not overlook the fact that most of these projects are in their initial stage of implementation. Moreover, the absolute majority of these proposals has been presented by Western or international institutions (the Council of Europe, the OSCE and others), whereas, with the exception of infrastructure development projects, very few have come from the region itself. This is particularly evident in the case of Working Tables I and III, in which international rather than local organisations clearly dominate.

Moreover, the bulk of cross-border co-operation initiatives presented by NGOs involves western NGOs. There are not many local NGOs that are actively involved in cross-border co-operation with other regional partner NGOs and that are applying for funds themselves to implement them. The relationship between Western and domestic NGOs can still be described as "paternalistic", in the sense that it is mostly western NGOs who provide financing for these projects, but they obviously depend on co-operation with local organisations for their implementation. The local initiatives and grass-roots groups themselves have not yet become significant players or partners to donors themselves. Due to the very unfavourable overall economic situation in most countries in the region, funds have been provided almost exclusively by foreign foundations and donors, rather than local ones.

Even though the Funding Conference at the end of March 2000 in Brussels resulted in pledges that were higher than the cost of submitted projects, pledges obviously do not guarantee effective provision of funds. The implementation of the individual projects will depend on the conclusion of contracts between parties involved. These packages, moreover, already take into account existing financing programmes of the EU, EIB, World Bank and EBRD and past commitments of some other donors. This explains why a number of projects are already fully financed, while others require limited additional financing.

IV The Stability Pact: From strategy towards implementation

The Stability Pact for Southeastern Europe intended to present a comprehensive strategy to support the institutional and economic development in Southeastern Europe with a broader perspective towards European integration. The structure chosen included the three Working Tables, which coordinate the activities in the different fields.

The *Working Table on Democratisation and Human Rights* (Working Table I) has been designed "to assist the countries of Southeastern Europe to develop and protect institutions and the sense of civic responsibility that is essential to bring the region closer to Euro-Atlantic institutions."[13] To develop priorities for activity in this field, the Working Table at its first meeting in October 1999 in Geneva designated the following specific areas to focus on, and identified a lead sponsor for each task force:
- Human Rights and Ethnic Minorities (Slovenia);
- Good Governance (Council of Europe);
- Refugee Return (UNHCR);
- Gender (OSCE);
- Media (UK);
- Education and Youth – The Enhanced Graz Process (Austria);
- Parliamentary Exchanges (Royaumont).

Within Table I, many projects are not explicitly related to cross-border co-operation, but due to co-operation among the different countries in identifying and applying national policies, they do have a cross-border dimension.

The sponsor of the *Human Rights and National Minorities* Task Force, Slovenia, in close co-operation with the Council of Europe, has developed a package of proposals highlighting the need for ethnic reconciliation in the region. The task force aims, among other things, to stress mutual respect among national groups as a way towards establishing more democratic government and institutions.

The return of refugees and displaced persons is an extremely important related issue. The recent political changes in Croatia suggest that it may be possible to carry out major new initiatives involving, in particular, the return of refugees to Croatia and Bosnia-Herzegovina. Since successful refugee return programmes demand the creation of infrastructure, including employment opportunities, the need for resources is particularly high. To ensure the broadest possible participation from action agencies and potential donors, and to encourage quick action to take advantage of improved circumstances, Bodo Hombach proposed the creation of a special steering board to focus on this issue.

---

13 Special Coordinator of the Stability Pact for Southeastern Europe: Report of the Special Coordinator for the Regional Funding Conference for Southeast Europe, Brussels, 29/30 March 2000, Brussels, 27 May 2000, p. 10.

The Task Force on *Good Governance* has developed three areas of concentration: local government, the creation of effective ombudsman institutions and public administration/administrative law. The task force identified institutional and training needs, and countries of the region presented their plans to strengthen the role of local government. It also explored the expansion of cross-border co-operation between local governments in an effort to promote functioning regions. A special meeting on the functioning of the ombudsman office was held in December 1999 in Budapest with the aim of helping to ensure that effective, independent ombudsmen will exist in all countries of the region in the medium-term future.

The *Gender* Task Force has given its highest priorities to national programmes to empower women politically, and increase the representation of women in political life. The initial meeting of the Task Force in Sarajevo was well attended by representatives from the region, including local NGOs dealing with problems such as the abuse of women. According to Hombach, "the mere existence of this Task Force is facilitating local NGOs' efforts to develop regional contacts and reinforce their self-confidence."[14]

The *Media* Task Force is negotiating a Media Charter that would protect the independent media and enhance its professional standing. It developed a number of proposals to help train, protect and improve the quality of the independent media.

The Task Force on *Education and Youth* has identified six priority areas including higher education, history teaching, general education and training, youth, vocational education and education for democratic citizenship. These activities build on the existing exchange networks between universities in the region and also in western Europe. These exchanges were and are of crucial importance to overcome ethnic hatred and to build a common future in Southeastern Europe.

The EU should work to promote more direct school exchanges between the different Southeast European countries by providing small funds for such events or longer travels to these countries. The funds should be provided for schools engaging in long-term cross-border co-operation with other schools in Southeastern Europe.

The *Parliamentary Exchanges* Task Force, within the Royaumont Process, has developed a priority list for promoting parliamentary co-operation with training and exchange programmes for newly elected members of parliament and staff. Other priority projects include a conference of speakers of parliament, proposed by Croatia, and an MP network for Southeastern Europe, proposed by the East-West Institute.

The Serbian democratic opposition and Montenegro are involved in the activities of Working Table I through the Szeged Process, initiated by the Hungarian government

---

14   Special Coordinator of the Stability Pact for Southeastern Europe: op. cit., Brussels, 27 May 2000, p. 11.

and the Stability Pact in October 1999. The overall objective of the Szeged Process is to incorporate the democratic forces of the country into the Stability Pact programmes, thus further contributing to the democratisation process of the whole region. The initial meeting of the Szeged Process provided an opportunity for democratically-elected opposition mayors from FRY to outline their needs and initiate contacts with potential partners. The Hungarian Government established a foundation to support this process on a continuous basis. At a meeting of the Stability Pact in Thessaloniki in mid-June 2000, the Serbian opposition, represented through the Group G-17 Plus, proposed a comprehensive package of measures to be taken after a change of government in Serbia.

Thus, under existing constraints, the only possible cross-border co-operation measures that can be promoted by the West in Serbia are direct humanitarian aid and political (material, technical) support of the democratic forces in Serbia – the opposition, opposition-held cities, the independent media and opposition NGOs. Although this type of measure is not cross-border co-operation in a strict sense, support of the opposition forces in Serbia can contribute to changing the overall political situation in the country, in this way also indirectly facilitating future cross-border co-operation between Serbia and its neighbours.

The strategic aim of the Working Table on Economic Reconstruction, Development and Co-operation (Working Table II) is to "promote greater prosperity and confidence throughout the region and progressive integration into the European and global economy."[15] The first meeting of Working Table II, which took place in October last year in Bari, focused on a variety of processes in many different fields: regional development, integration into European structures, infrastructure, private sector development, and trade and investment. In January 2000, the Business Advisory Council of the Stability Pact, a body comprising about 20 top-level representatives of major private sector companies from Europe, the US, Canada, Japan and Southeastern Europe, held its first meeting in Berlin.

A large number of infrastructure projects of the Working Table has been presented by the European Investment Bank. Out of the 400 initial submissions, 35 projects were chosen for the "Quick Start Package", whereas 50 submissions were qualified as short-term projects. The projects have a marked regional character (either because they have a direct effect on more than one country or for their demonstration value which will benefit all the countries in the region). They can reasonably be expected to be implemented in the next couple of years (therefore some long-term programmes, such as on

---

15 Special Coordinator of the Stability Pact for Southeastern Europe: op. cit., Brussels, 27 May 2000, p. 11.

the Adriatic Highway, are not included). Most of these projects include road and railway construction and rehabilitation, building of power grids and pipelines, waste water clearing systems, construction of bridges, etc.

Infrastructure development and to a lesser extent the protection of the environment play a significant part in the Stability Pacts plans. Better infrastructure will facilitate the exchange of goods and services; it will bring people closer together and out of their geographic and psychological isolation. Environmental protection will increase the tourist industries' chances to get back on their feet. Furthermore, it contributes to economic development, especially in those countries lacking foreign direct investment due to bad infrastructure and high risks. Thus, the building of secure power grids, roads, railroads and telecommunications lines remains among the most important measures to provide the basis for economic recovery. A considerable change of quality can be noticed with regard to most of the infrastructure projects. While throughout the 1990s many of these projects seemed unlikely to be implemented due to lack of public funds, many of them have already been launched within the quick-start-package.

The European Bank for Reconstruction and Development, within its strategy to promote Private Sector Development in Southeastern Europe, has also proposed initiatives with a regional dimension, such as guarantee and insurance schemes lowering the risk of cross-border trade and investment, facilities strengthening bank financing for local businesses bidding for infrastructure projects and a variety of financial and technical support schemes for small businesses. Most of these schemes can be implemented relatively quickly (in 2000 and 2001).

There has also been a major initiative on trade liberalisation. A first meeting of the countries of the Stability Pact on the elimination of trade barriers and enhancing trade co-operation was held in mid-January 2000 in Skopje, where a working group was created to evaluate current trade regimes in Southeast European countries, promote greater accessibility of trade-related information, explore the means for facilitating border crossing procedures and improve customs services. Five specific tasks of the working group have been specified: the promotion of the transparency of trade regimes and the identification of impediments to trade, the examination of existing and future regional trade arrangements, the identification of projects focusing on trade facilitation and promotion of intra-regional trade, the monitoring of progress in the facilitation of trade in the region, and the exchange of information on the development of trade relations between the EU and Southeastern Europe.

Finally, the *Working Table on Security Issues* (Working Table III) has been designed to promote mutual trust and security in Southeastern Europe. The aim is to enhance transparency and predictability in the military field and the internal security sectors. It is particularly committed to strengthening co-operation and good neighbourly relations in the region. The Working Table focuses on the following key areas: defence economics and demobilisation; arms control and non-proliferation; the fight against illicit transfers of light arms and small weapons; the augmentation of military contacts and co-operation and de-mining activities.

The Working Table has also created a sub-table on Justice and Home Affairs. This sub-table supports the creation of a legitimate, fair and effective network of police authority, an accessible, independent and impartial judicial system, and a transparent and legitimate penal system.

The Stability Pact has created a great deal of enthusiasm among many local politicians. It is clearly visible that there are already numerous contacts at the political level. Many NGOs are involved in projects in neighbouring countries and will play an important role in that regard in the future. Such a role would also be applicable to the political scene of some Southeast European countries where NGOs perform important functions presently not yet handled by the opposition parties.

From the overview of ongoing or planned projects on cross-border co-operation within the Stability Pact initiative – a more detailed list of proposed projects is given in the appendix – it emerges that in many specific areas there are very similar, if not identical, initiatives and proposals advanced by different institutions, resulting in overlaps without any clear coordination or division of competencies among the various institutions. The Stability Pact offices are trying to act as a global coordinating body, but they are obviously also dependent on the willingness to exchange information on the donors. Nevertheless, the mentioned overlap of initiatives may not necessarily be a handicap, as the enormous amount of similar projects may finally produce more permanent and more valid forms of cross-border co-operation in Southeastern Europe.

With respect to those undertaken in the past, present initiatives on cross-border co-operation are much more numerous. International donors, the EU and the Stability Pact are favouring projects with a cross-border dimension and have begun to make funding dependent on joint projects. However, given their initial phase of implementation, their impact is yet to be seen.

A crucial problem remains financing. The dependency on project funds under which many NGOs work often makes it difficult for them to maintain a sustainable strategy over a long period of time. This leads to rivalry between NGOs for funds, which is detrimental for co-operation. Indeed, projects have proven to bring actors from different countries together only when such exchanges were paid for by the donors. Domestic interest for such co-operation remains generally weak unless encouraged from the outside. Thus, it has become part of the Stability Pact strategy to include cross-border co-operation dimensions in the definition of different projects in which local NGOs can participate.

The spill-over effects of many ongoing initiatives on cross-border co-operation will not be visible before some time, but they are still extremely important for strengthening links among Southeast European countries in the medium and longer term. A number of cross-border regional projects for the improvement of infrastructure in the whole Southeast European region, as proposed at the Funding Conference in Brussels in March 2000, should indeed facilitate the achievement of these longer term objectives, which represent the core of the new approach of the international community towards Southeastern Europe. In the field of economic co-operation, similarly, the implementation of the EU recommendation on general trade liberalisation and the creation of a regional free trade organisation ought to prove beneficial for intensifying trade and other economic links among these countries. Many enterprises are already establishing contacts with firms in neighbouring countries; contacts which are likely to intensify in the future.

V EU policies and cross-border co-operation in Southeastern Europe

With respect to instruments available to promote cross-border co-operation in Southeastern Europe, in addition to all the on-going projects within the Stability Pact, there are others implicitly incorporated in the EU Stabilisation and Association Process. In this newest phase of the relations between the EU and Southeastern Europe, strong emphasis is again placed on promotion of all forms of co-operation among Southeast European countries in the immediate future, while these countries are preparing for eventual EU membership. The European Commission is in the process of establishing a single EU assistance programme for Southeastern Europe through its Reconstruction Agency. As already mentioned, the new CARDS assistance programme for Southeastern Europe is to replace the existing programmes Phare and OBNOVA. An essential feature of these EU programmes is that they are conducted under strict rules of conditionality, which ought to be an important mechanism for influencing the participants to implement their contractual duties, but also for carrying forward the main objectives of the Stability Pact and intensifying various forms of cross-border co-operation.

Nevertheless, on the negative side, we should also consider the manifold consequences for cross-border co-operation of the process of EU enlargement. One of the main problems Southeast European (but also Central and East European) countries face before EU accession is that they are being flooded with EU agricultural products (which are usually subsidised under the Common Agricultural Policy). The agricultural producers in Southeastern Europe face harsh competition which they often cannot cope with. The countries themselves are hesitant to introduce protectionist measures, because that would jeopardise their accession to the EU, despite the fact that the EU has maintained a number of restrictions on agricultural imports from Southeast European (but also Central and East European) countries.

A second issue concerns the border and visa regime. While waiting for EU membership, several Southeast European countries have introduced visas for citizens from neighbouring countries. In this way, these countries are closing their outside borders, while expecting the enlargement of Schengen, although this has an obvious negative impact on cross-border co-operation. Visas are particularly difficult to obtain for some Southeast European countries which are presently negotiating a Stabilisation and Association Agreement with the EU. This would be an ideal moment for the Commission to obtain a more flexible approach that could well serve as an example for other neighbouring countries.

A third area of problems concerns the poor state of the economy in most Southeast European countries. If the country which is presently in the most unfavourable position – Croatia – continues its policies of overvalued currency and lack of structural reforms, it will have difficulties in competing on EU markets. Since the situation in most other Southeast European countries is even less favourable due to the absence of more radical measures to increase competitiveness, EU accession is likely to severely harm domestic production.

A fourth problem regards the conflicting nature of bilateralism and regionalism. To what extent have EU policies actually stimulated regional and cross-border co-operation among transition economies? Variable-speed integration policies, based on strict conditionality and bilateralism have been the main features of EU policies towards transition countries throughout the 1990s, but by de facto imposing competition – not co-operation – among these countries (e.g., through the Copenhagen Criteria), the attainment of some key objectives of regional co-operation have frequently been undermined.

A final problem concerns the effects of the fragmentation of some existing regional groupings – cross-border links that have been established during the past decade – once accession takes place.[16] Given the variable-speed integration policies of the EU, the division of the applicants into different groups will also split existing regional groupings when various phases of EU enlargement take place. The first group of transition economies entering the EU will have to renounce to their free-trade agreements with other countries once they join (e.g., Slovenia with Croatia, Bosnia-Herzegovina and Macedonia). In this way, external barriers on trade will be introduced among countries which have had a free trade agreement for several years. The variable EU enlargement process will therefore imply the introduction of various trade restric-

---

16 M. Uvalic: Regional Co-operation – Lessons Learned, op. cit.

tions, which might have adverse effects, at least in the short run: "It is thus ironical that the European Commission sought to promote regional arrangements in the early 1990s only to destroy them through the enlargement process itself."[17]

VI Recommendations

Considering the large variety of beginning activities in the field of cross-border co-operation, it is still too early to give overtly general conclusions. The process of Southeast European integration is a long-lasting process, and small efforts help forge the regional consensus for moves in this direction. Most of the cross-border initiatives are such efforts.

Cross-border co-operation among Southeast European countries can contribute to the solution of some existing problems in the region, and the EU can do a lot to stimulate such efforts through the easing of customs and visa regimes, promotion of cultural exchanges, language and technical training, coordination of inter-parliamentary co-operation, creation of joint institutions of professional organisations (chambers of commerce, trade unions) and by offering other forms of technical assistance. The Southeast European countries can themselves offer a major contribution to such efforts through the creation of a Southeastern Europe free-trade area, intensifying political contacts, cultural exchanges, increased border traffic and institutional co-operation among governments regarding law enforcement and the implementation of common rules against money laundering, smuggling or corruption.

Agreement on promotion of cross-border co-operation as an objective, however, cannot mean that all such initiatives are effectively useful, as clearly illustrated by past experiences. There is a need to increase efficiency in cross-border co-operation and avoid potentially counterproductive effects. The following is a list of concrete recommendations for future policies.

1. *Regional structures*: It would be useful to promote the creation of regional institutions specifically designed for Southeastern Europe. New forms of regional economic linkages, as was the case in post-war Europe, would facilitate cross-border co-operation among countries in the region. As the Marshall Plan was designed to foster regional integration and was backed up by the creation of new Europe-wide regional institutions which were to facilitate intra-regional trade (such as the OECD and the European Payments Union), regional structures are also needed in South-

---

17 M. Lavigne: The Economics of Transition – From Socialist Economy to Market Economy, 2nd edition, Houndsmill, Basingstoke: Macmillan Press, and New York: St. Martin's Press, p. 210.

246

eastern Europe today, structures designed to facilitate and promote the expansion of trade and other economic links among Southeast European countries. A multilateral credit mechanism would be particularly helpful, with the function of extending credit facilities specifically for such purposes, backed by some credible financial organisation (e.g., the EBRD). Alternatively, as suggested in 1996 by the former governor of the National Bank of Yugoslavia, Dragoslav Avramovic, a common regional fund could be created, whose initial capital would consist of the still undivided foreign exchange reserves of former Yugoslavia that would serve as collateral to attract additional capital on international financial markets.[18]

2. *Inclusion of Serbia*: One of the major problems remains Serbia, which is still not included in the large majority of the present cross-border initiatives. The exclusion of Serbia (FRY) is at the root of many deep contradictions that severely limit the effectiveness of current initiatives.[19] Regional structures in Southeastern Europe will not function unless a way is found to include Serbia as well in all undertakings, as this will indeed determine the success some current regional projects in Southeastern Europe. While this is partly already being done through the Szeged Process, keeping the complexity of the present situation in FRY (not just in Serbia, but also in Kosovo and in Montenegro) in mind, political change and the democratisation of the country is the only permanent long-term solution to the numerous problems it is presently facing. These can be seen as the necessary condition for implementing more intensive economic, political, and other forms of co-operation in the whole Southeast European region as well. More substantial Western support of the democratic opposition in Serbia is therefore strongly recommended.

3. *Trade liberalisation*: The EU can contribute further to intensifying cross-border co-operation by lifting trade barriers in a more generous way than has been the case to date. Southeast European countries are insignificant partners for the EU, so it can easily afford major trade liberalisation. Although a lot has already been done, especially with the recent EU measures on trade liberalisation adopted in mid-2000, which also included duty-free entry of certain products from Montenegro, the EU should consider granting further trade preferences, as the effects would be marginal for the EU while extremely beneficial for Southeastern Europe, particularly in the agricultural sector where most of the restrictions still remain.

4. *Visas*: The EU should similarly consider relaxing visa requirements for all Southeastern European countries, in order to keep the borders open between those countries

---

18 M. Uvalic: Regional Co-operation in South-East Europe, op. cit.

19 D. Heimerl, Y. Rizopoulos, N. Vukadinovic: Contradictions et limites des politiques de reconstruction dans les Balkans, in: Revue d'Études Comparatives Est-Ouest, Vol. 30, No. 4, pp. 201–244.

who eventually will become Schengen territory and their neighbours in the region. In addition, given that some Southeast European countries have maintained rather stringent conditions for obtaining visas for neighbouring countries, the EU should also consider explicitly requesting, from countries negotiating a Stabilisation and Association Agreement, the relaxation of visa requirements for their Southeast European neighbours.

5. *Decentralised governance*: The example of positive experience in cross-border co-operation from outside Southeastern Europe cited before – close collaboration between the fire departments in the German-Polish border town of Guben/Gubin – suggests that it is paramount to strengthen the local governments and administration. Local and central officials from Southeastern Europe should therefore be invited to existing Euro-regions to study the positive experiences made so far, and to help them apply similar policies in their respective countries.

6. *Bottom-up approach to financing*: The level of EU assistance obviously depends on the concrete area of action, although in many cases the local level is likely to be most effective, showing results down the line. But considering the functioning of the EU itself, it would be unrealistic to expect that a wise distribution of funds will necessarily take place. Therefore, it would be advisable that much of the funding be channelled through local NGOs or the local administration, or that projects be implemented through city partnerships. This does not mean that there is no need for substantial assistance at the central and regional levels as well, especially in certain key areas such as infrastructure development which can only be handled at a higher level, but so far these have been the dominant channels of assistance and therefore must be supplemented, whenever possible, by funding of local institutions.

   In recommending a bottom-up approach to financing cross-border co-operation initiatives, experience has shown that all too frequently information on the availability of funds offered by Western governments, institutions and NGOs does not circulate if sent to central ministries or even the relevant competent offices in Southeast European states. Information on Western funding frequently does not arrive to the main potential beneficiaries which are usually the most active in developing cross-border co-operation. It remains in drawers and arrives after the expiry of deadlines, or it is passed on only to selected institutions and individuals. Certainly there must be ways to increase the transparency of information on available funds – via the Internet for example –, which could contribute to more competition in applying for funds and a better channelling of resources.

7. *Minimal self-finance*: In this context, it could also prove useful to introduce the principle of obligatory minimal self-finance. However unpopular this measure may sound at first sight, it could be required from local NGOs when applying for West-

ern funding to secure a minimum amount of own funds. Even a very small percentage of contributions of their own would increase responsibility in the use of resources, thus also contributing to more effective implementation of projects.

8. *Preference to local projects*: Presently there is a general dominance of projects implemented by international organisations and western NGOs, and much less from the countries in Southeastern Europe. Though the quality of submitted projects has most frequently determined such a choice, it seems even more important to involve national agents from all over Southeastern Europe in projects on cross-border co-operation more actively. Therefore, projects submitted by institutions from Southeastern Europe should be given priority in the future.

While the EU, its member states and the international community can certainly help promote cross-border co-operation in many ways, the main tasks necessarily rest with the Southeast European countries themselves. All of the discussed areas of cross-border co-operation are essential for further developing links in Southeastern Europe, but the key to the success of such initiatives remains the political willingness of states, NGOs and other local institutions to collaborate and implement cross-border co-operation. Solutions imposed from the outside have their obvious limits, as clearly illustrated by the Bosnian experience during the past four years. For various reasons – many of which have been determined directly by the events of the past decade – in Southeastern Europe today there is a strong need for "national ownership" of policies. This problem must not be underestimated. Externally imposed solutions, which have become rather popular,[20] risk to be ineffective or to produce very limited or counterproductive results.

Appendix – Current projects and proposals on cross-border co-operation

Within the framework of the Stability Pact for Southeastern Europe, a number of initiatives have been launched which ought to stimulate cross-border co-operation in the forthcoming period. Below, a list of current and planned projects is given, grouped into seven main subject areas. This list is obviously not fully comprehensive, but includes only the most important initiatives.

---

20   CEPS: A System for Post-War South-East Europe, Working Document No. 131, Brussels.

1. Civil society and media

Under the umbrella of the Task Force on Human Rights and Minorities of the Stability Pact, the Council of Europe proposed holding a series of Civil Society conferences. These conferences are intended to bring NGOs together in order to contribute substantially to the process of democratisation in the countries of the region – especially by enabling civic participation in social and political processes.

The European Training Foundation and the Royaumont Process proposed an action plan to promote the culture and practice of social and civil dialogue. They intend to achieve this aim by reviewing the current situation in each of the countries or regions, organising study visits, preparing cross-country analyses, holding a regional conference and national seminars in each of the countries, publishing surveys and cross-country reports and by developing an electronic network and a Website. It is too early to judge whether this strategy will show concrete results.

Since minority issues are of particular importance to good neighbourly relations and thus for cross-border co-operation, the Stability Pact has made these issues one of the top priorities of its activities. It tries to compensate for the previous lack of contacts in the region over minority rights through a variety of projects.

The Council of Europe and the OSCE High Commissioner for National Minorities have taken over the coordination of a campaign to raise awareness, aiming to improve ethnic relations in multiethnic societies of the region (although this runs counter to the present de facto tendency to create ethnic states in the region). The campaign is designed to promote the multicultural nature of societies – especially the awareness of the values and principles of multiethnic and multicultural society – and democratic citizenship. The campaign will rely mostly on structures in participating countries themselves. The intention is to set up a campaign committee in each country.

The Council of Europe also presented a project to review positive practices to promote full equality. It aims to promote and stimulate the positive practices of legal and de facto solutions of protecting minority rights. The countries will be invited to undertake a comprehensive and thorough review of their laws, policies and practices with a view to identifying and removing all discriminatory aspects.

The Republic of Slovenia proposed a project on the creation of an International Centre for Interethnic Relations within the Institute for Ethnic Studies in Ljubljana. One of its main objectives will be the creation of a network of different research and other relevant institutions (local, regional, national, international) in this field.

The OSCE Office for Democratic Institutions and Human Rights, the Council of Europe, Slovenia and the United States proposed a comprehensive programme aimed at promoting the status of the Roma population. While not being a clearly identified

250

project, the idea is to create an office that functions as a clearing house and can co-ordinate projects in the fields of education, gender issues, refugee return and good governance. The Council of Europe and Slovenia offered to advise national governments on forging bilateral inter-state co-operation in the area of protection of minority rights, using the experience of different countries.

The Office for National Minorities of the Croatian Government proposed a Seminar on the Rights of National Minorities, which would provide the participating countries of the Stability Pact with the possibility to discuss and review the national legislation and practice and subsequently reinforce the relevant mechanisms related to the protection of minorities.

The Open Society Institute proposed a project on "Managing Multiethnic Communities". The project will publish a textbook for schools of public administration on theory and practice of local multicultural policy-making using the best practice database, and is preparing the publication of a volume on Governance in Multiethnic Local Communities in former Yugoslavia. It also plans to support Elected Roma Leadership Training Programs, which are intended to empower elected Roma leaders and to arm them with skills and knowledge to participate effectively in the local decision-making process on behalf of their communities (in Hungary, Slovakia, Czech Republic, Ukraine).

The Stability Pact has also identified the under-representation of women in political and economic life as a key development problem in Southeastern Europe, so the support of women has become a priority of international strategy.

The Women in Politics Program Co-ordinator of the OSCE presented a media project, which intends to raise citizen's awareness of gender equality issues through TV/ radio programmes, publishing of basic information material and production of new "Best Practice"-based programming, combating the stereotyping of men and women roles in society.

The Central and Eastern European Network for Gender Issues (Hungary) and the Gender Task Force of the Stability Pact have proposed a training programme "Women Can Do It/Capacity-Building of Politicians". The project aims at offering seminars and assisting women in their participation in elections.

ODIHR, the International IDEA Institute, with the Gender Task Force Clearing House and national experts from the respective countries from the Southeast European region have proposed a project on Legislative Review/Reform, focusing on electoral legislation systems. The project offers region-wide international and regional best practices and know-how in providing a legal framework for equal opportunities of women and men to enjoy their active and passive voting rights.

The Task Force Clearinghouse, the Governmental Office for Women Politics in Slovenia, the Council of Europe and governments in the respective countries of the region presented a project which concentrates on electoral legislation in an attempt to begin addressing the issue of discrimination against women's participation in Southeastern Europe.

The BBC World Service, in co-operation with Deutsche Welle and Radio Netherlands, proposed setting up a European Centre for Broadcast Journalism in Podgorica to the Stability Pact's media task force. The Centre will be equipped to provide journalists with essential on-the-job training, both on-site in Montenegro (fixed equipment) and within the framework of the outreach programme (mobile equipment).

The European Centre for Common Ground proposed a project on "Bridges for the New Balkans". The project aims to break down media ghettos by: encouraging the exchange of information from original sources between the media of different languages, ethnic groups and countries; promoting co-operation and the exchange of opinion between journalists from different ehtnic groups; increasing non-negative and non-politically based programming; training journalists; identifying and covering issues of common concern; and by increasing public response to media outlets, and strengthen independence of media. It will involve television, radio and print media in the Southeastern Europe and will consist of workshops, training sessions and production assistance. In the case of newspapers, it will create an editorial board with representatives from Albania, Bulgaria, Greece, Macedonia, Montenegro and Kosovo and offer assistance in various areas. The project will be based in Macedonia, but its activities will involve Albania, Bulgaria, Greece, Montenegro, Kosovo and FRY.

The AMARC Europe office in Budapest has presented a proposal for the Development of an Independent Radio Network. The three-year project for capacity and network-building of independent electronic media will seek to contribute to a diverse and pluralistic media landscape in the region by linking and training independent radios and helping them to harness their efforts to the new communication opportunities offered by the Internet, satellite and digital production.

The BBC Albanian Service proposed the creation of Albanian Language Schools for Journalism. An innovative and sustainable radio learning package will be created for the Albanian-speaking children of Albania and Kosovo, Macedonia and Montenegro, which will combine interactive learning in the form of a Children's Radio Service and a monthly children's magazine, with local syllabus development and teacher training to ensure project sustainability.

The South East News Service Europe (SENSE) intends to develop into a news service directed toward the countries of Southeastern Europe (Bosnia-Herzegovina, FRY, Croatia, Macedonia, Albania) from news bureaus in Brussels, The Hague, Strasbourg/ Paris, Washington/New York and other cities. It intends to become a regional agency providing its services to independent media in all Southeast European countries.

The World Association of Newspapers (WAN), in liaison with its appropriate member organisations in the region, intends to build distribution networks and professional associations throughout Southeastern Europe. WAN proposes to launch a major programme of management training and assistance to ensure the emergence of a new generation of commercially competent press managers. Intensive workshops, multi-phase follow-up consultations, both on-site and via the Internet, and the creation of manuals and case studies, tailored to emerging democracies, are also in preparation.

The European Broadcasting Union to plans to set up a Partnership Project "Southeastern Europe Television". The main objective is to support public sector television stations in Southeastern Europe. The partnership project involves the co-operation of Southeast European TV journalists with TV journalists from established Western European broadcasters, such as BBC, ARD (Germany), France 3, RAI, NOK (Norway). Six hours of TV programming will be produced daily and sent via Eutel Sat. All regional Southeast European TV stations will be able to receive the programme, modify it and broadcast it regionally. The duration of the project is five years.

The Alternative Information Network (Alternativna Informativna Mreza – AIM) has asked for additional support within the Stability Pact to support media development. The Open Broadcast Network and the Office of the High Representative in Bosnia-Herzegovina has proposed a feasibility study on a regional independent television network. The primary goal of the study is to assess the viability of engaging in a long-term project creating an independent, multinational television network in the region.

The Institute for War and Peace Reporting intends to set up a Media Development and Strategy Program, offering production support, journalist training, media monitoring and a variety of special projects.

The OSCE office for the Freedom of Media, the OSCE Mission to Bosnia and the Council of Europe proposed a Conference on the Contribution of Media to Conflict Prevention.

Croatia and the Republika Srpska have agreed on a joint project in the framework of the Stability Pact, providing for the mutual return of refugees, with expected donor support amounting to US-$ 50 million, which will be used to support the necessary infrastructure for the returned population.

At a conference in mid-June, the Serbian opposition, through G-17 Plus, an NGO, presented a comprehensive action plan for the democratisation of post-Milosevic Serbia to representatives of the Stability Pact and the international community. It remained unclear, however, whether donors would respond to the action plan.

2. Security

In the field of security, we can see a clear shift in policies from containing military crises (such as in Bosnia or Kosovo) to the integration of defence forces through increasing practical co-operation (through the Partnership for Peace). The additional co-operation proposals merely complement the work of NATO and add a specific regional dimension to the effort. Especially the Kosovo crisis and the understanding by most players in the region that they want to participate in NATO's security umbrella points at the future perspectives of the security arrangements in the Balkans. The contacts through such an integration is already an essential part of practical cross-border co-operation.

A security-related project proposed by the Macedonian Government (Ministry of Foreign Affairs, Ministry of Defence, Ministry of Interior) to Working Table I of the Stability Pact provides for the creation of an International Centre for Preventive Activities and Conflict Resolution in Macedonia. The Law Faculty in Skopje and Columbia University's International Conflict Resolution Program developed the project which aims at sharing UNPREDEP's positive experiences in implementing preventive diplomacy. The centre intends to hold seminars and other forms of training of public officers and students; local, regional and international conferences; workshops and round-tables, with the aim of conducting research and maintaining permanent communication and dialogue with NGOs, as well as setting up an information system to mobilise public awareness.

At Working Table III, in the field of defence economics and demobilisation, NATO and the World Bank presented a plan to offer vocational training to unemployed military officers in Romania and Bulgaria. Furthermore, the government of Bosnia-Herzegovina and the World Bank prepared a project which is to offer assistance for the reduction of the armed forces in Bosnia-Herzegovina. These initiatives are extremely important. Although they appear not to have an obvious direct cross-border dimension, they contribute very substantially to regional stability, and therefore ought to be extended as soon as possible to other countries in Southeastern Europe.

The German Foreign Office's Arms Control Directorate is planning the creation of a Regional Verification Centre for Southeastern Europe, which ought to assist the Southeast European states to participate more effectively in the implementation of the arms control agreements they have concluded. The Foreign Ministry of France proposed setting up a regional aerial observation system.

The Norwegian Ministry of Foreign Affairs and the US State Department have offered to send a team of experts to assess technical requirements and recommend options for the secure storage and destruction of small arms and light weapons to any member of the Stability Pact. The Greek Ministry of Defence made available the Kilkis Multinational Peacekeeping Centre, near Thessaloniki, which will host seminars and training in specific areas of peace support operations and humanitarian aid missions. The Austrian Federal Ministry for Foreign Affairs plans to organise a seminar on "Structures of Armed Forces in Multi-Ethnic States". The German Foreign Office presented a proposal to organise a seminar on the "Democratic Control of Armed Forces."

3. Good governance

Recent efforts to promote cross-border co-operation in the field of good governance focus on legal reform, local government, the creation of ombudsman offices and parliamentary co-operation. The OSCE, under the umbrella of the Stability Pact's Task Force on Human Rights and Minorities, intends to set up a Regional Legal Aid Network. It will coordinate the numerous NGOs and private practitioners providing legal services in Southeastern Europe.

In the field of minority rights, there are three basic strategies: to support projects of capacity building and empowerment, to work towards better legal standards and to conduct further research. No doubt the two first are among the most efficient ways of supporting minority communities, while research, in particular in the field of legislative practise, is certainly useful to offer solutions for particular problems of minority rights.

The Council of Europe supports the creation of ombudsman offices throughout the region, a process that has already resulted in the creation of such an office in Albania in 1998, embedded in the constitution. Similar offices have also been created in Bosnia-Herzegovina. It launched a new project on "Independent National Human Rights Protection Institutions, including Ombudsman".[21] The aim of the project is to spread the process of establishing and reinforcing independent national human rights protection institutions in the countries of Southeastern Europe. Such bodies are key institutions for promoting accountability and good governance, representing an effective non-judicial means of human rights protection. They can play an important role in fostering stability.

The Deutsche Stiftung für internationale rechtliche Zusammenarbeit e.V. plans to launch programmes offering assistance in legislative and justice reform to all of the Southeast European countries. The project has been presented to the sub-table on Justice and Home Affairs of Working Table III.

In the same framework, the Council of Europe is planning three programmes: reforming criminal legislation in Southeastern Europe in the framework of the ADACS

---

21   Special Coordinator of the Stability Pact for Southeastern Europe: op. cit., p. 43.

programme of legal co-operation; strengthening the independence and efficiency of the judiciary; and helping the organisation and operation of the prison system. Similarly, the OSCE is planning a programme to support prison service reform in Southeastern Europe. The Greek National School of Judges plans to offer seminars for young magistrates on relevant legal issues.

The Centre for European Security Studies in Groningen is planning a project on "Democratic Control: Parliament and Parliamentary Staff Education". The objective of this three-year project is to strengthen legislative oversight of defence and security structures and of democratic control in this area.

The East West Parliamentary Practice Project presented a proposal on "Legislatures and Citizens", aimed at developing a true working relationship between parliaments and NGOs in seven countries of Southeastern Europe.

The International Institute for Democracy proposed a programme intended to promote parliamentary co-operation in Southeastern Europe. The Action Plan covers a period of 18 months,[22] consisting of training and exchange programmes for newly elected members of parliament, parliamentary staff, MPs of specialised committees, conferences for young members of parliament, a newsletter and an electronic discussion forum, aimed at sustaining the network.

The International Foundation for Promoting Studies and Knowledge on Minority Rights (IFPSKMR) plans to promote inter-parliamentary dialogue, through a university-based masters programme over a period of one year. Lectures and case studies will promote ideas of peaceful and pluralistic coexistence of different nationalities and ethnic groups.

The Committee on Foreign Affairs of the Croatian State Parliament is planning a summit of speakers of parliaments of the Stability Pact for Southeastern Europe to discuss "The Role of Parliaments in the Implementation of the Stability Pact and Strengthening of European and Euro-Atlantic Integration Processes."[23] With this initiative, the Croatian Parliament intends to participate actively in the implementation of the Stability Pact and, at the same time, to deepen the relations between Parliaments of all Stability Pact subjects – participants, facilitators, observers.

The Committee on Foreign Affairs of the Croatian State Parliament plans to set up a Centre for Parliamentary Co-operation and Education in Croatia. The objectives of the Centre are to strengthen inter-parliamentary co-operation among the participating countries; provide training courses for MPs and parliamentary civil servants from the Stability Pact countries in parliamentary procedures and practices of other countries; share the

---

22   24 months in total. A six-month pilot phase for which funding has been secured starts soon.
23   Special Coordinator of the Stability Pact for Southeastern Europe: op. cit., p. 152.

experience of the European Parliament and EU parliamentary standards; exchange information, visits and experience; and organise training courses in the form of multilateral seminars and training programmes for young parliamentarians following national elections.

Under the Council of Europe's initiative, the sub-table on Justice and Home Affairs of Working Table III intends to establish a Legislative Clearing House and creating of a Web page.

The East West Institute in Prague proposed the development of an MP network for Southeastern Europe. It is designed to help the practical implementation of the goals of the Stability Pact. The network will be composed of members of parliament from Southeastern Europe and selected Members of the European Parliament.

The main projects for the support of the local government have so far come from the Council of Europe's experts, who advised regional governments in drafting legislation which would increase the authority of the local institutions. Most efforts have gone into legislation, much less into implementation and capacity building. The Council of Europe has now changed its focus and intends to increase its efforts for strengthening local self-government. It has drawn up a variety of proposals to address the issue. One such proposal to the task force on local government of Working Table I aims to establish the Southeastern Forum, as a platform to monitor the development of local democracy in the region. It also intends to bring together the ministers of the countries of Southeastern Europe responsible for local government, and to raise awareness on the most sensitive issues relating to local democracy. The task force thus aims to promote the principles enshrined in the European Charter of Local Self-Government.

The Council of Europe also presented a project to develop a legal framework for local self-government. It intends to create joint working groups with Council of Europe experts, ministries responsible for local government and, where appropriate, a parliamentary committee on local government and national associations. It will organise workshops and seminars on problems of the implementation of a legal framework for local self-government and regional conferences.

The Council of Europe has proposed a project on enhancing financial management and service provision at the local level. The project aims at promoting sound budget procedures and methods at the local level, effective management of the local financial resources, property and assets, and effective management and delivery of public services at the local level, through the dissemination of best practices relating to financial management and management of municipal real estate. It also intends to provide assistance to local authorities that undertake organisational and managerial reforms of their administrations, in order to improve the skills and knowledge of the managers of key local public services.

The Council of Europe furthermore proposed an action plan to foster transfrontier co-operation. It shall do so by offering legal assistance concerning the ratification of the European Outline Convention on Transfrontier Co-operation Between Territorial Communities or Authorities and by providing assistance regarding the conclusion of interstate agreements on transfrontier co-operation and the adoption of the necessary legislative reforms in domestic law.

Another project presented by the Council of Europe aims at developing democratic "citizenship" and intercultural dialogue at the local level. The project shall develop a network of Local Democracy Agencies (LDAs) so as to encourage, in particular, inter-cultural dialogue and co-operation at the local and regional level. Furthermore it plans to establish pilot projects in a number of countries, encourage and support development and activities of NGOs and to conduct study visits. The Council of Europe presented a proposal to promote partnerships between towns and regions, by organising field visits (groups of representatives of European cities and regions – i.e., mayors and/or their representatives – interested in establishing partnerships with cities in the region); organising exchanges between the partners involved, bilateral and multilateral round tables, meetings and conferences.

The Ministry of Justice, Administration and Local Self-Government of Croatia proposed the organisation of conferences on local self-government to promote the exchange of experience and contribute to the standardisation of legislation in the Southeast European countries.

The Open Society Institute proposed setting up a Local Government Information Network, with the intention of promoting transparent, accountable, responsive and efficient governance. It intends to prepare a report on the Status of Local Democracy, in order to provide indicators and evaluation of local governance in selected countries of the region. It is part of the Fiscal Decentralisation Initiative Indicators project to develop benchmarks on different aspects of local government systems.

The Foundation in Support of Local Democracy (FSLD), set up in Poland with the support of the Polish Foreign Ministry, proposed a project designed to help Southeast European countries to share the Polish experience in building a democratic state. The Project aims to establish mechanisms for transferring knowledge and experience on the use of foreign assistance funds and on key barriers and problems existing in this area in post-communist countries.

The OECD plans to conduct surveys on fiscal design across all levels of government. The World Bank's Fiscal Decentralisation Initiative and the Metropolitan Research Institute (Hungary) intend to deliver courses in governance (i.e., on decentralisation and local financial management).

The Center of Studies and Programs for Development proposed a project on "Citizens: Pillar for good governance in Southeastern Europe." The project shall promote and develop partnerships between local and regional authorities and establish "local democracy agencies."

The Foundation for Local Government Reform in Bulgaria proposed a Local Government Expert Exchange Programme for Southeastern Europe. The project aims at increasing the expertise and capacity of local governments to manage local affairs effectively through promotion of partnerships (technical twinning) and transfrontier co-operation between towns and regions in Bulgaria, Romania and Macedonia.

The "Eurocities" project and the Royaumont Process office presented a programme for the Development of Democratic Systems of Local Authorities. The Action Plan provides for the creation of networks aimed at establishing and reinforcing stable links and co-operation between cities of the EU and cities in Southeastern Europe; developing co-operation projects aimed at strengthening institution building at the local level and targeting various community groups such as youth, women and the elderly; exchanging experience and good practises within and among the networks; and promoting the principles and the institutions of EU integration among the local partners in Southeast European cities.

Among other projects presented by the Council of Europe is a project for improving public administration and administrative law procedures. It intends to introduce sound and efficient civil service systems, administrative procedures in conformity with predefined legal standards (Council of Europe's international instruments), to help guarantee judicial control of compliance with the law by administrative authorities, and to introduce alternatives to litigation between administrative authorities and private parties.

The OSCE Mission to Bosnia-Herzegovina presented a Capacity Building Project for Government Offices. The project aims to help states developing strategic capacities to reorient their role in order to strengthen systems of democratic governance based on the rule of law, and to develop mechanisms to detect and manage both domestic and international crisis in the region. The same office proposed setting up a Regional Association of Elected Officials, with the intention of supporting and strengthening independence. It also promotes ethics and professionalism among election officials by creating a regional Association of Elected Officials in Southeastern Europe. A founding assembly of the new regional Association was tentatively scheduled for September 2000.

The Public Administration Reform Section of the Ministry of the Interior of the Czech Republic proposed a programme on "Transfer of know-how and exchange of experiences with public administration."

The Ministry for European Integration of the Republic of Croatia presented a proposal to create an International Public Administration Training Centre. The Centre would train the participants in Euro-Atlantic integration issues through lectures by professors and professionals from participating countries and international organisations. Training would be organised in the form of general and topic-specific seminars, lectures, and short and medium-term courses.

The Secretary of the European Commission for Democracy Through Law proposed setting up the UNIDEM (Universities for Democracy) "Legal Training for the Civil Service". The project aims at ensuring complementary training for civil servants with responsibilities, young civil servants at the start of their career and possibly also administrative judges as well as other categories of lawyers. The programme's scope is to ensure that these persons, when executing their tasks, apply the principles of democracy, human rights and the rule of law.

4. Economic development

Even before the Bari meeting of Working Table II in October 1999, the UK and the USA took the initiative to launch the Investment Compact Initiative. A three-phase approach to implement the project has been set up: diagnosis of current investment conditions in the countries of the region; development of country-specific policy recommendations; and design of regional policy initiatives. Support and monitoring of progress in policy implementation for improving investment conditions and investment performance in the region are also planned.

SECI intends to promote co-operation among securities markets in Southeastern Europe, including setting up a list of companies whose securities are listed/traded in the participating stock exchanges.[24] These companies may constitute the initial candidates of the potential list of companies to be traded on a Common Trading Platform (CTP). These companies also may form the basis for the construction of a SECI Index. Albania, Bulgaria, Croatia, Macedonia, Romania, Slovenia and Turkey have signed a memorandum of understanding on the exchange of information on security markets.

A number of projects are being launched by the EBRD to support private sector development in Southeastern Europe, particularly small and medium-sized enterprises, but these initiatives have usually taken a unilateral direction, from Western donors to Southeast European countries, rather than adding to a cross-border co-operation dimension.

---

24   However, the present stock exchanges in SEE are so insignificant that this initiative for the moment seems highly immature. It may gain ground only once capital markets in SEE countries develop further, which is bound to take some time.

The Carl Duisberg Gesellschaft, Cologne, presented a trainer programme for business-related administration bodies to Working Table II, supporting the rapprochement with EU structures. While these projects will be offered to all Southeast European countries, they will also help cross-border co-operation by supporting the adjustment of regulations among countries during the process of preparing for EU membership.

The ILO office in Europe presented a project on employment creation through entrepreneurship development and business start-ups. The European Training Foundation plans an Integrated Transnational Programme of Support for small and medium-sized enterprises.

The Macedonian Chamber of Commerce intends to set up a human resource development project which would have a regional perspective. It will train managers and staff of small and medium-sized enterprises and provide professional education for all countries in the region.

5. Crime and corruption

So far, the main cross-border initiatives in the field of police co-operation have come from SECI, which is planning to set up a Regional Center for Combating Trans-Border Crime. SECI will seek to link the Center's system to that of INTERPOL and WCO. The SECI Crime Center is co-operating with the Stability Pact in the area of organised crime. Other initiatives in this field include the deployment of policemen in the framework of IPTF in Bosnia and of the MAPE mission in Albania. Cross-border co-operation also developed in the field of customs control between Albania and Italy, with the Italian Guardia di Finanza taking over essential controlling tasks at the Albanian coast and harbours.

The sub-table on Justice and Home Affairs of Working Table III has launched additional cross-border co-operation projects. In this context, the Association of European Police Colleges (AEPC) is working on a training programme for the countries of the region, which ought to increase the institutional capacities in the different fields of policing.

Another training programme comes from the German government, which plans to offer multinational police-training programmes for police and border police officers from Southeastern Europe, as well as academic and practical instructions, including on-the-job training, in Germany.

The Office of the High Representative in Bosnia-Herzegovina presented a proposal to create a National Information Network to the Ministries of Interior of Bosnia-Herzegovina, linking both entities of the federation. The Ministry of Civil Affairs and Communications of Bosnia-Herzegovina presented a proposal aimed at improving the international criminal law enforcement co-operation in the region by installing equipment enabling permanent contact to INTERPOL (it is not clear to what extent this overlaps with the SECI initiative).

UNDCP intends to launch assistance programmes aimed at fighting drug trafficking and an International Drug Control Program, while the Council of Europe plans to organize a seminar on Combating Trafficking in Human Beings in Southeastern Europe.

One of the key cross-table issues of the Stability Pact is the Anti-corruption Initiative, which aims at assisting countries in the region to lay the foundations and build efficient mechanisms for a sustained fight against corruption, by applying more transparent administrative structures as well as accountability. This will be done through assistance and advice in institution building. The initiative is designed to "coordinate the efforts of the international community and work with recipient countries through a true and responsible dialogue."[25] The Council of Europe has taken the lead in the programme.

By and large the efforts of the international community have focused on co-operation in exchanging information between the police forces of the Southeast European countries, while at the same time there is a strong focus on training and democratic education, both essential parts of building transparent and democratically controlled police forces. It is essential that these training programmes address trainers in order to multiply the effects in the countries.

6. Education

In Croatia, there has been a project proposal to be funded by UNESCO on "virtual teaching of national subjects," which brings together schools from Croatia, Serbia, Macedonia, Bosnia-Herzegovina (both entities). "Virtual" refers to the Internet, while national subjects are history, literature and other sensitive subjects, which need a more flexible approach (i.e., liberated from nationalistic interpretations of the "other"). The project was launched by a Croatian association through the Croatian UNESCO Commission, and received support from the Slovenian UNESCO Commission.

The PETNICA centre in Valjevo (Serbia) intends to create a Regional Education Improvement Centre.

In Slovenia, the Open Society Institute (Soros) is in the process of establishing an information network on educational developments and innovations based in Ljubljana,

---

25   Special Coordinator of the Stability Pact for Southeastern Europe: op. cit., p. 10.

which will serve the Southeast European countries (Albania, Bosnia-Herzegovina, Croatia, Macedonia, Romania and Slovenia and FRY).

Numerous new initiatives have been proposed to the Task Force on Education and Youth of the Stability Pact within the so-called Enhanced Graz Process. In co-operation with partners represented in the Task Force (Council of Europe, Open Society Network-Soros, OECD, UNICEF and UNESCO), a seminar on strategies for educational reform in Southeast European countries was organised in Bled from 8–10 June 2000 bringing together policy-makers and practitioners.

Several other projects have been presented by the Task Force on Education to the Donors Conference in March. Within the European Commission, the General Directorate for Education and Culture proposed a comprehensive action plan on higher education. The package consists of activities by various institutions within the framework of the overall action plan of the Enhanced Graz Process, including several cross-border projects.

The Council of Europe presented a package of measures, intended to promote and help young people to improve the opportunities of developing their full potential and of contributing positively to the development of civil society and a project on Education for Democratic Citizenship which aims to promote a culture of human rights, pluralism, democratic principles, citizen participation and responsibility.

The European Training Foundation presented a proposal to create a Network for Post-Graduate Education in Southeastern Europe. The five-year project aims at strengthening the provision of post-graduate education at existing higher education institutions in Southeast Europe, particularly in the social sciences. The network will give support to innovative projects which link the teaching and learning processes across several institutions in the region, together with a limited number of key partners in the rest of Europe. These projects will therefore create a regional network for post-graduate education.

The same foundation presented a project for Vocational Education and Training and Democratic Citizenship. The objective is to assist countries in Southeastern Europe with the upgrading of their vocational education and training systems as a means of promoting social dialogue and ensuring that democratic principles are implemented at all levels. The package has been put together by the Working Group on Vocational Education and Training Systems and Democratic Citizenship of the Enhanced Graz Process.

The OECD, together with the Center Education 2000 in Romania and the Kosovo Foundation for Open Society (KFOS), presented a project for General Education Policy and System Improvement. The project will organise a summer university on education policy and strategy development, building human capacities at the level of governmental and non-governmental organisations by training experts from Southeastern Europe countries. It aims at strengthening and improving teacher education and establishing a Kosovo Education Centre. The OECD has also presented a Programme for International

Student Assessment (PISA), which will monitor a broad range of curricular and cross-curricular learning outcomes on a regular basis within an international comparative framework, in collaboration with the OECD countries. The OECD, within its thematic reviews of education, is also preparing a comparative thematic review of education policy in Southeastern Europe.

The Council of Europe's Education Policies and European Dimension Division presented a proposal aimed at the improvement of history teaching. This includes the establishment of a Board of Historians and of a co-ordinating committee of experts and government officials for managing a coherent strategic framework for action in the region. It also intends to develop a network of schools to conduct joint projects on historical and archaeological sites, summer schools, competitions in history research and essay writing, multicultural history education, etc.

The Stability Pact's Task Force on Human Rights and Minorities also came forward with an education-related cross-border co-operation project, proposing the creation of a Postgraduate School in Economics for Southeastern Europe. The task force intends to set up an International University in the long term, located somewhere in the region. Nevertheless, considering the time needed to achieve this goal, the establishment of the Postgraduate School of Economics for Southeastern Europe has been proposed as a quick-start project. The project can, in turn, lead to the improvement of inter-state relations and better protection of minorities in the region.

7. Infrastructure

The main field of activity of the Stability Pact's Working Table on Economic Reconstruction, Development and Co-operation (Working Table II) has been in infrastructure projects. The projects are now divided into:
1. A Quick-Start Package of projects for which implementation is likely to start, or for which a tender will be awarded by 31 March 2001;
2. A Near-Term Package of projects which appear prima facie economically justified and do not present major sector or project issues; projects for which preparation (including tendering) should thus be accelerated; and
3. A Medium-Term Package of projects that require further investigation or analysis on specific issues which must first be solved.

The World Bank launched a project on Trade and Transport Facilitation in Southeastern Europe (TTFSE) following the SECI initiative. The project aims at helping six countries in Southeastern Europe improve customs procedures. A World Bank loan will be used for three main areas: physical improvement of border stations, management information systems, and scanning equipment. Also included as part of the package is technical assistance for the customs services. The United States has made a total commitment of US-$ 9 million for Romania, Bulgaria, Macedonia, and Croatia. Albania and Bosnia-Herzegovina will receive technical assistance from the European Union.

SECI has set up a project to support the development of links between electric power systems of participating countries, with the aim of improving their integration into the European power grid. The project plans to set up a tele-information system among national dispatch centres in Southeastern Europe. The project was presented to Working Table II in Bari. The US Agency for International Development (US AID) has agreed to sponsor this project and to provide expert services.

SECI also launched an Energy Efficiency Demonstration Zones Network in Southeastern Europe. The goal is to enhance regional co-operation among the countries of Southeastern Europe by encouraging joint and co-operative solutions and sharing economic and environmental problems. The SECI energy efficiency project group receives technical support from the UNECE Energy Division.

SECI also has a project on the Recovery of Rivers, Lakes and the Black Sea. So far Bulgaria, Croatia, Hungary, Macedonia, Moldova, Romania and Slovenia are participating. In addition, Greece, Macedonia and Albania have started a trilateral process of co-operation on environmental protection and on supporting tourism in the Prespa and Ohrid Lake region.

The Working Table II of the Stability Pact has agreed to implement a Regional Environmental Reconstruction Programme (RERP). The priority areas include institution building, regional co-operation, rehabilitation of environmental damage and the development of civil society. RERP has established an open-ended ad-hoc group on environmental issues which is co-chaired by the European Commission and one country from Southeastern Europe.

The UNEP Balkans Task Force plans to create transborder nature protection areas. A first project is the creation of a Prokletije National Park situated on the borders of Kosovo, Montenegro and Albania. Studies for post-conflict environmental assessment in Albania and Macedonia are also planned among future UNEP Balkans Task Force activities. As an example of a prominent municipal initiative, the Ohrid and Prespa Lakes regional cross-border co-operation initiatives on environmental protection should be mentioned.

Map

Key Documents and Web Sites

(as of 26 October 2000)

International organisations

Central European Initiative
   http://www.ceinet.org/CEIForum/
Council of Europe
   http://www.coe.int/
European Union
   http://europa.eu.int/
   Kosovo
   .../geninfo/keyissues/kosovo/index_en.htm
European Councils – Presidency Conclusions
   http://europa.eu.int/off/conclu/
EU Directorate General for Enlargement
   http://EUROPA.EU.INT/comm/enlargement/
   Progress reports October 1999
   .../report_oct_99/
EU Directorate General for External Relations
   http://europa.eu.int/comm/external_relations/see
   Regional Approach
   .../see/docs/reg_approach_96.htm
   Bosnia-Herzegovina
   http://europa.eu.int/comm/external_relations/see/bh/index.htm
   Stabilisation and Association Process
   http://europa.eu.int/comm/ external_relations/see/intro/index.htm

EU Phare

http://europa.eu.int/comm/dg1a/phare/

EU and the World Bank – Southeastern Europe Reconstruction and Development

http://www.seerecon.org/

NATO

http://www.nato.int/

KFOR

http://www.kforonline.com/

NATO Partnership for Peace

http://www.nato.int/pfp/

NATO Kosovo/Operation Joint Force/Guard

http://www.nato.int/kosovo/jnt-grdn.htm

OSCE

http://www.osce.org

Kosovo

.../kosovo/

Bosnia-Herzegovina

http://www.oscebih.org/regstab/eng/regstb-main.htm

SECI – Southeast European Co-operation Initiative

http://www.unece.org/seci/

Stability Pact for Southeastern Europe

http://europa.eu.int/comm/dg1a/see/stapact/10_june_99.htm

http://www.seerecon.org/KeyDocuments/KD1999062401.htm

Stability Pact Office

http://www.stabilitypact.org/

UN

http://www.un.org/

Security Council Res. 1244

.../Docs/scres/1999/99sc1244.htm

Kosovo

.../peace/kosovo/pages/kosovo1.htm

World Bank

http://www.worldbank.org/

Kosovo

.../html/extdr/regions.htm

Western governments (USA und EU-15) and Russia

Austria, Bundesministerium für auswärtige Angelegenheiten, Vienna
  http://www.bmaa.gv.at/politik/konflikt.html.de
Belgium, Ministerie van Buitenlandse Zaken, Brussels
  http://www.diplobel.fgov.be/Politics/policy_beleid_1_2_NL.htm
Denmark, Udenrigsministeriet, Copenhagen
  http://www.um.dk/udenrigspolitik/oesteuropa/balkan/
Finland, Ulkoasiainministeriö, Helsinki
  http://formin.finland.fi/netcomm/news/
France, Ministère des Affaires Étrangères, Paris
  http://www.france.diplomatie.fr/europe/index.html
Germany, Auswärtiges Amt, Berlin
  http://www.auswaertiges-amt.de/&_archiv/inf-kos/
Great Britain, Foreign and Commonwealth Office, London
  http://www.fco.gov.uk/news/dynpage.asp?Page=10096&Theme=19
Greece, Ipourgio Exoterikon, Athens
  http://www.mfa.gr/foreign/a3en.htm
Ireland, Department of Foreign Affairs, Dublin
  http://www.irlgov.ie/iveagh/
Italy, Ministero degli Affari Esteri, Rome
  http://www.taskforcebalcani.com/
Luxembourg, Ministère des Affaires Étrangères, Luxembourg
  http://www.gouvernement.lu/gouv/fr/gouv/minist/aececd.html
Netherlands, Ministerie van Buitenlandse Zaken, The Hague
  http://www.minbuza.nl/Content.asp?Key=302342&Pad=305942,305943,305945
Portugal, Ministerio Nestrangeiros, Lisbon
  http://www.min-nestrangeiros.pt/mne/portugal/dgac.html#topo
Russian Federation, Ministerstvo Inostranych Del, Moscow
  http://www.ln.mid.ru/WEBSITE/BRP_4.NSF/ENG?OpenView
Spain, Ministerio de Asuntos Exteriores, Madrid
  http://www.mae.es/mae/portadas/documentos.htm
Sweden, Utrikesdepartementet, Stockholm
  http://www.ud.se/inenglish/policy/index.htm
USA, State Department, Washington, D.C.
  http://www.state.gov/www/regions/eur/index.html

International think tanks and NGOs

Bertelsmann Foundation, Gütersloh
  http://www.bertelsmann-stiftung.de
Brookings Institute, Washington, D.C.
  http://www.brookings.org
Center for Applied Policy Research, Munich
  http://www.cap.uni-muenchen.de
Center for European Policy Studies, Brussels
  http://www.ceps.be
Copenhagen Peace Research Institute, Copenhagen
  http://www.copri.dk
Council on Foreign Relations, Washington, D.C.
  http://www.cfr.org
EastWest Institute, New York/Prague
  http://www.iews.org
German Council on Foreign Relations – DGAP, Berlin
  http://www.dgap.org
Institute for Security Studies, WEU, Paris
  http://www.weu.int/institute
Institute for Southeast European Studies, Munich
  http://www.bicc.de/coop/fiv/suedost/info.html
International Crisis Group, Washington, D.C.
  http://www.crisisweb.org
International Helsinki Federation for Human Rights
  http://www.ihf-hr.org
Istituto Affari Internazionali, Rome
  http://www.iai.it
U.S. Institute for Peace, Washington, D.C.
  http://www.usip.org
Vienna Institute for International Economic Studies – WIIW, Vienna
  http://www.wiiw.at

Governments and political parties in Southeastern Europe

Albanian Government
http://www.albgovt.gov.al

Bosnia-Herzegovina Government
http://www.gov.ba

Croatian Government
http://www.vlada.hr

Democratic Opposition of Serbia DOS
http://www.dos.org.yu

FRY Government
http://www.gov.yu

Macedonian Government
http://www.gov.mk

Serbian Radical Party SRS
http://www.srs.org.yu

Serbian Renewal Movement SPO
http://www.spo.org.yu

Socialist Party of Serbia
http://www.sps.org.yu/index-ne.htm

Abbreviation Index

BPK	Banking and Payments Authority for Kosovo
BSEC	Black Sea Economic Co-operation
BSP	Socialist Party (Bulgaria)
CAFAO	Customs and Fiscal Assistance Office
CARDS	Programme of Assistance for the Reconstruction, Development and Stabilisation of the Western Balkans
CCP	Common Commercial Policy
CEFTA	Central European Free Trade Agreement
CEI	Central European Initiative
CESDP	Common European Security and Defence Policy
CFSP	Common Foreign and Security Policy
CIS	Commonwealth of Independent States
CMEA	Council for Mutual Economic Assistance
CoE	Council of Europe
CSCE	Conference for Security and Co-operation in Europe
CSEE	Conference on Stability and Good Neighbourliness in Southeastern Europe
CTP	Common Trading Platform
DA	Democratic Alternative (Macedonia)
DPA	Democratic Party of Albanians
DPS	Democratic Party of Socialists (Montenegro)
EAPC	Euro-Atlantic Partnership Council
EBRD	European Bank for Reconstruction and Development
ECHO	Humanitarian Aid Office (EU)

ECHR	European Convention on Human Rights
EFTA	European Free Trade Association
EP	European Parliament
FRY	Federal Republic of Yugoslavia
FYROM	Former Yugoslav Republic of Macedonia
G-7	USA, Germany, France, Great Britain, Italy, Japan, Germany
G-8	G-7 and Russia
G-17	Opposition Group of Economic Experts in FRY
ICG	International Contact Group or International Crisis Group
IFI	International Financial Institutions
IFOR	Peace Implementation Forces
IGC	Inter-Governmental Conference
IHF	International Helsinki Federation
ILO	International Labour Organisation
IMF	International Monetary Fund
IPTF	International Police Task Force
JAT	Yugoslav Airlines
JHA	Justice and Home Affairs
JIAS	Joint Interim Administrative Structure
KFOR	Kosovo International Peace Implementation Force
KLA	Kosovo Liberation Army (UCK)
LDA	Local Democracy Agency
LDK	Democratic League of Kosova
LSCG	Montenegrin separatists
MAP	NATO Membership Action Plan
MAPE	Multinational Advisory Police Element
MPFSEE	Rapid Reaction Force of Southeastern Europe
NGO	Non-Governmental Organisation
NS	People's Party (Montenegro)
NSF	National Salvation Front (Romania)
OBNOVA	European programme for the rehabilitation and reconstruction of Bosnia-Herzegovina, Croatia, the Federal Republic of Yugoslavia and the Former Yugoslav Republic of Macedonia
ODIHR	OSCE Office for Democratic Institutions and Human Rights
OECD	Organisation for Economic Co-operation and Development
OSCE	Organisation for Security and Co-operation in Europe
PCA	Partnership and Co-operation Agreement

PDK	Democratic Party of Kosova
PDP	Party for Democratic Prosperity
PfP	Partnership for Peace
Phare	Programme of Aid for Eastern and Central Europe
RERP	Regional Environmental Reconstruction Programme
SAA	Stabilisation and Association Agreement
SAP	Stabilisation and Association Process
SDM	Social Democrats of Macedonia
SDP	Social Democratic Party (Montenegro)
SDS	Serbian Democratic Party
SECI	Southeast European Co-operation Initiative
SEDM	Southeast European Defence Ministers Group
SEEI	Southeastern Europe Initiative
SENSE	South East News Service Europe
SFOR	Peace Stabilisation Forces
SID	Foreign information and documentation service (FRY)
SIGMA	Program for Support for Improvement in Governance and Management in Central and Eastern Europe (OECD)
SNP	Socialist People's Party (Montenegro)
SNS	Serb People's Party (Montenegro)
SPO	Serbian Renewal Movement
SRS	Serb nationalists (Montenegro)
SZP	Alliance for Change (Serbia)
TCA	Trade and Co-operation Agreement
TEMPUS	Trans-European Mobility Programme for University Studies
TRAFKO	European Commission's Task Force for the Reconstruction of Kosovo
TTFSE	Trade and Transport Facilitation in SEE
UNDCP	UN International Drug Control Programme
UNDP	UN Development Program
UN-ECE	UN Economic Commission for Europe
UNEDIM	Universities for Democracy
UNEP	United Nations Environmental Programme
UNHCR	United Nations High Commissioner for Refugees
UNMIK	United Nations Mission in Kosovo
UNPREDEP	United Nations Preventive Deployment Force
UNSC	UN Security Council
USAID	United States Agency for International Development

VRMO-DPMNE	Internal Macedonian Revolutionary Organisation-Democratic for Macedonian National Unity
WAN	World Association of Newspapers
WCO	World Customs Organisation
WEU	Western European Union
WTO	World Trade Organisation

About the Authors

Lucian Boia is Professor and Director of the Centre for History of the Imaginary, Department of History at the University of Bucharest. Areas of interest: history of historiography, history of ideas and mentalities, history of the imaginary. Selective bibliography: Istorie si mit in constiinta romaneasca [History and Myth in Romanian Consciousness], Bucharest 1997; Pour une histoire de l'imaginaire, Paris 1998; Jocul cu trecutul. Istoria intre adevar si fictiune [Playing with the Past: Truth and Fiction in History], Bucharest 1998; Doua secole de mitologie nationala [Two Centuries of National Mythology], Bucharest 1999; La mythologie scientifique du communisme, Paris 2000.

Martin Brusis is a Research Fellow at the Centre for Applied Policy Research, Munich University. His work currently focuses on public policy reforms in Central and Eastern Europe, the eastern enlargement of the EU and the transformation process in the Balkans. He studied political science, sociology and Slavic languages at the Universities of Marburg and Berlin and received a Ph.D. in sociology with a thesis on policy analysis on privatisation in Hungary. Recent publications: Governance Capacity as a Key Factor in Preparing Accession to the European Union: A Survey of the Discussion, in: Perspectives 14, Summer 2000; Internal Problems of the European Union That Might Obstruct an Enlargement Towards the East, in: H. Tang (ed.): Winners and Losers of EU Integration. Policy Issues for Central and Eastern Europe, Washington, D.C., 2000; Negotiating EU Accession: Policy Approaches of Advanced Candidate Countries from Central and Eastern Europe, Munich 2000; Verhinderte Nationen. Über den Umgang mit ethnischen Minderheiten, in: Internationale Politik 9/1999.

Kinga Gál is a Research Associate at the European Centre for Minority Issues, Flensburg, Germany. She is a specialist in international human rights law and minority legislation in Central and Eastern Europe, as well as within the context of the UN, OSCE and Council of Europe. She studied Law at the Eötvös Lóránd University in Budapest, Hungary, and received a degree in International Comparative Human Rights at the International Institute for Human Rights in Strasbourg, France. She has also worked as legal adviser to the Chairman of the Democratic Alliance of Hungarians in Romania (RMDSZ) in Bucharest (1992–1994). She is currently working towards her Ph.D. in international law on the role of bilateral treaties at the University of Kiel, Germany.

Nathan Galer studied international politics and international law at the Walsh School of Foreign Service in Washington, D.C. For the past year, he has been a Research Associate at the Center for Applied Policy Research in Munich, recently returning from studying at the Ludwig-Maximilians-University. He has worked on conflict in Eastern and Southeastern Europe at the United States Department of State, where he served as the Congressional Liaison for peacekeeping missions. He is currently continuing his study of international relations in a European context at the Center for German and European Studies at Georgetown University in Washington, D.C.

Daniela Heimerl studied political science, history and Slavic studies at the Ludwig-Maximilians-University (Munich), Institut d'Etudes Politiques (Paris) and Marc Bloch University (Strasburg), where she received her Ph.D. in 1998. Since 1990 she has been an analyst at the Center for East-European and CIS Studies (CEDUCEE-La Documentation française, Paris) and a member of the editorial staff of the Courrier des pays de l'Est. Her areas of responsibility include the successor states of former Yugoslavia and the enlargement process of the European Union to the East. She has been an associate analyst at the LASP Research Center (Laboratoire d'Analyse des Systèmes Politiques-CNRS) since 1996 and lecturer at the Nanterre University (Paris X) since 1999. Selected publications: Le Pacte de stabilité pour l'Europe du Sud-Est: les Balkans en point de mire, in: Le Courrier des Pays de l'Est, September 2000; Serbie-Monténégro 1999–2000: échec et mat?, in: Le Courrier des Pays de l'Est, June–July 2000; Contradictions et limites des politiques de reconstruction dans les Balkans, Revue Comparative Est-Ouest, 4, 1999 (with Nebojsa Vukadinovic and Yorgos Rizopoulos); Elargissement à l'Est de l'UE: procédures et enjeux des négociations, in: Le Courrier des Pays de l'Est, June 1999; Les coopérations transfrontalières dans les PECO: nouvelles géographies économiques, in: Le Courrier des Pays de l'Est, October 1996 (with Jaroslav Blaha).

Kostas Ifantis is an Assistant Professor of International Relations in the Department of Public Administration and Political Science of the University of Athens. He studied Law at the Aristotle University of Thessaloniki and International Relations (Ph.D.) at

280

the University of Bradford, UK, where he worked as a lecturer (1991–1993). From 1993–1995, he was a lecturer for international politics at the University of Portsmouth, UK. He has also served as a Special Advisor to the Directorate of Security and Defence of the Greek Ministry of Foreign Affairs (1997–1998). He has been a Research Fellow with the Hellenic Foundation for European and Foreign Policy (ELIAMEP) since 1997. Selected publications: NATO in the New European Order, London 1996 (with Fergus Carr); Greece in a Changing Europe, Manchester 1996 (with Kevin Featherstone); Theory and Reform in the European Union, Manchester 1999; Current Issues of International Relations. State Sovereignty: Threats and Challenges, Athens 2000 (with Michael Tsinisizelis, in Greek).

Iris Kempe is a Senior Research Fellow at the Centre for Applied Policy Research, University of Munich, where she serves as director of the project "Direct Neighbourhood" and co-ordinator for the CIS and the Baltic States. She received her Ph.D. on problems of social policy and the Russian transition at the Free University Berlin. Project manager and expert in international assistance programmes such as Tacis and Transform since 1993; 1993–1996 project assistant at the Friedrich-Ebert-Foundation, Moscow. Selected publications: The EU Accession States and Their Eastern Neighbours, (ed.), Gütersloh 1999; Direct Neighbourhood. Relations between the enlarged EU and the Russian Federation, Ukraine, Belarus and Moldova, Gütersloh 1998; Rußland am Wendepunkt. Analyse der Sozialpolitik von 1991 bis 1996, Wiesbaden 1997; The European Union and Ukraine: Interest and Strategies, in: K. R. Spillmann, A. Wenger and D. Müller (eds.): Between Russia and the West: Foreign Policy of Independent Ukraine, Bern 1999; Die Ukraine und Europa, in: W. Weidenfeld (ed.): Europa Handbuch, Gütersloh 1999.

Wim van Meurs is a Senior Analyst at the Center for Applied Policy Research, University of Munich since 1997, in charge of Southeast European affairs. He received his M.A. (1988) and Ph.D. (1993) in International Relations and Russian and East European Studies at Utrecht University in the Netherlands. Post-doc and lecturer at the Free University and the Humboldt University in Berlin (1994–1997 and 1997–1999). Selected publications: The Bessarabian Question in Communist Historiography, Boulder, Colo., 1994; Carving a Moldavian Identity out of History, in: Nationalities Papers 26/1, 1998; J. Kempe, B. von Ow (eds.): Die EU-Beitrittsstaaten und ihre östlichen Nachbarn – The EU Accession States and Their Eastern Neighbours, Gütersloh 1999; Social Citizenship and Migration: The Immobility of the Russian Diaspora in the Baltics, in: R. Munz, R. Ohliger (eds.): Ethnic Diasporas, Berlin 2000; The Club of Three and the Balkans, The Balkans and New European Responsibilities, Gütersloh 2000.

Plamen Pantev is a graduate of Sofia University "St. Kliment Ohridsky", Law Department. He received a Ph.D. in International Relations and International Law. Founder and Director of the Institute for Security and International Studies (ISIS), Sofia, since 1994. He is Associate Professor at Sofia University "St. Kliment Ohridsky", lecturing on theory of international relations and theory and practice of international negotiations. Member of the International Advisory Boards of the Journal of International Negotiation and Journal of Southern Europe and the Balkans. Editor-in-chief of the monthly e-periodical Balkan Regional Profile and the quarterly e-periodical Black Sea Basin Regional Profile' [*www.isn.ethz.ch/isis*]. Relevant publications in English: Coping With Conflicts in the Central and Southern Balkans, Sofia 1995; Bulgaria and the Balkans in the CFSP of the EU, Sofia 1995; Strengthening of the Balkan Civil Society: the Role of the NGOs in International Negotiations, Sofia 1997; Pre-Negotiations: The Theory and How to Apply It to Balkan Issues, Sofia 1998; Legitimizing Subregionalism: Evolving Perceptions, Initiatives, and Approaches to Subregional Relations in South-Eastern Europe, in: R. Dwan (ed.): Building Security in Europe's New Borderlands: Subregional Cooperation in the Wider Europe, New York/London 1999; Peacekeeping and Intervention in the Former Yugoslavia: Broader Implications of the Regional Case, Sofia 1999.

Ivanka Petkova is Executive Director of the Economic Policy Institute and Assistant Professor at the Technical University, Sofia. She received a Ph.D. in Economy from the Academy of Science, Sofia. Her particular expertise lies in drafting economic transition laws for Bulgaria and the management of projects on EU accession and NATO membership. Selective bibliography: Securities Transactions, Sofia [1]1994, [2]1998; (co-author) Reforming the Financial System in East and West, Dordrecht/Boston/London 1993; (co-author) Die kleinen und mittelständischen privaten Unternehmen in der bulgarischen Tourismusindustrie, in: Südosteuropa 44 Heft 3–4/1995; Stanovisko Bulgarii wobec drugego etapu otwarcia NATO, in: Polska i dalsze otwarcie NATO, Krakow 1998, pp. 139–145; Country Reports on Bulgaria, in: Central European Quarterly, Vienna 1996, 1997, I/1998; Regional Cooperation on Capital Markets, in: Regional Cooperation on Central and Eastern Europe, Sofia 2000, pp. 125–130.

Fabian Schmidt is a Research Analyst on the former Yugoslavia and on Albania at the Südost-Institut in Munich. He worked at the Open Media Research Institute and at Radio Free Europe/Radio Liberty in Prague and was Director of the Albanian Media Monitoring Project in Tirana at the Institute for War and Peace Reporting, London. Selective bibliography: Menschenrechte, Politik und Krieg in Kosovo 1989 bis 1999 [Human Rights, Politics and War in Kosovo 1989 to 1999], in: Zur Diskussion gestellt: Der Kosovo-Konflikt, Bayerische Landeszentrale für Politische Bildungsarbeit, München

2000; Generationskonflikte in Albaniens großen Parteien [Generation Conflicts in Albania's large Parties], in: Südosteuropa 49 Heft 1–2/2000; Enemies Far and Near: Macedonia's Fragile Stability, in: Problems of Post-Communism, 45/4, July–August 1998; Upheaval in Albania, in: Current History, 97/617, March 1998; Pyramid Schemes Leave Albania on Shaky Ground, in: Transition, 3/4, 7 March 1997.

Predrag Simic is Foreign Policy Adviser to the President of the Federal Republic of Yugoslavia. He received his Ph.D. (1998) from the Faculty of Social Sciences of the University of Belgrade. Presently, he is also Professor at the Faculty of Political Science (University of Belgrade), Member of the Advisory Board of the International Institute for Peace, Vienna, and Member of the Editorial Board of the International Politics, The Hague. Previous positions: Director of the Institute of International Politics and Economics, Belgrade (1988–1997); Deputy Minister for Economic Relations in the Interim Government of Serbia (2000–2001). Selective bibliography: Socialist Modernization: Continuity and Change in Contemporary China, Belgrade 1988; Socialism and Modernization in the P.R. of China (1978–1988), Belgrade 1988; American and Yugoslav Views on the 1990s, Belgrade 1990; Veränderungen in Europa – Vereinigung Deutschlands – Perspektiven der 90er Jahre, Belgrade 1991; Towards a new Community, Belgrade 1993; Crisis and reform – State and Civil Society in Transition, Belgrade 1994; The Road to Rambouillet – Kosovo Crisis 1995–2000, Belgrade 2000; European Union, NATO and Their South Eastern European Neigbors, Belgrade 2001; Do the Balkans Exist?, Paris 2001 (in print), The Last War of the XX Century: USA, NATO and the Yugoslav Crisis, Belgrade 2001 (in print).

Milica Uvalic is Professor of Economics at the University of Perugia. She studied at the University of Belgrade (B.A. and M.A.) and the European University Institute (Ph.D.), where she also worked as Research Fellow (1989–92) before coming to the University of Perugia. She has been Consultant to the Commission of the European Communities for Former Yugoslavia and for Employee Participation in Western Europe, and more recently to the ILO and to Governor Avramovic of the National Bank of Yugoslavia. She has published some 90 articles and several books, including: Investment and Property Rights in Yugoslavia, Cambridge 1992; The Pepper Report (Commission of the-European Communities), Brussels 1992; Impediments to the Transition in Eastern Europe, Florence 1992; Privatisation Surprises in Transition Economies, Cheltenham 1997; The Balkans and the Challenge of Economic Integration, Ravenna 1997; Equality, Participation, Transition, London 2000. Together with Will Bartlett, she edits Economic Analysis – The Journal of Enterprise and Participation.